JANE DOE NO MORE

Jane Doe No More

My 15-Year Fight to Reclaim My Identity—
A True Story of Survival, Hope, and Redemption

M. William Phelps

National Best-selling Author
Star of the Investigation Discovery series *Dark Minds*

with Donna Palomba

Founder, Jane Doe No More, Inc.

LYONS PRESS
Guilford, Connecticut
An imprint of Globe Pequot Press

*For those who have been sexually
assaulted but are afraid to come forward—
and for the hope that this book helps,
in some small way, to begin the
process of healing.*

To buy books in quantity for corporate use
or incentives, call **(800) 962-0973**
or e-mail **premiums@GlobePequot.com.**

Lyons Press is an imprint of Globe Pequot Press.

All photos courtesy of Donna Palomba unless otherwise noted.

Project editor: Meredith Dias
Layout: Sue Murray

Library of Congress Cataloging-in-Publication Data is available on file.

ISBN 978-0-7627-7880-5

Printed in the United States of America

10 9 8 7 6 5 4 3 2 1

CONTENTS

Authors' Note

The book in your hands conveys a true story. It is a research-backed, collaborative memoir, mostly supported by the documentation and recollections of one woman, Donna Palomba, and suffused with her very own words. A working mother of two, Donna was living her version of the American dream—family, husband, kids, a good job—when the unthinkable happened: Her home was invaded by a masked intruder.

What took place in Donna's bedroom next was horrifying, tragic. Yet what she endured after she had been sexually assaulted is where the tragedy turned to heroism. I do not want to delve too deeply into Donna's incredible tale of determination, survival, and triumph here; I simply want to say a few things about how and why I decided to get involved in this story and tell it in this manner.

Over the course of twelve months, Donna dictated her story to me, and I put that story into a narrative with the added help of the documentation available—thousands of pages of police reports, trial transcripts, depositions, personal notes (throughout my career I've never seen more comprehensive, detailed entries from a victim of a crime, including conversations, thoughts, and quotes, recorded on the day of each incident), and many other forms of research. In some cases there is documentation to back up Donna's story directly; in others, the story relies solely on Donna's memory of the event(s). I conducted several interviews for this book, but did not set out to speak to all the people involved. My aim with Donna was to tell this story through her eyes and her memory. She lived it. This book is *not* one of my usual pieces of investigative journalism. It is Donna's version of the events of her life, told by me.

Throughout the book (beginning below my author's note) the reader will find sections—the more personal aspects of the narrative—told in Donna's first-person voice and set in italics. This dual storytelling is not a new literary device; but it is rather uncommon. Donna and I wanted to give the reader that all-important personal connection, beyond simply the quoting or paraphrasing of a source, that a story such as hers demands. To convey exactly how emotionally trying and altogether frightening Donna's life became took courage on her part, and I wanted Donna to have a distinct voice, especially as she related her battle against the system and her discovery of the shocking identity of her attacker.

This story is about Donna Palomba's life. My role was to frame her narrative and point out various aspects of the case the reader needs to understand.

I pored through literally thousands of pages of documents, interviewed Donna at length, studied her notes and diaries, exchanged hundreds of e-mails, got to know her on a personal level, and spoke to several of the people deeply involved in this case. Whenever someone is quoted, that dialogue was taken from those documents, trial transcripts, interviews I conducted, and Donna's recollections.

Even without all the research, anyone would know that Donna Palomba is a fighter, an unbelievable woman, and a survivor. She is not a victim.

When tragedy strikes, some of us—perhaps myself included—might cower into a fetal ball. We might allow the enduring trauma to envelop every sense of our being. Very few would stand up to that misery and look it in the eye. Fewer still would continue to fight when victory did not seem possible. Donna is one of the brave few. Faced with defeat time and again, with nearly an entire city against her, Donna persevered. When the identity of her attacker was exposed, Donna did not lose her strength; she held her ground in defense of truth and justice, and continued her fight. Donna did not want to see another human being have to go through what she did.

What follows is her incredible journey. Donna lived as a "Jane Doe" for nearly fifteen years. Her identity was stolen from her. If you are a rape survivor (or know someone who is), or if you have been sexually assaulted and have not reported it (or know somebody who was), please read Donna's story and visit the Jane Doe No More website. The information there can help you recover your identity and take back your life.

—M. William Phelps
June 2012

Rape is the most misunderstood and underreported crime. The first step to healing is talking about the assault. Yet hundreds of thousands suffer in silence.

Every Jane Doe is a person with hopes and dreams and talents. I want to let everyone know that he or she is not alone and invite them to become part of what is a vocal, vibrant, and visible survivors' community.

No more blame. No more shame. No more fear.

This mission found me; I did not seek it. In a million years I would not have dreamt that I would be doing what I am doing today. And yet, I would not change a thing. This challenging journey has brought countless blessings and surprises and dared me to reach farther into my soul than I ever thought possible. I have found a greater purpose. Each day brings affirmation that something very special is in play— and I truly believe it is all part of God's greater plan.

—Donna Palomba
June 2012

Injustice anywhere is a threat to justice everywhere.
—MARTIN LUTHER KING JR.

Chapter One

A Stranger in the House

THE DARKNESS ENVELOPED HER THAT NIGHT, AND IT MAY HAVE BEEN the absence of light that saved her life.

The first sound thirty-six-year-old Donna Palomba could recall later was muffled, a squirrel-in-the-attic rustling. Nothing obvious or particularly loud. Still, it was enough to startle her awake. Initially she thought the sound may have come from a closet down the hall. We've all been there: jolted from a deep sleep by a sudden noise in the dead of night, no idea what the sound is or where it's coming from. Donna couldn't establish what time it was with any accuracy, only that it had to be after midnight and into the very early morning of September 11, 1993.

After collecting her thoughts and listening closer, Donna was certain she heard footsteps: the creak of her wooden stairs that led to the second floor, where she and her children slept in separate rooms.

Those are not the tiny footsteps of children, she thought. The noise, now distinct and frightening, was definitely not the pitter-patter of a child rushing into her mother's room to snuggle after a bad dream. Quite the opposite, actually, this was positively an intruder's stride: heavy and obtrusive, yet stealthy.

The house was pitch dark, and since everything seems different late at night, Donna's fear was magnified. Every sound was augmented and sustained. That internal filter between fear and reality, generally always there and functioning, was still sleeping. Alone in the house

1

with her children, the comforting sound of crickets, and the late summer breeze outside the window, the last thing Donna wanted to hear were footsteps coming up the stairs toward her bedroom—and now it was too late to do anything about it.

Acclimating herself to her surroundings, Donna realized that someone was now quickly moving around the front of her bed.

Donna hadn't been sleeping well earlier. Her husband, John, was away for the weekend at a friend's wedding in Colorado. She would have gone with him had it not been for a business partner's wife who gave birth that week. Donna had spent some time on September 10 at the hospital, smiling, laughing, and holding the ten-pound newborn in her arms. What a wonderful moment and testimony to God's grace. Everyone was so happy. The talcum-fresh, clean smell and swollen redness of a newborn, gurgling and twisting her small balled-up fist in her mouth—it reminded everyone how such natural, everyday miracles can bring so much joy to life.

Now, merely hours later: an unfolding nightmare. It was the first time in twelve years of marriage that John and Donna had been apart. She was alone in a small community—the Overlook section of Waterbury, Connecticut—inside a big house. Her five- and seven-year-olds were sound asleep in their rooms down the same second-floor hallway. Donna had no weapon. No way to protect herself. No idea what to do.

It took a moment for Donna to register what now happened so suddenly. She had been sleeping on her stomach and did not have the opportunity to turn over before he was on her back, violently holding her down, the two of them struggling for position, man against woman—not a fair fight.

The random thoughts that popped into her head when she found herself fighting to survive baffle her to this day: *Blue jean material . . .* During the struggle she felt the scratchy crisscross-patterned fabric of denim. She kept thinking: *He's wearing blue jeans. If you live through this, remember that.*

She glimpsed some sort of mask concealing his identity, although she would not have been able to see him clearly in the dark anyway.

Instinct and reaction took over. Donna screamed as loud as she could. Her window was open. Maybe a neighbor would hear and come running to her rescue.

But her attacker buried his knee deeper into her back, then reached around and put his gloved hand over her mouth. Donna could smell the fabric: greasy, synthetic, musty.

She bit down on his hand.

That set him off. He took one of her arms and cranked it around her back, wrenching it up toward her long, full, curly mane of auburn hair, holding her down even tighter. Then he leaned over Donna's back and approached her ear. It would be the first of several times he threatened her life.

"If you don't cooperate, you are going to get hurt."

His voice was raspy. She first thought he had a Jamaican accent. Regardless, she believed him and knew then what he wanted.

If I scream again, my kids will wake up and find us . . . Then what?

Obedience. Obey and live. Fight and die.

Donna's senses ratcheted up. She couldn't see, but she could certainly hear, smell. This is how she would later recall the sexual assault—through a series of sounds and scents. Like a blind person, Donna began to see with her ears and nose.

She heard him reach into the dresser drawer beside her bed (as if he knew where to look?) and pull something out. Next he placed a pillowcase over her head and secured it by tying nylons over her eyes like a blindfold. He bound her hands behind her back with the same material. She figured the nylons were the reason for his reaching into the dresser drawer.

After he finished tying Donna's hands behind her back, he jammed his knee into her spine again to hold her down. Donna could smell mechanic's grease and oil on him. Maybe it was tar, she considered, the same stuff they use on the roads. These simple, everyday smells were overpowering, stagnant in the balminess of her bedroom. Later those same odors would send Donna into traumatic spells of depression and anxiety whenever she encountered them in the world.

As he held her down, she felt a forceful tug on her nightshirt and panties, and then heard the fabric tearing as he cut her panties with a knife. The ripping of the fabric seemed amplified.

Then she heard a heavy clank: metal against wood.

In her mind, Donna Palomba saw her attacker placing a gun on the floor.

My husband, John, and I were married on October 10, 1981. It was one of those large Italian-Catholic weddings with bridesmaids, ushers, tuxedoes, limos, a simple, elegant gown made of satin in an off-white candlelight shade, along with all the other amenities little girls dream about all their lives. I was a twenty-four-year-old college graduate from Southern Connecticut State University looking to start a family and a career in marketing. We lived in an apartment that first year. Then John found a house he'd had his eye on for a long time a mere block from where he had grown up in Overlook, a section of Waterbury named for its commanding view over the city. John's parents still lived there, as did his friends, cousins, several of his siblings. There was a pond a few blocks away where kids played hockey during the winter months and fished during summer. Overlook was one of those Norman Rockwell–type of blue- and white-collar neighborhoods centered on family, community, and God—a melting pot of many different nationalities, most with large families. John knew and loved everyone. His mom used to say John was the only kid she knew with three hundred close personal friends.

The neighborhood was so tight-knit that even as John and his buddies matured and went out into the world as adults, they kept

their ties and got together any chance they could. The words family *and* friend *meant something to these guys. They depended on one
another. Everyone in Overlook seemed to carry on the traditions of
the family business, be it insurance, roofing, financial, construction,
electrical, whatever. Your grandfather started the business, passed
it down to your father, and you carried the torch until your son or
daughter took over.*

*The fact that we had kids within the first few years of the marriage kindled our spirits; we enjoyed and adored being parents, same
as our fathers and mothers had before us. Our kids would go to Catholic school, same as we had, and grow up being coddled, loved, cared
for. Having kids was a gift I had waited for all my life, yet I never
realized or considered how much that experience was going to change
me and teach me about love and the will to survive.*

~~

Believing her attacker had a gun, which he had just placed on the floor
beside the bed so he could free himself up to rape her, sent Donna to
an emotional place she had never been: a cage of survival and mortality. She was now only *mother*, protecting her kids, telling herself not to
scream or make any noise whatsoever.

She thought, *I will give this man what he wants. God willing, I will
walk away with my life.*

"As long as the children remained asleep," Donna recalled, "and
I could convince him to leave afterwards, I felt I could come back. I
could heal. This man was going to rape me. There was nothing I could
do to stop him. The only possible silver lining holding me together was
the basic maternal instinct to protect my children and live through this
for their sake."

"Please, take anything you want," she pleaded with her attacker.
"My diamond is on the dresser. My pocketbook is in the closet. Take
my money . . . please . . . please. Just *don't* hurt me."

Without saying a word, he tied another pair of nylons around her mouth. She was totally incapacitated at this point, bound and gagged.

The thought she had at that exact moment stung all her senses: *How can I survive this? How am I going to convince this man that it is okay to rape me and leave without harming my children?*

For the next several minutes he sexually assaulted her.

When she believed he was finished, Donna spoke through the nylons covering her mouth. She realized later that "God had placed the words in her mind." Looking back, going through every moment of that night, she had no idea where else they could have come from. Donna simply opened her mouth, and the words were there: "Please . . . it's okay. This is between you and me. I will never tell anyone what happened here tonight. I don't know who you are. I know you're a good person. I sense that from you. I'm okay. I couldn't even identify you if I wanted to."

Words were all she had left.

From him, however, utter silence.

Her heart pounded with anxiety. Without warning he placed the barrel of his gun up to Donna's mouth through the pillowcase. The steel was hard on her teeth. With the chamber of the pistol butted up against her lips, Donna and her attacker were at an impasse. This moment—when she believed he was going to fire that weapon into her mouth and blow the back of her head against the wall—made Donna's mind burn as though on fire, a throbbing that grew as she waited for the end of her life.

~ ~

I could feel the anticipation of death growing, a slow and agonizing approach. It was paralyzing. He was finished with what he had come for. He didn't need me any longer. I expected death to be quick and painless, though the fear of not knowing when made me shiver and sweat. This is it . . . I'm thirty-six years old, and I am going to die. My kids are going to wake up and find my bloodied body on this bed.

I needed to prepare myself for death.

◄──►

After he took the barrel of the gun away from the area near Donna's mouth, she spoke again: "Please, God, absolve me of all my sins." The words came out shaky but swift. Donna desperately wanted to, but could not, cross herself, as she would when walking into a Catholic church, dipping a finger in the holy water font.

Her attacker had other plans. Without warning he placed the gun against her left temple. Then he snarled, "If you call the pigs, I will come back here and *kill* you."

It was the first time Donna believed she might survive.

Later Donna said that at this point she felt she needed to "*will*" him down the stairs and out of her house. "That sounds crazy, I know," she would later say. "But it had worked so far. I was disoriented, however. I had no idea where he was at any given moment. He was off the bed—that much I knew."

Yet something told her he was still standing at her bedside, staring, his gun pointed at her head, debating whether to pull the trigger or flee the scene. What could she say to this man who had just raped and threatened to kill her that would comfort him enough to leave?

"Thank you. Thank you. Thank you for not hurting me," Donna said, certain again that the words were not her own. "I promise I won't tell anyone."

She was sure the words sounded too desperate, shallow.

The most horrifying period of silence she would ever know settled over the room. Just silence and the subtle hum of the house pulsating and the whisper of the New England night outside her open window.

As Donna considered her options, and perhaps again prepared for death, she heard something.

7

Footsteps.

This time they headed down the stairs.

Then the front door of her house whined open.

He's leaving, she thought.

An immense sense of gratitude washed over Donna. A moment ago she had believed death was her destiny. But she had survived.

The kids?

The front door shut. He was out of the house. Donna was overcome with a sense of relief, yes, but more than anything, *gratitude*.

◄━ ━►

This man had allowed me to live. This was all I needed. I could overcome the rape and heal. I had my life, which was enough to convince me that I had decades ahead of me to live. Minutes before, I didn't think I was going to have a life. What will I do with this life now? I was transformed then and there. Every day, I knew, would be a gift I could not ignore.

Quickly I broke free from the nylons by stretching and slipping one hand out, leaving them on the other hand like a wristband. I pulled down the nylons covering my eyes and my mouth over the top of the pillowcase and let them slip onto my neck like a handkerchief or scarf. Only then was I able to take the pillowcase off my head.

I ran down the hall to check on the kids.

They were both still sound asleep. I knelt down beside my daughter's bed as her boney chest moved slowly up and down—a metronome to the faint whistle coming from her nose. I dropped my head, closed my eyes, sobbed, and thanked God my children were untouched.

I wondered if he was outside, waiting to see what I was going to do. I needed to call for help.

Family, I thought. Call someone from the family . . . he told you not to call the police.

Donna went back to her bedroom and picked up the telephone.

No dial tone.

She rushed downstairs.

The phone line in the kitchen, like the one upstairs in Donna's room—the only two phone lines in the house—was also out of service.

In an age without cell phones, Donna felt trapped inside her house with her kids, with no way to communicate with the outside world and no idea if her attacker was outside waiting for her to emerge.

Chapter Two

Blindfolded

DONNA HAD BEEN BOUND, GAGGED, AND SEXUALLY ASSAULTED. A GUN had been placed to her mouth by her attacker, but she had somehow talked him out of killing her. Throughout the entire ordeal, Donna's children slept like angels just down the hallway. Now, though, she was downstairs in that same house, roaming around, certainly in shock, her adrenaline pumping, finally realizing that the phone lines to the house had been cut. She had no way to call out. Her attacker, Donna thought, could be just outside the door, maybe reconsidering having left her alive.

What now?

There was only one thing Donna felt she could do: run like hell out of the house to a neighbor's. After contemplating her options for about ten minutes, Donna slipped into a bathrobe, checked on the kids one last time (they were still sleeping), locked the door behind her, and took off.

Running west on Leffingwell Avenue, Donna stopped at the first house with lights on. It was the home of her husband John's third cousin, Cliff Warner, a man Donna knew only in passing, a friendly hello in the neighborhood.

Donna banged as loudly as she could on Cliff's back door while peering into the house, trying to spot someone.

"Come on . . . someone answer," she whispered.

Overwhelming anxiety. There she stood on Cliff's back porch, knowing that her sleeping children were home alone (five houses away) while her attacker was on the loose. Donna kept looking back toward her house, that chilling warning he had given her echoing . . .

If you call the pigs, I will kill you.

Donna later said that Cliff came to the door, recognized her, took one look, and immediately knew something was wrong.

Donna explained the situation as best as she could: "Someone broke in . . . attacked me . . . I was raped. My God, the kids, Cliff. The kids are still there."

Donna ran into the house behind Cliff as he picked up the phone and dialed 911.

"I'm calling from 500 Farmington Avenue," Cliff said hurriedly after a dispatcher from the Waterbury Police Department (WPD) answered. (In Waterbury 911 calls went directly to the police department.) "We have an assault—a sexual assault, on Leffingwell Ave, um . . ."

In the background Donna yelled, "A burglary!"

The dispatcher asked where the sexual assault had taken place.

Cliff didn't know Donna's address off the top of his head. His voice was broken. He sounded nervous, shaken.

Donna grabbed the telephone from Cliff's hand: "I'm the victim . . ." She came across as fairly calm at first—maybe even in control. But she had been frightened to her core, unsure whether she was even doing the right thing by talking to the police. She added, "Listen, he told me if I called the police he would be back to kill me. He cut my phone lines, so I'm at a neighbor's. My children are okay, but they're in the house by themselves."

The mere mention of her children sent Donna into hysterical crying.

"Where?" dispatch asked.

Donna gave her address.

Dispatch asked her to spell out the name of her street.

She did that, adding, "But please . . . he told me—"

Dispatch interrupted, "What apartment?"

"What?"

"*What* apartment?"

"...It's a home."

"Okay. How old are the kids?"

"Seven and five." By now Donna sounded as though she was out of breath. She was hyperventilating. Her voice carried one message: Get someone over there to protect her children, fast.

"Seven and five?" dispatch confirmed.

"Please, I don't want to leave them alone ... what ... *what* should I do?"

"Okay," dispatch said. "You were sexually assaulted?"

Donna was speaking so fast—in a manic state of panic—it was hard to follow, but she said quite clearly at one point: "It was an attempted rape ... and ... and ... he burgled ... I don't even care ... I just want my children safe from him."

Why "attempted rape," and not "he raped me," would become an issue in the months that followed. Later Donna explained the rationale behind the ostensibly odd choice of words: "I believe part of the reason is because he prematurely ejaculated even though he penetrated me with a finger, and the other part is probably because I couldn't bring myself to say or believe that I had been raped at that point." And indeed, coming up with the correct words—*any* coherent words, for that matter—or an explanation for what had just taken place would have been nearly impossible for anyone in this same situation.

"Can you meet the police outside [your home]?" dispatch asked.

"Is George Lescadre in?" Donna asked. This seemed like a strange request to the dispatcher. But George, a detective with the WPD, was a family friend. Donna was desperate to speak to someone she knew; she felt the urgency she'd hoped to convey wasn't getting through to the dispatcher. She was terrified her attacker would go back to her home and harm her children. She didn't know what else to do. Getting George on the line seemed like the best idea at the time.

"George Lescadre . . . I . . . I really don't know him," the dispatcher said.

"He's a detective!" Donna said, breathing heavily into the phone.

"Okay, can you hold on, ma'am?"

"Yes."

There was a long pause. Lots of beeping and static.

Donna waited. A minute went by. To Donna it felt like forever.

"Hi, I'm Sergeant Rinaldi, can I help you?" a man's voice said.

Meanwhile, Cliff Warner, the neighbor, emerged from his basement with an ax. As Donna repeated her request to Sergeant Rinaldi, Cliff signaled to her that he was heading up to the house with the ax to protect the kids and wait for the police.

"No, he's not working now," Rinaldi said.

"All right, listen," Donna explained. "I've just been attempted raped and burglarized . . ." She repeated her address and explained why she was at Cliff's, with as calm a tone as she could muster, hoping Rinaldi would take her seriously, adding, ". . . my children are home sleeping. I wanted to have . . . I don't know what to do. The gentleman that did this said . . ."

Rinaldi cut her off, asking, "Do you *know* him?"

Gentleman was perhaps a strange way to refer to a man who had just brutally raped Donna and threatened her life, but she was in a state of pure panic. She really had no idea what words she was using—they were just coming from a hyperactive, fevered mind.

"What?" Donna asked.

"Do you *know* the guy?"

"No, I don't know him at all. He covered my head. Thank God he left me alive. He just said that if I killed . . . if I called the cops he would kill me, and I am very afraid."

"Listen to me," Rinaldi said, trying to take control of the conversation. "The kids are in the house?"

"Yes!" Donna answered.

"Okay. You stay on the line with me, okay? I'm going to dispatch—"

Donna interrupted him. She sounded terrified and desperate, crying out in between her words: "But listen . . . he told me that if I called the cops . . . he would kill me . . . I don't want to—"

"He cannot *kill* you. You're not there, are you?"

"No," Donna said through her tears.

"Well, aren't you concerned about your kids?" Rinaldi asked, again trying to keep Donna focused.

"Of course I am."

~~

I had always lived my life a certain way. My devout Catholic upbringing and resilient faith had gotten me through every possible interruption and hardship: death in the family, argument with my husband, other traumatic moments. I didn't know it then, but the night of September 11, 1993, was going to erase my identity. I became a Jane Doe the moment I stepped out of my Leffingwell Avenue house. Still, after being raped, escaping death, and having my life and my children's lives threatened, I believed in the depth of my soul that the worst part of my nightmare was over. My attacker, I thought, had left the house and disappeared into the darkness of the night. I thought that after this 911 call ended, the police would come, begin an investigation, and ultimately find him. I would initiate the process of healing—all while being grateful for the second chance at life that God had given me.

My home had always been one of a few places I considered a safe harbor; somewhere to hide from what could be a dangerous, evil world, a carefree dwelling, essentially, protecting my family from what at times could be a dysfunctional culture filled with monsters. That all changed on this night. In fact, the local WPD, which I had previously measured on a similar scale of safety, became a space I would despise more than anything, each subsequent visit prompting an emotional reaction I did not think even existed inside me.

I had no idea, obviously, that nearly fifteen years would pass—the worst of my ordeal ahead of me—before I would be able to reclaim my identity and take back my life from the police and my attacker.

The idea that her kids were not her main concern as she spoke to the WPD rattled Donna. What was Rinaldi implying with that last question? Did he think that she had left her children alone because she was worried only about herself?

Rinaldi told Donna to remain calm. He said he was going to get "some police" dispatched to her house immediately. He asked again for the address. Then, strangely enough, the officer said, "You're sure, you're *sure* you live in this house?"

"Yes."

Rinaldi told her to stay put. "Hang on a second."

There was a pause. Donna's labored and heavy breathing took over the dead air space. She was hyperventilating again.

A minute or more went by. Rinaldi came back. "Okay, ma'am . . . we got some officers going to your house right now."

"Yes," she said. "Should I meet them there? I'm down the street. I locked the door. The guy's out of the house. He's gone."

Rinaldi was speaking to someone in the background, repeating certain details Donna was giving him. Then, addressing her, he said, "Okay, stay where you are. There's nothing you can do right now . . ." There was a pause. Then: "You don't know this gentleman—he just *came* into your house?"

"I couldn't get a look at him. He came in while I was sleeping, and he put a thing over my head."

"You don't know if he was white, black, or anything?"

"He smelled like grease . . . I don't know if he was black. He had kind of a black accent," she added. "That's very vague. I wouldn't be able to tell. My main concern is my children."

"Okay."

"I begged and pleaded for my life, and he was kind," Donna said, surprising herself with her use of the word *kind*.

They spoke about addresses and doors being locked. Then Rinaldi explained that an officer was on the way to pick her up at Cliff's.

"Don't change your clothes or anything," Rinaldi advised. Important evidence, the officer suggested, could be on her person and clothing.

"I'm all ripped," Donna said, referring to her attacker cutting her clothing.

"Listen," Rinaldi said, "don't *wash*."

"I know."

"Try to stay calm. There's nothing you can do."

"I just want my children safe."

Rinaldi promised Donna that they were working on getting the children.

Donna was beginning to lose total control of her emotions. She had kept things in check for quite a while, but now Rinaldi was losing her. In tears, she said, "This is the most frightening thing I've ever . . . I'm just so grateful—I cannot tell you—that he left me alive."

"That's the main thing . . ." Rinaldi agreed.

For the next several minutes, Donna and Rinaldi talked about what had happened inside her bedroom. Donna explained why she believed her assailant had a gun—the sounds of metal and the fact that he had pressed what she thought was the barrel against her lips and to her temple. As soon as Donna said something important, Rinaldi repeated it to someone else in the room with him. Donna kept saying, "Oh, God . . . I cannot believe it . . ."

Interrupting, Rinaldi told her that an officer had arrived at her house.

"Are my kids okay?" Donna asked excitedly.

Rinaldi said the cruiser had just pulled up; no one was inside the house yet.

Donna asked that they not enter the house without her there. She was firm: "Don't scare the children!" She also warned Rinaldi that there would be a guy standing in the yard with an ax, but he was not the perpetrator. He was there to protect the children. "Don't hurt him."

This got Rinaldi's attention: "Pardon?"

She explained what Cliff was doing up at the house. Rinaldi understood and relayed the information.

Some time went by, and Rinaldi continued to comfort Donna, telling her that their main concern was getting the children into a safe environment.

Donna was eager to get out of Cliff's house and up to her home. She wanted to be there when the children woke up.

"The best thing you can do right now is give me as much information as you can," Rinaldi said. The information regarding her attacker was fresh in Donna's mind. Looking back later, she assumed the WPD wanted to get the details from her so they could begin to search the area for the man who had attacked her.

Rinaldi asked Donna if she knew which way her attacker went when he left the house.

"No . . . out the front door, I believe." Donna was crying now, again losing her composure. She sensed the impact this incident was going to have. The gravity of the situation was beginning to make sense to her. The thought that her kids were almost in the arms of safety was overwhelming. She was waiting to hear that the police were inside her home, protecting them.

"Do you know which way he went down?"

"My . . . my eyes were blindfolded. It took me a while to work them off."

"Are you positive that he left the house?"

"Yes." Donna said. She had heard him walk down the stairs and shut the door.

"He cut the phone lines?" Rinaldi asked.

"Yes."

"How do you *know* he cut the phone lines?"

She explained how she couldn't make any calls. The line was dead. It made sense that he cut the line. That's why she left the house.

At this point Donna saw a police officer at the back door of Cliff's house. "The police are here," she said to Rinaldi. Then, to the officer that entered Cliff's kitchen: "I am the victim."

Donna handed the phone to the responding officer, saying, "My children. I need to get my children."

"Yes," he said to Donna, then, addressing Rinaldi, "Hello?"

"Is she all tied up?" Rinaldi asked the responding officer. There was a problem with the connection. "Is she all ripped up?" Rinaldi asked again after getting no response.

"Yeah," the officer said.

After a few words: "This sounds real serious," Rinaldi said.

"I know it is."

Rinaldi explained that the kids were still in the house up the street.

"I'm going to get the key from her and head up there," the responding officer said.

"Okay."

They hung up.

CHAPTER THREE

Jam Sandwich

DONNA WAS IN SHOCK. THE PRESENCE OF THE POLICE, LIGHTS FLASHING, radios squelching, the entire neighborhood, it seemed, waking up in the middle of the night, amplified the event, made it all too real. She was crying now without realizing it, wandering around Cliff's house in a daze, wondering what was going on at her house and if her children were safe. Had the police woken them up and frightened them?

The responding officer hung up with Sergeant Rinaldi and asked Donna for the key to her house. They needed to get in.

She handed the officer the key and followed him as he walked toward the door to leave.

"Listen," he said, "you have to stay here . . . and don't remove any of that," pointing to the nylons on her neck and wrist.

Donna wondered why she had to stay behind—alone. But she did as she was told. Within a few moments the officer pulled out of Cliff's driveway and sped off, en route to her house.

Donna was now by herself at Cliff's house. Why hadn't they brought a second officer to stay with her? It didn't make sense.

She walked back inside and called her cousin. The one person she did not want to call was John. He was in Colorado. Sleeping. What could he do? In a day without cell phones, to notify John, Donna would have to phone the hotel and ask the desk clerk to wake him up and tell him there was an emergency back home. News like that would only spread the anxiety and fear she felt to Colorado and ruin

John's flight home. He would be home later the next day. She could tell him then.

"I'll be right there!" Donna's cousin, Nick Gugliotti, said. Nick lived in Watertown, a neighboring city only minutes away.

The separation anxiety I felt as I waited at Cliff's grew with each passing moment. I had no idea what was going on at my house, or if the police had woken my kids up. I wanted to see and hold my kids. There were all these people—the police, Nick (my cousin), Cliff, even my neighbors—waking up, arriving at my house, and I am at another location. With that playing in my mind, along with the trauma of having just been raped, feeling a sense of urgency, and not knowing where my attacker was, I felt like I could no longer stay at Cliff's house. So I made a decision.

Inside Cliff's kitchen, unfamiliar with the layout or where Cliff and his family kept things, Donna frantically searched through cabinet drawers for a knife. If she was going to run back to her house, she was not going to do it without having something to protect herself with. She was certain he was out there, watching her, now upset that she had involved the police when he had given her specific directions not to.

Arming herself with the "biggest knife" she "could find in the drawer," Donna ran the five houses back to her home. Approaching the yard, she could see people mingling, neighbors looking out their windows. Police lights. The front door wide open. All this activity gave her a fleeting sense of relief that she was safe. But still, the children. Were they okay? Were they waking up wondering where she was?

A police officer approached Donna as she walked up to the front door. She asked him where her kids were.

"I need to take that knife, ma'am," he said.

Donna's mother- and brother-in-law, who lived nearby, had just received a call from Nick, who had explained what was happening. Now they walked up and hugged Donna.

Within a few moments, Donna was inside, running up the stairs to check on her kids.

Remarkably, the kids were still sleeping.

The house filled with people and Donna calmed down, if only slightly. She felt less threatened. Police were now inside her house, going up and down the stairs, sizing up a crime scene that had grown crowded, even bustling. Meanwhile, friends and family consoled Donna.

"We checked the inside and outside of the residence," noted a report written by the WPD about this crucial period of the night, "and did not find anything but the victim's kids sound asleep in their bedrooms upstairs . . ."

Describing Donna arriving at the scene, the report noted that she "appeared to be a little upset and had a knife in her right hand . . ."

One of the first things Donna told police when she arrived, in describing her attack, was that she "might have heard" a noise "coming from one of the closets and then spotted a shadow." She then described the attack in detail. In the police report the WPD said she "did not appear to have any marks . . ." Donna described her attacker as having a "Jamaican accent." She said he "smelled of oil." He "cut her panties, then tried to rape her, but couldn't for some reason, then left the scene . . ." Even more interesting, when placed within the context of Donna's ensuing case and how the next few weeks would play out, was the report's description of Donna's bedroom, the scene of the attack: ". . . Palomba's pocketbook, wallet . . . were neatly on her bed. Residence appeared to be very neat."

Upstairs, inside Donna's bedroom, according to the report, a pair of officers collected "2 floral pattern pillow cases, 1 silver earring, gold earrings, 2 pearl necklass [sic], 1 silver heart pendant . . . 1 black panty, torn . . . 1 grey sweatshirt with writing . . ." which were all, the report added, "turned in as evidence."

Police also took the panty hose that were tied around Donna's neck and wrist, but not the clothing she was wearing. They confiscated more jewelry downstairs, "sheets, cases . . . ," and also a "bat" (as in baseball), which they found on a chair in the living room.

On that night, not one neighbor was interviewed by the police. The neighborhood itself was not canvassed for Donna's assailant. Besides those obvious items the police collected, the house was not cordoned off with yellow police tape and processed. Most important, there was no record of the WPD's CSI unit being called in to fingerprint and photograph the house, or to search and collect trace evidence from inside or outside the house or from Donna's body that night. Those procedures are part of crime-scene 101, regardless of circumstances. It was as if this was the first time an event of this nature had occurred for the WPD, and they were unprepared to deal with it. Why weren't officers out scouring the neighborhood for an alleged rapist who had tied Donna up, brutally assaulted her, and threatened her life?

"Looking back," Donna said later, "I just don't think they knew what they were supposed to do."

Donna was in a daze for the next twenty-four hours. She was saying and doing things out of the norm, but it was behavior that should have been expected from a victim of a sexual assault. When Nick had arrived earlier with his wife, Dawn, he was amazed when he first saw Donna.

"When I got there," Nick said later, "the image that comes to mind when I think of what Donna looked like is a scarecrow. Donna was standing in the doorway, her arms stretched out, those nylons hanging from her wrists and her neck . . . It was a bizarre picture to see someone you love standing there that way: pale as could be and shuttering."

Nick wanted to hug Donna, but he was told he could not because such contact could transfer evidence.

"I saw a beautiful young lady that looked terrorized," Nick added. "One of the things, however, that was literally bungled by the police was that they allowed me to go through the house without stopping me."

For Nick, to see his business partner, his friend, a family member, torn apart by an unspeakable crime, was gut-wrenching. Nick idolized Donna in many ways.

"She is an exceptional, unique individual," Nick said later. "I've known her since she was a baby. We grew up together. We were in business together. So I've seen her just about every single day of her life. She is the epitome of a lady. Respected by our clients. No one in our family expected Donna to be anything but honest—she's always been kind to a fault. So what was torturous to me was to later see what happened to Donna in the weeks after, as the police got hold of her. What they would say about Donna was so contrary to who Donna is and her life's experience."

While at the house, Nick said he walked upstairs to check on the kids. Then he went from room to room, looking at windows, inside closets, all over, to see if anything stood out to him. He was curious to find out how the intruder had entered the house.

As the police finished at the scene, a female officer suggested to Donna that she go to the emergency room for treatment. "I believe," Donna recalled, "one officer might have asked to take me, but I wanted to go with Nick."

"She didn't even want to go at first—she was obviously in shock and couldn't make decisions," Nick recalled later.

Despite everything that had occurred, there seemed to be no frantic hurry to get Donna to the hospital. But by about 2:30 in the morning of September 11, 1993, Donna's eye was swollen, throbbing badly, and tearing up. She felt as though her attacker might have scratched the actual eyeball. While she hadn't been beaten, her wrists had ligature marks where the nylons had been tied by her attacker. Her emotional state was deteriorating rapidly as the morning progressed. As she absorbed more and more of what had happened, the idea of being a rape victim began to consume Donna. Granted, she was grateful to be alive and even touched with gratitude toward her attacker for allowing her and her children to live. But the violence and her suffering during the ordeal were now overriding everything else as she wandered about the scene of the crime. She was starting to think in terms of . . . *I was raped during a home invasion. I'm a rape victim.* The totality of the night hit Donna as she prepared to go to the hospital after her cousin Nick and his wife Dawn offered to take her.

"You know, you really should go," the female police officer advised.

"I know," Donna said. "But my kids. I don't want them to wake up and be scared. I'm worried about the kids."

After some time spent debating what to do, it was decided that Cliff and Donna's brother-in-law would carry the children down the street to Donna's mother-in-law. They would be safe there.

This female officer, Donna later said, also told her to make sure she asked the hospital to conduct a sexual assault examination.

Ultimately this advice would change the entire investigation.

—◦—

This place I called home, Waterbury, Connecticut, was a community of wonderful people, close, always willing to help one another. I grew up in the north end until I was about six or seven, and then we moved to the west end. My family was super tight, both sides 100 percent Italian. My mother was born in Italy. She came over when she was five years old and met her father for the first time. Life revolved around family. Sundays were always at my grandparents, where I learned about hope, faith, and perseverance at an early age. They had a grape vine. They crushed the grapes, made wine. My noni would make bread, pasta, and sauce from tomatoes we grew and harvested. They had a three-family house with a big garden in the back. The whole family lived in the house. We lived just up the street, my mother, father, my sister, Maria, and I. Life was all about family and food—the great Italian culture. My grandfather, Nonno, emigrated from Italy to America in 1924 at age twenty-three, leaving behind his young bride, who was pregnant with their first child. He came here to make a better life for his family, and finally by 1936 he had saved enough money to bring [everyone] over.

After John and I met in college and married, life became that same Italian cliché of family, family, family. We had kids and lived among all our siblings and relatives in what was a town then centered on community. John's family, the Palombas, were quite well-known in town. Whereas we, the Cappellas, came from north of town, the Palombas lived in Overlook, which was a more prestigious area. John grew up with five siblings—two sisters, three brothers. You can look at a photo of them when they were all young kids and, with mom and dad, they truly look like the all-American family. Fred Palomba, John's father, was a Fordham graduate; he worked for Army Intelligence as well as owning multiple businesses. My father-in-law was even mayor of Waterbury (1965–68) until he had a heart attack. The four boys worked in—you guessed it—the family business: insurance.

As we began our own life together, John worked as an insurance inspector in the family business while I worked at various marketing jobs, including one at the Republican-American *newspaper in the advertising display department. We had the life. Love. Children. House. Great families. The community. The American dream, really.*

—〰—

Under the fluorescent lights of Waterbury Hospital's emergency room hallway, it was clear to Nick and his wife that Donna had sustained serious injuries. She had not yet washed or changed her clothes. By now her eye was not only throbbing, but almost totally closed. There was no reason for Donna to imagine that the police were not systematically searching the neighborhood and the town for her assailant. When she left the house with Nick and Dawn, escorted to the hospital by a single police cruiser, Donna thought that additional law enforcement would take over and process the scene. She believed that everything within the WPD's power was being done to make sure the man who had attacked her would eventually be brought to justice.

Donna was led into an examination room. The nurses explained that they would be taking a sexual assault kit from her. This entailed fingernail scrapings, swabs from her vagina, blood samples, head and pubic area combing, a saliva sample, a nasal mucus swab, and several additional and invasive—but important—procedures.

"My eye," Donna said to the nurse. "It's my eye that is really hurting me."

"Ma'am, I'm sorry, but we have to do evidence collection for a sexual assault kit first."

As they completed the kit, it seemed to Donna that "it took forever."

What became obvious as she was being checked out was how badly her wrists had been marked up by her twisting out of the nylon restraints. And it turned out that Donna had suffered a scratched cornea and her eye needed to be patched up. It would be some time before the swelling went down and the pain went away.

Police came in, took all of Donna's clothing, and placed it in a paper bag.

"Please come down to the police station when you're ready," an officer requested, "and give us a voluntary statement."

She agreed to the WPD visit, but her mind was wandering. Just hours before she found herself sitting in the ER being poked and prodded, now a victim of a brutal crime, she had been in this same hospital visiting her friend and celebrating the new life her friend had brought into the world. The juxtaposition of good and evil was overwhelming as Donna sat, staring at the police officer talking to her, Dawn and Nick beside her for support, and the business of the

ER going on around her. It was all a blur, really, life happening in slow motion.

"The birth of my friend's baby was the reason why I wasn't in Colorado with my husband," Donna said later. "I stayed behind because the baby was supposed to be born. I had experienced God's miraculous power of life and the terrible evil in the world all within a twenty-four-hour period."

And what an innocent night it had been before the home invasion and rape. Donna believed she'd done everything right.

I remember the children and I making only one trip from the car (something John had always told me to do when I was alone so I would not go back out) into the house when we arrived home. The kids had their book bags. I had my briefcase from work and a change of clothes, leftover pizza from Pizza Hut. We all did our part in carrying everything and making it in one trip, just as John had said.

Funny thing, I also remember that we bought a cassette of the music from "Jam Sandwich," the children's concert we were at earlier that evening at Judson School in Watertown. The kids loved it, and truth be told, so did I. We popped the cassette in on the way home, and I remember the kids and I singing the entire way. When we left the car to walk into the house, we sang one of the songs, "Tra la la the Fracasaur," a story about a dinosaur. I was very aware it was dark and John wasn't with us, and singing the song put us all at ease. I still have that cassette somewhere.

Waiting in the hallway of the ER for a preliminary report of the sexual assault kit (lab results would take weeks), Donna had trouble regaining control of her thoughts. She told herself everything would be okay. She had survived. Her children were safe and with her mother-in-law. She could overcome the emotional hell that was undoubtedly her future. Yet sitting there, not allowed to take a shower, she could still smell this man who had attacked her.

"I stunk," Donna remembered. "All the anxiety and perspiration throughout the night felt so disgusting on me. I could not wait to take a shower."

The first round of medication that Donna was asked to ingest consisted of a massive dose of antibiotics. Her assailant was unknown. He could have the HIV virus that causes AIDS. Or hepatitis. Or any number of other diseases. The best way to combat that, according to the doctors at the hospital, was to load up on antibiotics.

Donna wasn't going to argue.

After a while, the nurse from the ER came out and asked, "Where are you in your menstrual cycle, Mrs. Palomba?"

Donna thought about it. Through tears, she said, "Right in the middle."

"Well, you should consider taking the morning-after pill," the nurse said.

Donna's assailant had left behind several samples of his DNA in the form of semen. She had been under the impression that he had not entered her with his penis, although she knew that he had tried. The sexual assault kit would ultimately determine traces of semen found in several places, including on the vaginal swabs taken in the ER that night.

A practicing Catholic who did not believe in abortion, Donna was torn. She didn't know what to do. The morning-after pill, to her, was an abortion. Yet she was not in the right psychological state of mind to make a decision. It was too much to think about.

"Nick, Dawn," Donna implored, explaining the dilemma to her friends, "what should I do?"

Chapter Four

Turning Tables

Nick and Dawn, part of Donna's extended support system of friends and both passionate, practicing Christians themselves, told Donna the best thing under the circumstances was to take the morning-after pill. She could deal with the moral and religious implications of her decision at a later time.

"Yes," Donna told the nurse.

The last police officer at the hospital reminded Donna that she needed to go down to the WPD at some point when she felt better, to give an official statement. She agreed. The impression Donna had, again, was that the WPD was busy searching for her assailant. She had no idea at the time that little was being done to find the man who had attacked her.

In fact, quite the opposite was going on behind the scenes: Police were beginning to think that Donna had invented the entire home invasion and rape to cover up something she had done.

The red flag, according to officers later, was no evidence of forced entry into Donna's house—no screen cut open, no door busted up, no lock tampered with. Nothing. The question became: How did her perpetrator get inside the house if he did not break in? Had Donna left the door unlocked? Had she let him in herself?

This puzzle would plague Donna for years to come: "I have gone over and over this again in my head," Donna said later. "And I can't imagine leaving the door unlocked. The house was built around 1910, and it was the original door. It locks upon closing, and then there is a second deadbolt lock, which I believe I turned and locked. Again, it was routine. I can't imagine I would not have, particularly when John was away."

What could have been an important clue early in the investigation was overlooked by the WPD. It was never unearthed because police did not interview anyone in Donna's family. Donna's mother-in-law, who lived just down the street, was missing her key to Donna's house.

～～

Donna's parents were at their beach house in Clinton, a Connecticut shoreline town about an hour and fifteen minutes from Waterbury. They had no telephone at the beach house. They had no idea what was going on back home.

The sun was about to rise on September 11, 1993, as Donna left the hospital. Nick and Dawn dropped Donna off at her mother-in-law's, where her kids were still sound asleep. There was no way, Donna said, that she was stepping foot back in her house at this point.

Dawn and Nick headed straight for Clinton to alert Donna's parents.

The first thing Donna wanted to do was take a shower, which she did before lying on the couch, exhausted, the ordeal of the night having sucked the life from her.

Soon after, Nick, Dawn, and Donna's parents arrived, just as the kids woke up. Everyone then drove to Donna's parents' house, where Donna said she would feel more comfortable. The dilemma became: How was Donna going to tell John what had happened once he came home later the next day? There were family members around. John's brothers were there. John was a man's man; he would want to go out and smash somebody's head for hurting his wife, as would Donna's father. Together, John and Donna's father would want to take action.

Throughout the morning of September 11, a Saturday, people stopped by the house as word spread among family members about what had happened. For the kids, shielded from the violent crime, it was like Christmas—all the family gathered around, doughnuts, coffee, sweets, people talking. The only thing missing was the festive spirits. Donna's brother-in-law went over to her house and installed new deadbolt locks on the front and back doors at some point that morning.

Around noon the drugs Donna had taken at the hospital began to affect her. She was vomiting violently, hour after miserable hour, her mother there beside her, holding Donna's hair back as she spent most of her time staring into the toilet. "I could not keep anything down." It was a combination of the morning-after pill and the antibiotics. Donna spent the day in the bathroom. After the vomiting stopped, she decided the family needed to get together and talk about how she was going to break the news to John.

Throughout that day, WPD Detective George Lescadre popped in to Donna's mother's house to see how Donna was doing. George wasn't officially involved in the investigation. He explained, however, that he had gone over to Donna's house earlier that Saturday morning to have a look around. That first time he stepped inside Donna's mother's house and said hello, it appeared to George as though someone had died. Donna's mother, father, and sister were devastated; they had a look of deathly despair. George picked up on this immense feeling of hopelessness coming from everyone but Donna.

"It looks like somebody died around here," George said to his friend. "Donna, you are going to be okay."

"I know . . . I know, George," Donna said. "I'll be fine. You have to talk to them."

George was encouraging and reassuring, telling everyone that in time everything would be fine. He also had no reason not to believe that his colleagues at the WPD were doing everything they could to find Donna's attacker.

That Sunday evening John made it back to Connecticut and drove directly home from the airport. Donna had spoken to him briefly over the phone before he left Colorado, not telling him anything about what had happened, doing her best to hide her emotions. But there was no hiding from it any longer. John was in town.

The first thing Donna's husband noticed were the new deadbolts on the doors; he couldn't get into his own house without knocking. Walking in, putting down his luggage, John worked his way into the kitchen, where everyone was gathered, and he knew immediately that something was wrong. Donna sat at the kitchen table. She wore sunglasses to cover her eyes. That sense of desolation, which George Lescadre had picked up on earlier, infused the air.

"What's going on here?" John asked. He looked around the room. It was odd to John that George Lescadre was there. The police? Family? Donna sitting at the table wearing sunglasses.

"We're all fine, John," Donna began. "But we had a break-in . . ."

"What . . . when?" John looked around at everyone for an answer. "What happened?"

"Friday night. I didn't tell you because you were away and it didn't make sense. The kids are fine. I'm okay, John."

"What did he want?"

Silence.

"What happened, Donna?"

Donna hesitated, then explained. "I was raped, John."

John turned and stormed out of the room. He was angry and confused and mumbling to himself. "I cannot believe this . . . the first time I am away and this happens . . . what the hell!" It was clear he was mad *at himself*. "How could this happen?"

It was important that John process the information in his own way. Donna knew him well enough to understand that he would need time to accept what had happened and return to being the husband he had always been.

"Throughout this time," Donna said later, remembering that Sunday evening when her husband returned and she broke the news to him, "we believe a major investigation is going on behind the scenes. I am confident that I will heal quickly, emotionally and physically. I am grateful to be alive and feel as though God has spared my life for some reason."

There was Donna's gratitude, again, and her knowledge that she would heal. And that John would too. The family would go on and maybe be stronger. Part of that healing, however, included getting Donna's attacker off the street so he could not harm another woman. This concern became a major focus for Donna—the welfare of other women. If this guy had attacked her so brutally, in a way that appeared so calculated and planned, how many other women had he done the same to?

A couple days passed before Donna and John headed down to the WPD so Donna could find out where the investigation was. She had not heard a word from the WPD, but she remembered that the officers on the scene had requested she provide a voluntary statement. There was never any question in her mind that she was going to do exactly what the police had asked her to. Donna had waited the extra days because she needed to see several doctors in the wake of her attack and get rechecked and retested. She also needed to regain her strength and composure. She wanted to feel comfortable and have a somewhat clear head before sitting down and talking about what had happened to her that night.

On Monday I had doctors' appointments, follow-up visits. We went down to the WPD on Tuesday to just reiterate everything we could, to make certain that they had every detail from us. I wanted to make certain I wasn't leaving out anything that might be important. I had gone over the night of the rape in my head again and again. I needed to relay that information to the WPD. John wanted to give them a layout of our house and talk about how my attacker might have gotten in without breaking in. It was hard to fathom, you know . . . that I had been attacked and raped like this. I was still trying to get my head around what was a surreal situation, and accept it. I was thirty-six years old. I had two children. A wonderful husband. A nice home. We both had great jobs. Our world had been shattered overnight, just like that. I thought this was the beginning to a road of healing and forgiveness and justice. Yet that was all about to change as I learned what was happening behind the scenes with the WPD.

⊷⊶

Detective Lou Cote greeted Donna and John as they walked into the WPD. The Waterbury Police had been formed under the supervision of Samuel Warren on July 28, 1853. Warren was the department's first police chief, overseeing twenty-five men on the force at that time. The department went through a multitude of changes throughout the century-plus leading up to the early 1980s, when it began to put its resources into fighting the drug war, which had hit Waterbury hard. By 1990, however, the focus was on computers and how they could help crime fighting efforts. According to its website, the WPD used its first desktop computer "network" in 1990, "allowing for local criminal history record checks, active arrest warrant checks, and the booking of prisoners." Computers were a major aid in criminal cases such as Donna's. They allowed for repeat offenders, for example, to be easily recorded and tracked. "Prior to this time," the department website continued, "police officers working the booking desk would have to record the name of each arrestee, go to the Records Division, and manually check paper-based files to determine if the arrestee had a prior criminal history. The police officer would then have to travel to the second floor and manually check the files of the Detective Bureau to determine if the arrestee had any outstanding local warrants."

Of greater importance to what would transpire in Donna's case over the next decade, in February 1992, after what was a long fight inside the Connecticut Supreme Court, was a ruling handed down concerning the "rank of Detective" within the WPD. Before the Supreme Court ruling, becoming a detective was "a promotion and not an assignment." After the ruling a candidate would be required to take "a competitive civil service examination." As far back as 1902, the gold badge position had been something of an assignment by the superintendent. Thus, "a dispute over the issue ensued between the Board of Police Commissioners and the Superintendent, who wished to maintain the position as an assignment, and the Civil Service Commission and the Police Union, who wished the position to become a permanent rank requiring competitive civil service examinations."

The year 1993, leading up to the day of Donna's attack, had been a busy one for the WPD, with gang-related warfare breaking out in the streets. The major problem was a rift between rival Hispanic gangs, the Latin Kings and the Los Solidos. The WPD had formed a new tactical unit on May 26, 1993, the Gang Task Force.

What did all this mean for Donna Palomba as she and her husband walked into the WPD on September 14, 1993? First, the WPD was certainly able and capable of an investigation such as the one Donna assumed had been initiated moments after her 911 call reporting the home invasion. Furthermore, the experience and technology within the Detective Bureau of the WPD should have been sufficient to solve Donna's case.

It was 3:20 p.m. when Donna and John sat down with Detective Lou Cote inside the WPD. Cote came across as friendly, but also a bit indifferent. He didn't discuss one theory in any more depth than another. He was there to collect information, Donna believed, so that the investigation could move forward. Cote did not mention if the WPD had any suspects or if there was a search ongoing. Cote simply sat Donna down and asked her to give a thorough account of what had happened, beginning when she had arrived home that night.

Donna explained the attack in as much detail as she could. Some of the more revealing sections of the account would give detectives plenty of information to go on—clues, in other words, to help them begin looking for a possible suspect or suspects.

⁂

I was laying [sic] on my stomach and I looked toward the door of my bedroom and I saw the shadow of a body coming into my room and turning toward me. At that point I saw his image lurching toward me, and his head was covered with what appeared to be some type of black mask or something, and he jumped on top of me.

⁂

Donna mentioned gloves made of a "thick type material . . . not leather or rubber." As she talked about the more physical moments of the crime, tears came to her eyes, but she remained strong. One of the important factors about this statement was that Donna's story never wavered or changed. Certain words she chose to use might have differed, but the substance of her account of what had happened stayed the same. Moreover, she gave explicit details regarding what the man smelled like, what he wore, what he said, the type of accent she believed he had, and the fact that she believed he had a gun, which he placed to her mouth and temple.

She concluded the statement by saying that her intruder took a "sterling silver puffed heart on a silver chain . . . that had a noticeable dent on one side of the heart . . . He also took $250 in cash, a full strand of pinky-tinted pearls, and a stone necklace of different colors . . ."

To Donna it felt like a weight had been lifted. She had openly talked about the rape itself, the threats made against her life, her attacker leaving as stealthily as he had appeared. John sat nearby, his arm around his wife, helping her get through it all. Donna was able to articulate the night and not lose total control of her emotions, a major step.

Cote explained that he had purposely misspelled several words as he typed out the report so Donna could circle the words and place her initials near each one. It was a way, Cote said, for the WPD to verify that the statement she had given was under her own free will and exactly what she had wanted to say. By Donna correcting the words and then initialing next to each misspelling, it showed on the document that she was in control of what was being written.

Donna considered the request strange, but she did it. Leaving the WPD, Donna and John had a sense that the case was moving forward.

I was feeling like they were continuing on the case, and they were doing whatever they could to solve it. Detective Cote seemed sincere. Even though John and I believed that Cote didn't come across as the sharpest knife in the drawer, we hoped—and certainly believed then—that he "got it."

Later that same day, Cote and a colleague showed up at Donna and John's Leffingwell Avenue home to have a look around. A one-paragraph report of that visit (three days after the crime occurred) offered what they found: "The scene of a past burglary and larceny and sexual assault. There was no sign of forced entry. [We] processed the scene for latent fingerprints and no identifiable prints were lifted."

The following day Cote and his colleague were back at Donna's house. They met a phone company field supervisor there to look around the outside structure. After locating the telephone line junction box "near ground level," they first photographed the box. In his report Cote documented what he found, writing: "This junction box was a result of the telephone line being cut by the intruder prior to entering the building." Then Cote and his team removed the junction box from the side of the house "in an effort to compare the cut marks with a cutting tool should it be recovered at a later date . . ." The entire structure was "entered as evidence . . ."

This activity was another indication to Donna that the case was getting the attention it deserved, not to mention moving forward. The WPD was working on it—collecting evidence and taking statements. A good sign. Donna felt they were getting somewhere. The fact that they dusted the house for fingerprints three days after the crime seemed strange to John and Donna, but maybe the police knew something they did not.

The initial theory, now being checked out by the WPD, was that a security company employee monitoring homes in the area, or a phone company employee who knew the neighborhood, was responsible. It made sense. The man would have known the layout of the houses in the community, where the phone lines were located, and how to cut the lines. The phone company performed a test for Cote on-site, demonstrating how hard it was to cut the phone line. You'd need a special tool, strong enough to get through a tough outer coating of wire that was manufactured to withstand New England weather.

Furthermore, the more Donna thought about it, the more she suspected that her attacker might have snuck into the house *before* she arrived home from her night out with the kids. Maybe he had hidden inside somewhere until everyone was in bed. Whatever the case, the man who attacked Donna must have known her routine, or even personal aspects of her life. Donna Palomba had been chosen as a target; she was not attacked at random, which could only mean one thing.

Donna knew her attacker.

CHAPTER FIVE

Life Goes On ... But Only for a Moment

DONNA PALOMBA'S GREATEST DESIRE WAS TO GO TO SLEEP ONE NIGHT soon with the consoling feeling that the man who had raped her was behind bars. But weeks after the attack, as she began the process of taking back her life, she realized that wouldn't be the case.

Donna was a successful marketing executive at a small advertising agency that she and two partners had started in 1987. The agency, GP&P, named for Nick Gugliotti (her cousin), Tom Peterson (a friend), and Donna, was the result of a dream and years of hard work.

❧

We had a handful of employees—a couple designers, receptionist, bookkeeper. We were truly like a family. I worked four days a week so I could be home with the kids on Tuesdays, and since I was working part-time and having babies when we formed the agency, I was a minority owner but always hoped one day to be an equal partner (which eventually happened). I remember when Johnny (our son) was born. The agency was young. I felt needed at the office. I came back to work two weeks after Johnny was born and turned my office into a nursery. I took him with me so I could nurse him and be with him.

❧

Now, after her attack, Donna would get counseling. There would be times of tremendous emotional struggle. But this assault was not going to defeat Donna Palomba. Part of the healing process, Donna knew, was getting back into the swing of everyday life right away and leaning on her Catholic faith. She had turned to her religion before in times of celebration and desperation. She knew her love and faith in God could carry her through what would be the toughest period of her life, and it was that inherent trust in God, Donna was convinced, that had been driving her since the very moment her world had been turned upside down.

It was amazing to me when I looked back on it later, that on the night of my attack, this immense feeling of gratitude had come over me. I never felt, Why me? Why did this have to happen? *From the first moment after the attack, I was overcome with a sense of gratefulness like I had never experienced. I was elated to be alive. He put a gun to my mouth and then to my temple. I absolutely believed that I was going to be killed. I did not think I would survive. And my children . . . my goodness, they slept through the entire episode. After I had a moment to stop and realize, okay, my children are fine . . . even as I stood there in my neighbor's kitchen, I knew I would be okay with what happened. The attack would not define who I am. I felt like a survivor, not a victim. This belief, along with my strong faith, would carry me through the worst days of my life, which would lie ahead. I had literally cried out to God that night in my bedroom, asking Him to absolve me of all my sins—because I believed my days in this world were over. Maybe that's why I was able to overcome this with so much gratitude. A family member said something about a week after the crime that I heard about, and it bothered me: "Donna will never be the same . . ." It was the total opposite of how I was feeling. I did not like that someone thought I would not be able to recover. I did not feel guilt. I did not feel shame. I felt free. I felt . . . thankful.*

Donna also had guarded hope that the WPD would someday find her attacker, and that she could stand in front of him, testify, and put the entire incident—at least from a justice standpoint—behind her. Healing would never be complete without that happening.

Yet Donna was well aware that this would not be an easy investigation. DNA was not the master evidentiary key—especially where rape cases were concerned—that it would become in the years that followed. It was one thing to have a DNA sample, but law enforcement needed somebody to compare that DNA to. DNA is only useful when there is another sample to make a comparison.

"I did feel in some respects as though we would find my attacker someday," Donna said later. "But I was also aware of the fact that we did not have much to go on."

At work now, Donna was taking back her life and moving on. It had been two weeks since the attack. As each day passed, she expected to hear something from the WPD about a suspect or any progress being made by investigators. Some sort of an update. Anything.

But no word came.

As the days passed, the memory of her assailant's shadow crept up on Donna, and his words came back to haunt her: *If you call the pigs, I will kill you.* Would he return to finish the job? Was he following her to and from work? Was he someone she saw during the normal course of her day? The guy who sold her coffee? The guy behind the lunch counter? She had even shied away from the WPD because she was scared that he was watching her—*If you call the pigs, I will kill you.*

Then Donna learned of something that had happened on September 9, 1993, two days before her attack. The incident on that day involved Donna's sister, Maria Cappella. Maria had left her apartment in Waterbury to pick up a friend in a neighboring town. As she drove down the street, a car driven by a man, Jeff Martinez,* who worked for a local glass company, approached from the opposite direction. Jeff

---

* Jeff Martinez is a pseudonym.

beeped his horn at Maria and motioned for her to pull over. Maria knew Jeff from years ago; he lived a few streets over and palled around with a group of familiar guys and girls from the neighborhood. She had seen him from time to time around town and always waved a neighborly hello. Her sister Donna had too. These days Jeff was married with kids.

Maria pulled over on the crest of a hill not far from her apartment; Jeff's car pulled in behind her. Jeff walked over to the passenger's side of Maria's car and leaned down.

"Hey," Jeff said through Maria's open window. "I saw Donna's picture in the newspaper!" He seemed excited, adding, "I didn't read the article. I only saw it because I was wrapping newspaper around some glass and there was Donna's picture."

That article, "A Dream Job with Benefits," had been published in the *Republican-American* on August 31, 1993. It was a cover story in a section of the newspaper called "Today's Woman," focusing on local women and their stories of triumph. A head shot of Donna accompanied the article. "Her job in advertising allows her creative juices to flow," read the caption. The photo showed Donna smiling, a happy, attractive, successful businesswoman. A sidebar near the photo listed some information about Donna: married with two children, lives in Waterbury, volunteers at St. Mary's School, and attends Immaculate Conception Church. The body of the piece centered on Donna's accomplishments in the world of advertising. Donna's strong personality and tenacious will came through in every quote. Donna talked about male chauvinism in the workplace and how she had dealt with it over the years. The article gave specific details about Donna's personal life, including certain parts of Donna's and her husband's schedules. One of her coworkers called Donna "Robowoman."

"She's not Superwoman, by any means," the reporter paraphrased Donna's explanation. "When things get rough, she relies on her faith in God."

"Some things seem so overwhelming," Donna told the reporter. "I always try to step back and take a minute to get through the situation."

Maria didn't think too much about her conversation with Jeff on the street until after Donna's assault. She remembered the chat—and especially him mentioning the article—as September turned into October. The thought occurred to Maria—if only subtly then—that perhaps someone—not Jeff, specifically, but *someone*—had read the article about Donna and developed a fascination or obsession with her. Maria explained to Donna what Jeff had said, and they considered that when the time was right, maybe the article would become important to her case. It turned into one more thing Donna had to keep track of as she waited to hear from the WPD regarding any new developments.

So the sisters put it on the back burner.

It would not be the last time Maria saw Jeff Martinez. Nor would it be the last time anyone considered that Donna's attacker was somebody she knew.

—~—

On October 6, 1993, Donna received a call at her office from a Lieutenant Douglas Moran, who explained that he had been on vacation during the time of her attack, but her case had been assigned to him. Moran had an associate's degree in science from Mattatuck Community College. He had studied psychology and sociology at a second community college and had joined the WPD in 1978 after a stint with an ambulance company in town. Moran's reputation within the department was rock solid—no suspensions or even reprimands on his record. He had been a patrol officer from 1978 until 1984, when he was promoted to sergeant. He held that position for about six years until, he later stated under oath, he was "reassigned to Vice and Intelligence" in 1990. Moran claimed to have been involved with "dozens" of sexual assault cases. By 1992 he had worked his way up to lieutenant, in charge of the WPD's Sexual Assault unit.

Moran explained that he was calling to ask Donna if he could come down to her office. He wanted to get caught up on the case and brief her about a few things the department was working on.

"I'm picking up the case from Detective Cote and need to speak with you."

A lieutenant, Donna thought. She was curious and nervous at the same time. Why was a lieutenant getting involved? It must mean something.

"Whatever I can do to help," Donna said.

"The results of the DNA came back," Moran explained at their meeting. "There was a lot of semen recovered. Some pet hair . . . Caucasian hair, and saliva." Moran emphasized how important the evidence would be regarding any "future suspects." Just the fact that the WPD had DNA was a significant piece of the investigation. As soon as they could round up a few suspects, the testing could begin. What's more, the DNA from Donna could be tested against known rapists with records in the system once investigators started looking more closely at potential candidates recently released from prison and offenders living in the area.

The words—*a lot of semen*—made Donna sick to her stomach. She trembled as she flashed back to what had happened that night. It was like a movie playing in her head in strobe-light fragments. At the same time, though, the thought that the WPD had what seemed like plenty of evidence was reassuring. It was clear that the WPD had trace and DNA evidence available, both of which were key factors in solving rapes. Donna and John had never owned pets because of allergies, and yet there was pet hair. This was a positive development, as far as Donna could tell.

A day or so later, Moran called Donna again. He said the WPD had "confirmed" that her "panties had been cut from the back and that one fact . . . had helped to verify" Donna's story.

It was the first time Donna considered that what she had told the police needed verifying. Still, it was good news.

But then Moran questioned the severed phone lines. "I've been to your house," he said, "and I inspected the outside wires . . . They were confusing." What he meant was that he had seen a tangle of various wires all bunched together outside the house. "How would the guy know which ones were the main phone lines to cut?"

Why would Moran ask such a thing—especially of the victim? Donna suspected something was wrong. But she had no idea what Moran was trying to accomplish, or if this was standard procedure.

Days later Moran visited Donna at her office again. He wasn't imposing or overwhelming in any respect, nor was he an overly friendly type of police officer. His "bedside" manner could have used some work, according to Donna, but she was pleased with having a lieutenant take her case, not to mention the recent progress with the DNA evidence.

"I have taken over your case," Moran reiterated after Donna invited him into her office where they could chat. "I just need to get some more details from you."

Donna recalled again what she could. Then she handed Moran the newspaper article Jeff Martinez had mentioned to Maria, saying, "I don't know if it means anything, but this was published two weeks before the assault."

Moran took the article. He didn't say much about it. It appeared to Donna as though he had his mind on other things. Moran thanked Donna and said he'd be in touch.

On or about October 12, 1993, Moran called Donna at work again. This would be Donna's first indication that there were problems with the investigation—problems, it would soon turn out, about the WPD's belief in her story of what happened inside her house the night of the attack.

"I was wondering if you would be willing to go under hypnosis," Moran asked. "It might help you to recall some more detail about the incident."

Donna was taken aback. *Hypnosis? Why would they need me hypnotized?* Donna had not been drugged or knocked out during the attack. She had repeatedly stated that her attacker had covered his face. What sorts of details could she possibly provide under hypnosis?

"I had told them everything—in great detail—that happened," Donna recalled. "I had left nothing out. The hypnosis request seemed so far out of left field."

"Why?" Donna asked Lieutenant Moran.

"Well, Mrs. Palomba, it might give us some additional information."

"I'll get back to you. I need to speak with my husband."

Donna hung up and stared at the phone. There was a certain shift, she felt, in the tone and pace of Moran's communication. Not that he was easy to read in this respect; he wasn't. But the investigation didn't seem to be a ticking clock—as if they were hunting some crazed, maniac serial rapist and every moment mattered—situation any longer. It was as if the WPD was thinking of alternative scenarios.

❧

A day after the hypnosis request, on October 13, Donna's sister, Maria, saw Jeff Martinez again, that old friend she had bumped into two days before Donna's attack. This time the encounter took on an entirely new meaning for Maria and—eventually—for Donna. In fact, where Maria and Donna were concerned, a prime suspect in Donna's sexual assault was about to emerge.

It was about 11:30 a.m. Maria was at home and heard a truck pull up outside her apartment. She looked through the blinds and saw that it was a truck from the glass company for which Jeff worked. Maria watched as Jeff "took a while" to get out of his truck, as if he was doing something inside the vehicle that she couldn't see. Then he approached the porch and knocked on the door.

"Who's there?" Maria asked.

"It's Jeff from [he gave the name of the glass company]."

Maria opened the door. "Hi, Jeff ... what brings you here?"

This was the second time she had seen this man within about a month. Up close and personal. What gives? It wasn't like they had seen each other much in the recent past or talked on a consistent basis.

Jeff leaned in and kissed Maria on the lips "for much longer than a friendly hello," Maria later explained.

Maria thought it was weird, aggressive. "I was extremely uncomfortable," she said.

Maria and Jeff chatted briefly about everyday topics; she mentioned some pain she had in her shoulder and told Jeff she was going to physical and massage therapy. Jeff seemed to have something to share and wanted to talk, so Maria thought that inviting him inside her apartment might help. She walked over to the couch and sat down. Jeff followed.

"Would you like a cup of tea or a cold drink?" Maria asked.

"No, thank you," Jeff said.

No sooner had Jeff declined the beverage offer than he moved toward Maria and began kissing her again, this time more aggressively.

Maria pushed him away. "That makes me uncomfortable, Jeff. Stop it. It's not right." Maria knew Jeff was married with kids. She had no idea what was going on. Jeff was not just coming on to her. He was being sexually forceful, overbearing. Maria was frightened.

"You don't always have to do things that are right," Jeff said. "So if it feels good ... well, you just do it."

"Massages are great," Jeff continued, going back to the massage theme they had discussed. "They feel so good. I could almost orgasm during a massage. I haven't had one in a while—a massage, that is." He laughed. "I have no trouble having an orgasm."

This made Maria even more alarmed.

"Where does it hurt?" Jeff asked. "Come on. Please let me give you a massage."

"No, Jeff ... this is making me very uncomfortable." Maria wanted him to leave, but she didn't know how to tell him without perhaps making him violently angry. There was no telling what he'd do if she demanded he leave right away.

"You know," he said, "I have every right to pick you up and bring you in the bedroom and make love to you. You're not the type to kiss and tell, are you, Maria?"

Maybe a bit naïve, Maria figured Jeff's "kiss and tell" remark was a reference to him not getting caught by his wife.

"Why didn't you answer your door yesterday when I knocked?" Jeff asked.

Maria said she never answered the door unless she was expecting someone, adding how "extremely cautious" she was because "You never know what might happen." Her sister being raped, of course, was now at the forefront of Maria's mind. To the outside world Donna was an anonymous Jane Doe. Nobody, with the exception of family and a few close friends, knew what had happened. The newspapers had reported the attack under the Jane Doe policy of not publicly announcing the victim's name or address. Where was Jeff taking this? What was Jeff trying to say?

Jeff said, "Hey, I know what you mean. I own a gun and bring it with me wherever I go."

Maria remembered Donna telling her that the man who raped her had a gun.

As the alarming conversation continued, Jeff asked about Donna and John's house and how much they were asking for its sale. The Palombas had recently put their house on the market.

"Not sure, Jeff," Maria answered. "But she recently installed an alarm system because of a burglary, so I assume it will go for more money."

The mention of a burglary piqued Jeff's interest. He asked when the burglary had occurred; he seemed to want to know details.

"About a month ago," Maria said. Although Maria didn't put it together right then, the questions Jeff asked seemed to fall in line with some of the particulars of Donna's attack.

"Was anyone home?" Jeff pressed.

"Yes—Donna."

"She must have been scared shitless."

For the next several minutes, Jeff tried to talk Maria into giving him a massage while he "made love" (his words) to her. As he talked, the neighborhood mailman walked up to the door and slipped Maria's mail into the door slot. The noise startled Jeff, and he jumped off the couch and said, "Who's that?"

Maria thought Jeff looked "troubled" and asked if he was okay.

"Yes," Jeff snapped. "Why do you ask—because I kissed you?"

Maria continued to refuse Jeff's advances. He finally got the message and asked if he should leave.

She said yes.

Jeff thought about it for a moment. Then he stood and approached Maria.

She was frightened as Jeff walked toward her, and later explained what happened next this way: "We then stood up from the couch and he held me close—at which point I smelled mechanical oil. Not overwhelming, but enough to notice the odor."

Oil. Donna had been certain about an oily smell.

"You can keep a secret, can't you?" Jeff asked in a decisive, almost coyly threatening manner. "This is between you and me, right?"

Maria nodded.

They walked to the door.

"Would it be okay if I stopped by every once in a while to check on you?"

"That's not a good idea, Jeff."

Jeff looked at Maria. "I need to know that you won't kiss and tell."

Maria finally got Jeff out of the apartment and closed the door behind him. Then she called Donna and explained what had just happened.

"Do you hear what you're saying, Maria?" Donna said right away, immediately considering Jeff a prime suspect. It all seemed to fit: the gun, Jeff's sexual aggressiveness, the smell of oil, the comment about the burglary, and one very important factor that Donna considered as Maria continued her account of Jeff's visit: the newspaper article Jeff had referred to before Donna's attack. Perhaps Jeff had seen the article and become infatuated with her. Donna felt certain that the article had given Jeff the idea to break in and rape Donna. Somehow Jeff must have found out when John was going away and planned the entire assault.

Chapter Six

Remain Silent

Donna and Maria decided to relay the information about Jeff Martinez to Lieutenant Moran and the WPD. This was explosive. Donna and Maria believed with little doubt that Jeff was—if nothing else—a prime suspect, someone who needed to be checked out. Donna did not want to tell John or her father about Jeff. Not right now. "They knew who he was and would have gone right after him," she explained later. Still, Jeff needed to be investigated. Did he have an alibi for that night? Could he be forced to give up a sample of his DNA? So many questions ran through Donna's mind that she began to experience major bouts of anxiety.

By now, after doing a bit of research, Donna had learned that 80 percent of rape victims are assaulted by somebody they know. She had also learned that many rape victims fear not being believed, or think they'll be blamed for the assault, and that because of these concerns, a large percentage of rapes are never reported. Donna, however, was not going to fall into a hole and go away. She was determined to see this through.

Donna again experienced that sense of something going on behind the scenes. When she called the WPD on October 14, 1993, and asked for Lieutenant Moran, the dispatcher on the other end of the line asked who was calling. Donna gave her name and explained who she was. Then she waited for a period of time ("longer than necessary") before Moran came on the line. It seemed odd to Donna. Then again, was she being overly paranoid? It was a constant balancing act for Donna: Were her anxieties about the WPD a consequence of the rape? Or were they legitimate worries? She didn't know. She had nothing to gauge her feelings against.

Donna's instincts were spot on, as she would only later find out. Moran had taken the extra time to get to the phone so he could set up to record the conversation.

"Lieutenant Moran, it's Donna Palomba." Donna and Maria were certain the WPD would be ecstatic to have this new information about Jeff Martinez. "I have something I need to talk to you about that happened to my sister . . . she'll be here too . . . I was hoping you could come down to my office today." Donna was certain Moran picked up on the urgency in her voice.

After a beat of silence, Moran said, "No. It's best that you come down here."

Donna was baffled. The last thing she wanted was to be seen by her attacker walking into the WPD—and Moran knew this. If she believed Jeff was her attacker, Donna had to think he was now following her and Maria, watching their every move. Maybe he was planning at that very moment to assault Maria. Even if Jeff wasn't her attacker, Donna was still certain that whoever the perpetrator was, he was keeping an eye on her, making sure she did not go to the police. Donna had explained her extreme nervousness to Moran on more than one occasion.

Nonetheless, Moran convinced Donna to come down to the WPD the next morning. He didn't seem interested at all in what Maria had to say, but did not discourage Donna from bringing her sister along.

At ten o'clock in the morning the following day, October 15, Donna and Maria arrived at the WPD. Donna still hadn't told John about Jeff or that she and Maria were heading to the WPD to talk to Moran. She saw no reason to alarm John, who she feared would track down Jeff and maybe choose violence over letting the police handle the situation.

This was not the first time that Donna and the WPD had worked together to catch a suspect. In mid-1992 the WPD had investigated a man who had been caught calling Donna's house and saying sexually explicit things to her over the phone. He later told police he had found Donna's phone number written in pen on the back of a porn magazine. Subsequently, he would phone the house and ask Donna what she was wearing. She would hang up before he had a chance to describe any sexually explicit acts. It disgusted Donna. She was terrified every time the phone rang. The WPD became involved, put a trace on her phone, and nabbed the guy. He was a security guard at a company across the street from Donna's office. The WPD had looked at the man during the previous month as a possible rape suspect, although Donna had not been given the details of how or why they had excluded him.

Now this visit, which Donna believed to be a pivotal moment in the investigation, with Lieutenant Moran, the man in charge of her case, would ultimately change Donna's life and the entire course of the investigation.

Moran came out of his office and said hello to Donna and Maria, who had come, as Donna understood it, to allow Maria to give a statement about what had happened with Jeff Martinez. They felt this could be the break in the case everyone had been waiting for. A bona fide suspect had literally walked into Maria's apartment.

"I'd like to speak with you privately, Donna," Moran said. He was uninterested, Donna felt as she stood and faced him, in what Maria had to say.

⌒

I wanted Maria to relay to the WPD exactly what had happened with Jeff. That was the reason why we showed up. Moran was such a cold guy that it was hard to read him. I didn't know what to think as he stated that he only wanted to speak with me. I had purposely not told

John or my father about any of this because there were times when my
father would just drive around looking for my attacker . . . as if he could
ever locate him. John and my dad would have gone crazy. I had no idea
this meeting was going to transform this case into something I could
have never imagined possible—the time I needed John by my side, I
didn't have him. And maybe Moran picked up on that, I don't know.

I walked into the elevator with Lieutenant Moran, and I felt so
uncomfortable. He seemed agitated; I tried to make small talk with
him to no avail.

As they approached the door leading to what was one of the WPD's
interrogation rooms, Moran hesitated. They stopped. Moran turned
to Donna and said, "When I investigate something, I just want you to
know, I stop at *nothing*."

"That's great! I'm really glad," Donna replied. "I really want you to
get to the bottom of this."

Moran had Donna sit directly opposite and in front of him, like
a suspect. He folded his arms over his chest. Moran had what Donna
viewed as a look of complete arrogance. He definitely had something
to share, but was withholding it for some reason—the cat with the
canary in its mouth.

There was a tape recorder sitting between them on the small desk.
Moran leaned over and pressed PLAY and RECORD. He did not ask
Donna if he could record the conversation.

This action confused Donna. She wondered why Moran would need
to record a conversation with her. Maybe it was standard procedure?

If that wasn't enough, what Moran did next threw Donna into
utter disbelief.

The lieutenant pulled out a folded piece of white paper. Clearing
his voice first, he began: "You have the right to remain silent . . ." and
concluded by reading Donna the Miranda rights warning.

"What are you doing?" Donna asked. "Detective Cote never did anything like this."

"This is the way *I* am handling the case," Moran said.

Donna ignored the comment and began her story about Jeff. As she talked through what had happened to Maria, detail by detail, Moran looked around the room as if he could not have cared one bit about what she was telling him.

"He rolled his eyes at me," Donna said later, "and at what I was telling him."

Donna quickly decided that Moran was "disinterested" in her story about Jeff, and that Moran had his own agenda for what was—Donna would realize in the coming days—a well-planned interrogation.

After finishing her story about Jeff, Donna took a breath and sat back, hoping to get some sort of response from Moran. Maybe the whole Miranda rights reading was a test to see if she would just drop the whole case and all the associated police work.

"A lot more information is now known about your case," Moran said. He stared at Donna. "The suspect you have talked about here is, in fact, *not* a suspect, Mrs. Palomba. I *have* a suspect!"

"Great," she said with sense of relief. "You have a suspect?"

"Yes, I do."

Donna nearly cried. This was it. They had found someone. Finally.

"Can you tell me who it is?" she asked.

"No."

"Is it a family member?" Donna thought it might be someone close to her if Moran felt he couldn't tell her.

Moran didn't answer.

"Am I in danger . . . is it someone I come in contact with that I should be aware of?" Donna was growing increasingly concerned. She couldn't walk out of there not knowing if her attacker was someone in her life. It seemed incredible that Moran would hold back such a potentially lifesaving piece of information.

The lieutenant looked at Donna with skepticism; she felt the disdain he had for her, a complete lack of empathy for her situation. It was surreal. She was a rape victim, and yet the police officer designated to arrest her assailant was turning the tables—and for what reason?

After a period of silence, Moran said, "Oh, I don't think so."

"Can you *please,* Lieutenant Moran, give me some more information about what was found out?" Donna was desperate, pleading.

"Why don't *you* tell *me!*" Moran snapped angrily.

"What?" Donna had no idea what he was talking about.

Before she could respond further, Moran broke into a story. "Today is a sad day, Mrs. Palomba. You know why? I have to go to court this afternoon . . . and there's this woman who did nothing wrong in her past but just happened to tell a white lie, and consequently she is losing her kids to the Department of Child and Youth Services and she is going to be convicted and go to jail."

Donna didn't pick up immediately on Moran's incredibly arrogant way of sending her a message. He was intimidating her, trying to scare her into telling what he presumed to be the truth of what had happened.

"That's too bad," Donna said. "And really sad. But it is unfortunate she lied in the first place."

"Is there anything you'd like to tell me, Mrs. Palomba?" Moran asked. He stared at her again.

"Like what?"

"Like what *really* happened that night."

"I've told you everything I can remember."

"I have proof that you purposely lied to us—countless interviews and photographs."

Donna, growing increasingly distressed by Moran's constant badgering, raised her right hand, as if testifying: "I swear to God the statement I gave was how I remembered it happening. If there were certain details that got mixed up it was because it was a traumatic situation and *I* may have gotten mixed up." She was asking for a little slack here. A man had broken into her home and raped her. Where was the sympathy?

"Oh, it's not the details that I am talking about here. Mrs. Palomba, you are a prominent person. You have a husband, two beautiful children, a business . . . please don't throw all that away."

"You're scaring me," Donna said, now in tears. "What are you talking about, Lieutenant?"

Moran shifted a bit in his seat. He settled, then replied: "Look, Mrs. Palomba, if you tell me what really happened, it will stay here right in this room confidentially"—he pointed down with an index finger on the table—"and I will keep this tape in a drawer . . ."

Donna's jaw dropped. She could not believe what she was hearing.

"If not," Moran said after a long pause, "I'll have to arrest you."

"At this point," Donna said later, "I became . . . weak, dizzy, nervous, disoriented."

And this was only the beginning. What Moran was about to say next would shatter Donna.

Chapter Seven

Your Lies Won't Leave Me Alone

THE ACCUSATION THAT LIEUTENANT DOUGLAS MORAN MADE AGAINST Donna—that she had yet to tell the real story of her alleged rape—combined with his threat of arrest completely blindsided her. What had she done wrong? What did they know that she didn't? Moran was calling Donna a liar. That was clear enough. He had made up his mind about her. What worried Donna more than anything was that if Moran was accusing her of being a liar, it meant her case was not being investigated. Her attacker was free to go about his business. The police were not searching for him. Crucial time was being lost.

Donna sat, stunned, thoughts racing through her mind. If she had been lying about that night, how could Moran account for the semen and pet hair and saliva, not to mention her scratched cornea? What was her motive for telling such an incredible untruth as a home invasion and rape? Had she scratched her own eye? Had she left her kids alone in the house and run to a neighbor's to begin constructing an elaborate fabrication?

Moran was about to address Donna's questions as the interrogation continued.

◆～◆

I felt like my heart was beating outside of my chest. I just could not believe this police officer was sitting across from me, turning the tables, and not willing to listen to one bit of information I was giving him about Jeff Martinez. Moran had totally disregarded my sister's account of what Jeff had done to her. As Moran continued, I became nauseous, the room started to spin . . . There's no way this can be happening. Blame the victim? *I could not get over how this was becoming my reality, and had no idea how much worse it would get. I kept thinking about what Moran was sitting there saying:* What photographs? What interviews? What is this guy talking about? I am being blamed for falsely reporting a rape, and I have no idea where it's coming from.

"You will not only be arrested," Moran said as Donna continued to cry, "but you will go to jail and your children will be taken away from you and dragged through the courts."

"What?" Donna felt like fainting, but was able to regain a small bit of her composure. "Look, Lieutenant, there is something very wrong in the information you have . . ." Donna pleaded with Moran to believe her. There must be some mistake, she kept saying.

"Oh, I don't think so," Moran continued, not letting up. "I have one hundred percent positive proof or I could not sit here and do this to you. I have spent many hours, as well as other officers . . . there are countless interviews—and I have rock solid evidence. Me, my team, and my captain are all in agreement on this."

On what? Donna wondered.

At some point the tape ran out, and Moran told Donna to hold on so he could flip the tape over and begin recording again. She watched him do this.

Donna felt so weak at this point, her body so incredibly numb and gummy, as if at any moment she would fall over, or collapse and melt off the chair.

Had someone planted something? Was someone setting me up? Why would someone frame me?

"You're going to be arrested, Mrs. Palomba," Moran said.

With that threat looming, Donna asked, "What should I do?"

"Tell me the truth!" Moran said, his voice growing loud and more intimidating. "Tell me what happened."

"I told you exactly what happened. This is what I recall happening."

"Fine," Moran snapped. "Then there is nothing left to talk about. You are going to be arrested, and you are going to jail."

—~—

Waterbury, the "Brass City," was my home. Waking every morning, I didn't have to go far to look out and see the immense white cross standing tall over the city from its place perched high atop a cliff just off the busy interstate. Holy Land, USA. Years ago it was a tourist trap and, although closed, is still a focal point today. People would flock to the cross located amidst two scaled-down replica cities of Jerusalem and Bethlehem. It was that fifty-foot-tall cross that I took with me every morning. There it stood, obvious and marvelous, towering over my shoulder as a comforting and divine shadow. At any time of the day, I could look up and get lost in this enormous symbol of suffering. It reminded me of who we were and why we were here; and became a reflection, honestly, of our lives, what we believed, how grateful for life I was, and how personal the Catholic sacraments I took so much pride in living were to my way of life. At one time fifty thousand people a year came from all over the world to stand at the cross and visit these "holy" cities; but we had it right here, overseeing our lives like a halo, staring down into our close-knit, seemingly trouble-free world. It prompted us to consider that the only expectation of a Christian was to follow the moral compass you absorbed growing up as a child of God; it would guide you through life. And if I allowed that to happen, I was certain, happily-ever-after would be the postscript to my life with John and the kids.

How could it not be?

And now, as I sat in front of this police officer, my world was coming apart. He was accusing me of being the polar opposite of the person I had worked so hard to become.

———

Where was Moran getting his false information? Was he protecting somebody? A cop, perhaps? Had they found out that one of their "brothers" committed the rape, and the cover-up was beginning right there in that room?

"Do you know that your neighbors are calling here," Moran said, "and they're scared to death?"

Again, Donna had no idea what he was talking about. "What are you saying?" she pleaded. "What do you mean?"

"A nine-month pregnant woman cannot sleep at night, Mrs. Palomba. How do you feel about that?" Moran was yelling, becoming even more aggressive.

"What in the world are you talking about? I'm the victim ... *I* cannot sleep at night." Donna was even more confused now. The guy—a police lieutenant—was beating up on a woman who had been sexually assaulted. She couldn't get over how surreal this entire interview had turned out to be—and she had volunteered to come down.

"She cannot sleep, and it's *your* fault," Moran raged.

"I'm sorry ... I feel awful about that, but it's not my fault."

Moran sat in silence, staring at her.

"What possible motive would I have to concoct this?" Donna said, breaking the silence.

"You tell *me*."

"Please stop this. Please, Lieutenant. I have told you everything. I beg you to stop. Think about this ... if I was your wife or daughter, how would you feel if they were being treated in this same manner. What would you tell them to do?"

"I would tell them to tell the truth. Look, I have twenty-seven cases on my desk, and one way or the other, this one is getting closed."

"If I had an alternative story to tell, why wouldn't I tell you—especially if you say that I am in danger of losing my husband, my reputation, my children. I would certainly tell you."

"You would think so," Moran shot back.

"Please, Lieutenant. Please. This doesn't make any sense." Moran had actually told Donna on the telephone earlier that two suspects had been 95 percent ruled out. "I came here today to give you more information . . ."

"Look, this is your last chance—or there *will* be an arrest. But I won't arrest you here. It will be at your home or at your work. Then I'll take you back here where you'll be fingerprinted and photographed."

Donna trembled. She had no idea how to get out of the situation. She was talking, but Moran refused to hear her. All Moran did was stick to his interpretation of the events, whatever that was. Donna had no idea what evidence he had against her. She just wanted to talk to someone else, someone willing to listen and understand.

"Can you give me till tomorrow?" Donna asked.

"Absolutely not!"

"Please believe me . . . I have nothing to hide. I'll take a lie detector test, whatever you want."

"I feel sorry for you, Mrs. Palomba. You're new at this. I think what happened was that you painted yourself into a corner and things got out of control and they snowballed and you made a mistake."

There had been a moment during the interrogation when Donna asked Moran about the DNA and any potential lab results. He had mentioned on the phone, she pointed out to him, that the DNA would become important down the road when they had any potential suspects.

"I intentionally gave you misinformation," Moran said. "It's one of my tactics."

———

I had never been more humiliated, betrayed, or sickened in my life. If I wasn't so strong, and if I didn't have the total support of my family through this period, I would have had a nervous breakdown. To take a victim who had been through the kind of trauma I experienced and to use the kinds of tormenting "tactics" that Moran used to intimidate me once he made up his mind about who I was, is something so unbelievable that I still have a hard time comprehending it.

———

There was a moment when Moran had Donna so perplexed and shaken up that she questioned her own memory. Maybe he was right. Had she been so traumatized that she had no idea what had happened?

"Do you think I could have been hallucinating?" she asked the lieutenant.

"Oh, I don't think insanity will work."

"What are you *talking* about?" Donna's tears flowed more intensely as she curled into herself, her emotions taking over. She slumped in her chair. "What could you be *thinking*, doing something like this to me?"

To her shock and disgust, Moran said, "I'm thinking about what I am going to have for lunch."

———

I sat there like an idiot. If I knew then what I know now, I would have gotten up right after he read me my Miranda rights and asked for an attorney. Walked right out of that room. I was just so determined on trying to set the record straight. I wanted him to believe me. I couldn't understand why he did not. Or what he was basing his argument on. He never told me then why he had come to this conclusion. I had no idea that he had been given erroneous information—gossip, basically—about me and was pivoting his entire case on this information.

Donna had been in the room with Moran for about an hour and fifteen minutes. A round of silence ensued as Donna sobbed quietly, staring down at her lap.

"I'll tell you what," Moran said. "I'll let you go, but only under the condition that you come back this afternoon and tell me what really happened inside your house that night." He paused before addressing Donna in a sharp, angry tone: "Or I am going to find you and arrest you."

Donna got up. Moran opened the door.

"Do you need to use the ladies' room?"

"No," Donna said. She wanted to leave.

"This is the part of the job I hate," Moran said.

Donna just looked at him.

Inside the elevator on the way downstairs, Donna trembled with anxiety and exhaustion. Moran did not say anything.

Maria was stunned as Donna approached. She stared at Donna and knew something was wrong. Donna looked rattled.

Maria expected Moran to sit down with her and hear her story. Donna knew he wouldn't, not after what she had just gone through.

Sure enough, Moran declined to listen to Maria's story of Jeff coming to her house.

"Let's just go," Donna said.

Moran watched as they walked out the door.

"Donna, I don't understand, what happened?" Maria asked as they got into the car. Maria thought perhaps the WPD had discovered who the perpetrator was, and that Moran had given that terrible information to Donna. It could have been the only reason why Donna was so upset.

Donna was still shaking. "He told me that I was going to be arrested if I didn't come back this afternoon and make up a story about what happened."

"What are you talking about?"

"They have something."

"What?"

As they drove away from the WPD, Donna thought she was going to have to go home and invent some fiction about that night in order to keep her kids.

—◆—

The theory that a cop was responsible for raping Donna became something she began to seriously consider as she and Maria drove toward their parents' home. Donna thought: *Maybe I was framed . . . Moran knows who did it and he's covering for him.*

Her mother and father sat and listened to her account of being verbally assaulted and interrogated by Lieutenant Moran. They could not believe what she was saying. The word Donna used later to describe her parents' reaction was "incredulous."

Donna's father was so disturbed by what his daughter had said that he left to go find John, who was at St. Mary's Catholic School, dropping off their boy at his afternoon kindergarten class. St. Mary's was across the street from the WPD.

Donna's father, with John in tow, went from St. Mary's directly to the WPD to see if they could get to the bottom of what was going on.

John demanded to see Lieutenant Moran.

Moran came down and escorted them upstairs to the third-floor hallway. It was afternoon. People were scurrying about everywhere, coming and going. The place was active and busy.

"What the heck," John said. "You're going to arrest Donna?"

"She's a good daughter. A great person. An incredible wife." Donna's father pleaded with Moran. "What are you people trying to do to her?"

"Look," Moran said calmly. "There *is* a threat of her arrest. John, her story is full of holes."

One of the forensic officers involved in Donna's case just happened to walk by while they were standing and talking. John called him over and said, "You hear what they're doing to Donna?"

He looked at Moran. Then at John: "I'm sorry, John . . . he's my superior." The man walked away.

What was going on? Was this some sort of conspiracy? John was dumbfounded, but growing angrier by the minute. What smoking gun information did the WPD have, and why weren't they telling Donna and John what evidence they were basing such scurrilous accusations on?

As Moran talked through some of the details he had discussed with Donna, John began to understand where the WPD was coming from. It started to make sense. Moran never came out and said it, but John now thought he knew what Moran had hung his entire theory on.

They left and drove back to Donna's parents' house.

Donna was still upset, and she didn't know what to do. There was no way she could make up a story to satisfy Moran and his cronies at the WPD, just so they could close the case and she could keep her kids. Donna was no liar. While John and her father had been at the WPD, she'd made up her mind that she would not succumb to Moran's intimidation.

"Donna," John said comfortingly, "is there *anything* you need to tell me about what happened that night?"

As John had listened to Moran, he realized that the implication—suffice it to say there was DNA evidence left behind—was that Donna had had an affair while John was away and felt she was going to get caught, so she made up the entire scenario to cover up the infidelity. The evidence the WPD had was apparently the word of someone who had made the allegation against Donna. But John was not told who that was.

"No, nothing at all."

John hugged his wife. "I believe you. I just had to ask. This is what they think," John said. "That you had an affair and you're making all this up to cover it up."

Donna was paralyzed by fear. The same people who were supposedly there to protect her from the monster who had entered her life were now against her too, chasing her down. She felt she had no one to turn to. Nobody to lean on, besides her immediate family and friends.

Outside of one tightly knit circle, Donna was alone.

"What do we do?" Donna asked her husband.

It had been two days since the interrogation, and I was still reeling. The rage I felt inside me would be hard to explain. Not only had I suffered the trauma of the rape, but then I had been pumped with antibiotics that made me vomit for hour upon hour till there was nothing left inside me. I had that severe scratch on my cornea, which was very painful and complicated things even more. Then I tried to pick myself up and move on, going back to work, beginning my routine of life. I had given a detailed statement to Detective Lou Cote, and he had never indicated to me that perhaps they did not believe me. I kept calling them inquiring about progress in the case and if lab results had come back and if there was a DNA hit on anyone. Now I realized all that was for naught. My emotional state was so fragile and maybe even broken. My therapist called it "homecoming trauma," the same suffering Vietnam veterans faced upon coming back home from the war. The people who were supposed to be protecting me were now the same people coming after me.

Not long after the interrogation, Donna's mother-in-law called retired police superintendent Fred Sullivan, a man the family knew quite well.

Mrs. Palomba explained everything. Sullivan told John's mother he would call the WPD and try to get some answers.

Not long after, Sullivan called Mrs. Palomba back. "They say Donna's story is full of holes," Sullivan told her. "That's about all I can say."

Sullivan advised her to tell Donna and John to set up a meeting with Lieutenant Moran's superior, the Vice and Intelligence Division's captain.

John and Donna decided that John would call to demand a meeting. They needed to know what evidence the WPD had against Donna and confront it. Maybe there was a major misunderstanding that Lieutenant Moran had taken completely out of context. Or maybe he had what anyone would consider a good reason to accuse Donna. It would not, however, excuse his behavior during the interrogation, but the shining of a spotlight in Donna's face and interrogating her like a terrorist could be dealt with at a later time. What Donna and John needed to do was get the WPD back to investigating her case. There was, after all, a rapist running around the community.

John called the captain—Captain Robert Moran—the lieutenant's own brother.

CHAPTER EIGHT

Something's Missing

JOHN SPOKE TO CAPTAIN ROBERT MORAN, LIEUTENANT DOUGLAS Moran's brother, and the captain, as John would later recall, "reluctantly" agreed to meet with them, while again repeating what his brother had said about "holes" in Donna's story.

It was the morning of Monday, October 18, when John and Donna arrived at the WPD. Donna had barely been able to sleep or eat since Douglas Moran had interrogated her. Her world had become what she later described as an "unsafe" place.

My healing, for which I was working hard, came to an abrupt halt. I had considered the police station a safe place, where good people who could help me resided. My bedroom used to be a comforting place to unwind and relax and sleep and read and play with the kids. Both of these places were now horrifying for me to even think about. They had become danger zones. Just seeing a police car drive by gave me such a profound sense of pain and fear that I was losing control of myself and those emotions I had spent so much time over the past several weeks coming to grips with. I was constantly praying now . . . and even that was losing its power.

Greeting John and Donna at the WPD's entrance was another lieutenant, Harold P. Post, whom people called Phil. He was there, along with Captain Robert Moran, to hear what Donna and John had to say. The Palombas had heard that Phil Post was part of Lieutenant Moran's team investigating the case. Post had been with the WPD since 1973. When John and Donna met him that day, Post was with the Vice and Intelligence Division. He seemed pleasant and quiet and didn't say much.

After they sat down in Captain Moran's office, John turned to the captain and said, "Thank you for meeting with us." Then he jumped right into it: "I . . . I don't know if you're aware of the line of [questioning when] . . . my wife came in Friday. I'm sure you're aware of the case and what's going on."

Donna interrupted, saying, "I can tell him myself, John. Do you have the tape of the interview between me and Lieutenant Moran?"

Captain Moran seemed unemotional, difficult to read, and monotone. Moran was the head of the WPD's Vice unit and his brother Douglas Moran's boss. He had assigned Douglas to Donna's case. A University of Connecticut graduate, he had wispy white hair, parted to one side, with noticeable strands of black, a pale complexion, and big tortoiseshell glasses. He wore a white shirt, dark tie, blue slacks, and a stoic gaze of indifference. Moran had been on the Waterbury force since 1970: He had started like everyone else, as a patrol officer, moved on to patrol sergeant, then became a sergeant in the Detective Bureau (1981–84), a lieutenant (1984–86) in that same division, and finally captain of Vice and Intelligence. According to Moran, when asked later under oath, he had not a blemish to his record.

The tape, Donna knew, would tell its own story. It was futile for her to try to explain the degrading way in which Lieutenant Moran had spoken to her and the trauma she had endured while being subjected to his accusations. She had seen Douglas Moran record the interrogation. If they all could just sit and listen to the tape, Captain Moran would see that his brother had taken things too far by threatening to have Donna arrested.

"Did you listen to [the tape] at all?" John asked.

Captain Moran said, "No."

"Can we listen to it together?" Donna said.

"No," Moran snapped. "No."

John said he would appreciate it if they *could* play the tape. "I'm totally disgusted by what [Lieutenant Moran] said. My wife, I know where she is at all times because I worry about, you know the way things are today, and I worry about where she is and I know where she is and she's out with business and stuff at times." John was getting himself worked up already. He wanted to clearly make the point that he trusted his wife, had no reason not to, and was appalled that she would be accused of stepping out on him and then making up a story to cover up an affair. Furthermore, hadn't anyone from the WPD conducted a background check on Donna and John? Had they interviewed friends, family, people from her past? How could she be judged without a dogged investigation of her character?

"I don't know that much about the conversation the other day," Captain Moran said to Donna and John's utter amazement. The captain sounded smug, as if he was going through the motions because he had to, but had already made up his mind, same as his brother. He made a comment that he was busy and indicated that he had had to move some appointments around to accommodate the meeting with John and Donna. The longer the conversation went on, the more Donna felt that she was being ignored and Captain Moran was talking to John, giving him more attention.

"I know a little bit about it," Moran said, "but . . . but what things specific, uh . . ."

"Okay, first of all, Captain," Donna said. "I came in on my own . . . with my sister, because she had an incident occur with this person that we both know . . . When I came down I noticed that [Lieutenant Moran's] behavior was very cold and very different than the nice man that I had dealt with earlier on when I was inquiring about the lab results and everything else."

From there Donna went through the entire story of what had happened between her and the captain's brother two days before. She left nothing out. Captain Moran listened, as did Post, but neither said much as Donna took the time she needed to go through the interrogation point by point. There were times when John would add something that Donna had left out.

After nearly fifteen minutes, the point Donna was trying to make became clear: There was no good reason why they were doing this to her. It was absurd to strong-arm interrogate the victim while a rapist was out running around the town.

"Let me explain to you, okay?" Captain Moran said. "In, ah, in certain cases, it is a legitimate line of questioning."

John said he understood.

"And we have to follow every possible avenue . . ."

"Right," John agreed.

Captain Moran then explained that after they had eliminated "all [the] other explanations" they could find (meaning those suspects the WPD had checked out), they had to "follow whatever other course that might be indicated."

Again, John said he understood.

"It's a . . . it's an investigative method, okay."

"So was there substantiation, 100 percent proof positive?" Donna asked. *Why was Captain Moran talking in circles here,* she wondered. Why not just reveal the alleged evidence they had? If they were so certain she had lied to them, where was the proof?

"As far as that sort of thing, uh, you know, there are statements that were made at different times." Moran claimed, referring to the allegations made against Donna. "If we were to put 'em together and we were to put them in a warrant, would a judge sign it? Yeah, probably. Are we going to do that at this point? No."

John stepped in and said, "But I mean, for something like this to happen to her, I mean, for another man to try to violate her, it was just totally, it just . . . I mean, you must have women who make mistakes, you know, statements that are just so confusing, I mean."

"We have women that make statements that are confusing," Moran reiterated before coming down hard on John, adding, "We also have women who *lie*."

Donna then made a very good point, saying, "To me, Captain, this could be used as a last resort. Nobody I know was interviewed. My [business] partners were not interviewed. My family—the males in my family—were not interviewed. None of my character was questioned . . ."

"No, we've been working very hard," Moran said, defending the department's investigation.

As they talked back and forth, getting nowhere, Moran said, "Listen . . . one of the things that we would like to do, okay, is interview the children. Uh, you feel they were sleeping?"

"I *know* they were!"

What was the captain implying, Donna asked herself. Later she would hear from a source that the WPD thought that she had perhaps drugged her kids so they would stay asleep during her supposed tryst.

"Well," Moran said, "we're also wondering if one didn't wake up and wander around the house."

"No," Donna said. "I know for sure because they were right next to me."

"I understand that. But when the incident happened, okay, *who* can verify that they were sleeping?" Moran asked.

"I can," Donna said.

"Well . . ." Moran answered arrogantly. The only part he left out was, *There you go!*

They discussed possible suspects for a few moments, and then Donna told her story about Jeff Martinez. Moment by moment, she recounted exactly what Maria had described to her.

Captain Moran said nothing.

John and Donna continued to defend themselves and Donna's story, but it seemed that Moran and Post were uninterested in the minutiae of it all. Post and Moran listened, apparently, but did not react. At one point Moran said, "I understand your frustrations, and I sympathize with them. If there were another, if there were some other way I could change them or solve this case, I certainly would . . . And, uh, sometimes we have to do things that even ourselves we don't particularly like to do."

John decided to call their bluff. "I'd like this cleared up," John said. "I don't want them [Lieutenant Moran and his boys] to waste their time going after this point of view. If he feels they have enough that the [judge] wants to sign the warrant . . ."

Donna piped in here, finishing for her husband, "Then let's do it!"

***

I had been feeling grateful. I realized that there were people in the world a heck of a lot worse off than I was. I could overcome this. I was alive. My husband wasn't buying into their "she had an affair" theory—which would have made my home life a hell I could not have dealt with. John's trust and love were carrying me over this new hurdle. But the mention of a warrant set me back. I was just blown away by the fact that he said a judge would sign a warrant for my arrest. I was feeling frustrated, discriminated against, misunderstood, angry, sad, bewildered, helpless. It was clear they were not going to back down from this theory Lieutenant Douglas Moran had obviously come up with. It was the blue boys club—they were all standing behind their boy.

"Well, I'll tell you, if you had come in the other day," Captain Moran said next, "and you would have said [she lied], and if that happens, uh, we probably would have dropped this, washed this, whatever."

John and Donna looked at each other. What was he saying? Was the captain now trying to talk Donna into making this all go away by simply admitting to an affair she never had?

After Moran talked about how the WPD was not in the business of breaking up families, but that there were cases where they could not control the outcome, Donna said something for the first time since the attack that was soon to become the pulsating, driving theme of her life: "I want to make sure this type of treatment never happens to anyone else."

This evoked an eruption of heated emotion from Moran. He started to say something, but they all spoke over one another and nobody could be heard.

Donna needed an important fact verified. She wanted to know about the DNA. She was confused after speaking with Lieutenant Moran. He had called *her* at work regarding the DNA, but then referred to the DNA during the interrogation as a misinformation tactic he used when investigating crimes of this nature.

She wanted to know: Was there DNA available or not? More pointedly, "Was there, in fact, enough information from the lab so that if we find a suspect he can be either eliminated or—"

"There's no way that we can tell that," Captain Moran said.

"Well, he told me that once for sure. Was that one of his *tactics*?"

"I really don't know," Moran said. "I mean, usually DNA is not done locally. It has to be sent to the FBI laboratory. And it takes a long period of time. We have one [case] now where a fellow was doing a series of rapes . . . and, you know, uh, we, uh, as a matter of fact, DNA eliminated one suspect."

"Right," Donna said.

"But it took several months."

Donna wanted to know, concretely, whether there ever had been DNA—semen—found on the back of her shirt and panties, as she had been told, or if it was just one more police "tactic" giving her false hope. She had no idea what to believe anymore.

Moran never gave them an answer. Instead he talked about how frustrating a case it had been for his men. He said one of the most disturbing factors of the case was that John had been away and the "fact that there was no forcible entry."

John started to suggest a theory, but was interrupted by Moran, who said, "These are some of the things that we are finding very frustrating in our investigation and, uh, you know, quite frankly, uh, it certainly made us look at you a second time [referring to Donna], as you know it makes us look, as you say, that it's gotta be a personal nature. Somebody that knew quite a bit about you people . . ."

John explained that he hadn't told many people he was going away, and that he had also asked his brothers to drive by the house to make sure everything looked safe, adding, "I had another friend, uh, one of my best friends from years ago, I had him call and see if everything was all right."

"Who was that?" Moran wondered.

John gave him the name, saying his friend was at least "260 pounds and, um, Donna would have known if it was him."

Moran wanted the friend's personal contact information so they could reach him and investigate whether he had the opportunity to commit the crime.

This request opened up a dialogue that included John mentioning other people the WPD should be talking to: friends and acquaintances of John and Donna's that they had assumed the WPD had already checked out. Come to find out, they hadn't.

Then Moran said, "We would also like to speak with your sister Maria about her contact with . . . [Jeff]."

It finally seemed like they were getting somewhere.

Moran said he needed to conclude the conversation because of an important meeting he had at the top of the hour, explaining, ". . . We're going to pursue what we feel are the most productive lines of inquiry. Uh, as those terminate, then we'll go to other lines that are, uh, perhaps, less promising." Then he said someone from the WPD would be in touch soon.

And that was it. Meeting adjourned.

Lieutenant Post escorted Donna and John out of the building. Post had played good cop to Moran's bad cop. Neither had taken many notes during the conversation, but Post had written a few things down, Donna suspected, to "make it look good."

As they walked toward the exit, Donna told Post to listen to the tape Lieutenant Moran had made. "This is very important to me," she said. "What is going to be done?"

"I'm very busy," Post said. "But since the captain asked me to sit in, I am now involved. I assure you, I will listen to all the tapes this afternoon."

Leaving the WPD, Donna and John believed Captain Moran was holding back a lot more than he had been willing to give up. But why?

To say the least, Donna left the WPD confused and shaken once again. What was going to happen next?

"I was right back to the night I was raped," Donna said.

CHAPTER NINE

Jane Doe

JUST FIVE YEARS BEFORE DONNA'S ATTACK, ONE OF THE MOST SENSA-
tional false rape allegation cases in history began as fifteen-year-old
Tawana Brawley went missing one day from her Wappinger, New York,
home. Brawley was found behind an apartment complex four days later.
She was covered in dog excrement and curled up in the fetal position
inside a black plastic garbage bag. Her hair had been partially snipped
off. Several racial epithets—including "nigger" and "KKK"—were written on her frail and bruised body. When authorities had the opportunity to speak with the terrified-looking fifteen-year-old, she claimed
that six white men—one of whom had a badge and was presumably a
cop—had raped her repeatedly in the backwoods of upstate New York.
The case heightened racial tensions across America. Not long after
Brawley came forward, outspoken African American rights advocate
Reverend Al Sharpton took over her case, speaking as an advisor for
Brawley and her family. Sharpton made several serious and shocking
allegations himself. In one protest, which he staged outside the state
building in Albany, New York, to show how disgusted he was with the
state's handling of the Brawley incident, Sharpton linked the treatment
of Brawley to that of the late Dr. Martin Luther King Jr., saying, "We
come because twenty years after they mercilessly shot down a man of
peace, we still have no justice." Then Sharpton said that a New York
prosecutor, Steven Pagones, "on thirty-three separate occasions . . . kidnapped, abused and raped" Brawley. A year after the accusations of rape

and assault had been lodged by Brawley, a grand jury looking into the case concluded that the teenager had invented the entire story with her mother's help. It turned out that Tawana Brawley "was not the victim of forcible sexual assault," but a pathological liar. Brawley's name soon became a punch line, as did Sharpton's. Brawley's was one of the most high-profile criminal cases of the 1980s. Police departments nationwide were miffed that a young girl, fueled by her mother's greed, could invent such a deleterious story with the thought of destroying lives and careers by playing off issues of race.[*]

Donna Palomba was no Tawana Brawley, although there was a racial footnote to her story: Donna had said her attacker could have had a Jamaican accent, she just wasn't sure. In any event, it's possible that the memory of a recent, nationally covered, false rape case still lingered in the air among law enforcement.

Yet Donna had no motive besides the truth. As she sat at home after that strange meeting with Captain Robert Moran and Detective Phil Post, still getting nowhere, Donna wondered what was going to happen next in the saga that had become her life. It was clear she was being blamed, but exactly how had these police officers come to think of her as the type of person to have an affair and then invent such an extravagant plan to cover it up? This thought—the question of her character—bothered Donna perhaps more than anything.

‹~~›

We had been thrown into a world we knew nothing about. This consumed our lives. I went to bed with it and then woke up with it. How was I going to navigate through this foreign field? Should I hire legal counsel? John and I could not turn to anyone in our community. On top of that, I felt protecting my identity—which had not been a problem since the attack up until that point—was all I

---

[*] According to the National Center for the Prosecution of Women: "Research has shown that only 2 to 8 percent of rape allegations are false, and yet the stigma of disbelief remains pervasive."

had left. I was Jane Doe. Imagine. I was just getting used to this new identity, and they were trying to strip me of it. I needed to stay unidentified. My business depended on me being in public, meeting with people. Potential clients would not take kindly to the idea of me being a "liar" who made up false rape allegations. The moment I was arrested under those charges, my name was going to be smeared across the media. I would be finished. I feared that if my name was dragged through the papers as a liar . . . a woman who made up a story, I was going to lose everything.

❧

John and Donna waited for Lieutenant Post to review the tapes and get back to them. It had been ten days since they had met with Captain Moran and Lieutenant Post, and the WPD had not so much as called to check in. The department's silence was overwhelming. Donna wondered if a sheriff, at any moment, was going to pull up to her door with an arrest warrant and cart her off to jail as the local media followed close behind. Moreover, during those ten days, Donna had repeatedly called the WPD and asked for Captain Moran and Phil Post, but had not received a return call.

Finally, on October 29, Donna got Post on the telephone—this after she had called and left him yet another message.

"Have you listened to the tape?" Donna asked.

"No," Post said. "I have not."

Why not? Donna thought. But instead of verbalizing this thought, she asked a simple question: "What is going on with the case?"

"I can tell you that you have nothing to worry about with Jeff Martinez," Post said. "We have 99 percent ruled him out. He agreed to take a lie detector and fluid [blood] test."

"What? Ruled out . . .? But how could you do that so quickly?" They had just told her that DNA testing took weeks, if not months.

"I assure you, Mrs. Palomba, Jeff Martinez did not attack you."

"Has he taken those tests?"

"No, not yet. Look, he acts a little strange, but you have nothing to worry about with Jeff."

What are they doing?

"The captain," Post said before hanging up, "will have some information for you on Monday or Tuesday next week."

Donna waited. The captain never called on either of those days. On November 5, Donna left Captain Moran a message to call her back as soon as he could. It was one of several messages Donna had left for the captain over the past three days. Why was she getting the runaround? What purpose did not returning calls serve?

"You must be very intuitive," Captain Moran said as the conversation began. "I was going to call you today." He seemed condescending, flippant.

"*What* is going on with my case, Captain?"

"We've interviewed people you know and people you don't know," Moran said. "Basically, Mrs. Palomba, the case is at a standstill."

Donna could not believe this. *Standstill?* How could it be at a standstill if the blood work from Jeff Martinez, for one, had not been collected yet?

"Captain, what do you mean?" Donna asked.

"This brings us back to your children."

"The children were asleep, Captain. I saw them. The officers at my house there afterward witnessed the children sound asleep. They never woke up."

"It is totally up to you and your husband. If you don't want us to interview them, that's fine. I'll wait to hear back from you on that."

Donna was thinking about what the WPD had done to her. Now Moran expected her and John to consider putting their children in the same hands. What could a five- and seven-year-old, sound asleep through the entire ordeal, tell them?

"What about Jeff?" Donna asked.

"Oh, the glass guy," Moran said sarcastically, almost with a laugh. "I don't have the specifics, but I can tell you that he has been thoroughly investigated and ruled out."

"Have you listened to the tape?"

"No."

That was all Donna needed to hear. "Okay, fine . . ." she said and hung up.

Donna drove to her church and sat with the pastor of her parish. She needed advice about what to do. After hearing her out, the priest said, "You need to hire yourself a lawyer."

She then sought the advice of the principal from her children's Catholic school, who told her the same thing. Every family member she and John turned to advised them to obtain legal counsel so they at least had an advocate working on their side. Right now, they had no one.

Donna didn't know it, but something else was happening behind the scenes at the WPD. According to a report filed by Lieutenant Douglas Moran on October 21, 1993, that tape of the interrogation he had conducted with Donna on October 15 did not exist.

"On this date," Lieutenant Moran wrote, "it was discovered that . . . [the] tape recordings of interviews . . . with Donna Palomba . . . had not been recorded as first thought due to a switch on the tape recorder having been set in the wrong position."

Donna would find it to be an incredulous turn of events when she heard about it. She remembered Moran turning the tape over and the actual wheels on the tape recorder spinning as she sat and watched. How could the tape not exist?

Another major piece of evidence in Donna's case came through on November 2, but she had not been told about it. The results of the sexual assault kit came back from the Department of Public Safety Forensic Science Laboratory in Meriden, Connecticut. Lead criminalist Mary Beth Raffin signed the report, along with lead criminalist

Beryl Novitch. The results were, if nothing else, clear that the evidence left behind at the crime scene told a very concrete and alarming story.

Spermatozoa—semen—was confirmed on all the vaginal swabs taken from Donna that night at Waterbury Hospital. Tests for the presence of acid phosphatase, an enzyme found in the kidneys, semen, and prostate gland, were positive on these tests, also indicating that Donna's attacker had left behind his DNA in the form of sperm. It was not mere speculation any longer; there was plenty of DNA.

Several tests conducted for the presence of amylase (saliva) were positive; yet there was no semen found in any of the saliva samples (including Donna's), an important factor, again backing up the fact that Donna never claimed to have been forced to perform oral sex. Her narrative of what had happened, the evidence seemed to be bearing out, was lining up.

Additionally, pubic hair had been found on several of the items submitted for testing. There was no blood found underneath Donna's fingernails, which would have been evident had she scratched her attacker (she had never claimed to). Semen was also found on swabs taken from the T-shirt Donna had been wearing and also on her labia majora (the outer lips on both sides of the vaginal opening). There was no semen found on the panty hose used to bind Donna's eyes, mouth, and hands, but human hair (Caucasian) had been uncovered on those same items. The report indicated—again backing up Donna's version of the night—that Donna's panties had been cut "along the back crotch seam area, from one leg opening to the other leg opening." There were "very small white stains noted on the inside of the crotch near the cut"—stains proven to be semen. There was additional pubic hair (Caucasian) found on the panties. On the back of the T-shirt, additional semen was found along with (Caucasian) human head hairs. There was no semen found on the pillows taken from Donna's bedroom. On the sheet covering Donna's bed, several areas contained samples of semen.

If one were to look at this evidence objectively and piece together a scenario—to re-create the crime scene—it would be consistent with the story Donna Palomba gave to police on the night she was attacked (and two days later), save for one detail: The results proved that her attacker was a white male, while Donna had said, but was not sure, that her attacker might have had a Jamaican accent. The evidence also proved that Donna's attacker had prematurely ejaculated as he was cutting her panties (just as she had said in her statement), thus spraying semen over the back of Donna's T-shirt, her panties, the bedsheet, and possibly himself, including his hands. He tried to penetrate Donna with his penis (without an erection) and then entered her with his fingers, which would explain how she ended up with semen on her labia majora and minora (inside vaginal walls). The evidence supported Donna's account nearly 100 percent.

But the WPD officers investigating Donna's case did not view this evidence in that manner. In fact, every indication was that no investigator working the case was even considering looking at the available evidence and matching it up to Donna's story. Because even a rookie crime-scene tech and first-year detective could have pieced together Donna's story and corroborated it with the available physical evidence.

❧

It became clear that none of the officers involved in the case bothered to look at the actual evidence to determine the truth. I will always wonder what would have happened had the responding officers and people in charge of my case on that first night investigated it properly from day one. Would the perpetrator have been found then?

CHAPTER TEN

Rumor Has It

MAUREEN NORRIS WAS EVERYTHING DONNA AND JOHN PALOMBA were seeking in legal representation. Maureen's firm, Kolesnick and Norris, handled many different types of law: personal injury, criminal defense, divorce, real estate and business transactions, contracts, and leases. Maureen, who had been practicing law since 1985, knew many of the players involved in Donna's case. While studying for the bar, Maureen had worked at the Waterbury State's Attorney's Office (SAO) under the regime of then–state's attorney Frank MacDonald. Before she had even passed the bar, Maureen was hired by the firm for which she would go on to become partner.

"Originally," Maureen said later, "I thought I was going into criminal law because I had that relationship with the state's attorney's office, but I ended up working for attorney Kolesnick."

John and Donna had known Maureen for some time because Maureen had dated John's brother for a few years prior to their calling on her. Around town, within city law circles, Maureen had already heard about Donna's case.

"Rumors were that she had been raped," Maureen said. "Being involved in the legal field, you'd hear things that others wouldn't normally be privy to."

At thirty-three, Maureen was a few years younger than Donna, but they could see things from the same woman's perspective, which was important to Donna. Maureen's soft-spoken demeanor was not to be taken as a weakness; she was a strong woman and even tougher lawyer, quite willing to stick her neck out where it mattered. When it came to litigation, Maureen was the type of attorney who relied on the facts to speak for themselves. As Maureen sat and listened to what Donna had gone through over the past several weeks after the rape, she knew Donna stood on a firm foundation of truth; and truth, Maureen had seen time and again inside a courtroom, had a way of rising to the surface once all the evidence was presented.

"If this can happen to you," Maureen said on that first day she spoke with Donna, "it can happen to anybody."

This statement was to become a mantra Maureen would chant over and over as the weeks turned into months, and Donna's case dragged on.

As Donna explained all that had happened, Maureen thought the Moran incident was extremely strange. "It's not necessarily that my jaw was on the floor," Maureen later said, "when I heard what she had gone through; stranger things have happened. I just felt so sorry for her. I never had a doubt that Donna was telling the truth. It never even entered my mind that Donna could be lying about what happened to her. I had known her for a number of years. She loved her husband. She was a wonderful mother. I had been at her house. I mean, let's be serious, Donna doesn't even curse."

That the police were considering Donna to be some sort of cunning, pathological liar, Maureen thought, was unbelievable, even repulsive.

"I am thinking early on that the Waterbury Police have made an assumption and that maybe I can facilitate things and get the investigation back on the right track."

Maybe a phone call. A meeting with the right players. The Morans get a slap on the hand. Donna gets an apology, and all is forgotten. And Donna can move on.

What Maureen sensed from the initial conversation was that John and Donna were not looking to sue the city or anybody else. That was not why they had sought legal representation.

"It was the furthest thing from their minds. They wanted this investigation to get back on track."

Maureen saw no other option but to contact the SAO and set up a meeting with state's attorney John Connelly, so they could—with any luck—get to the bottom of what was going on inside the WPD and move the case forward from there.

"We need to find the person responsible for raping you," Maureen told Donna. It was appalling to Maureen to think that an investigation such as this one was stalled. What message would this send to women who were raped? How many other rape victims were out there being treated by police as Donna was?

Donna agreed with Maureen. Sure, it had been upsetting and her life had been thrown once again into a tailspin, but the main issue here was that a rapist was still at large, maybe raping other women, and nothing was being done to find (and stop) him.

Their thought was that any man bold enough to commit a sexual assault during a home invasion had likely committed this type of crime before and would do it again.

State's Attorney Connelly had a long-standing reputation as a straight player within the politics of courtrooms and public opinion. He was in his late forties, a lifelong Waterbury resident whose parents had both been blue-collar workers within the massive manufacturing and textile industries that had sustained Waterbury throughout the 1950s and 1960s. Connelly, like many other local cops and politicians, had gone to Mattatuck Community College before doing his graduate work at Trinity College in Hartford. Maureen hoped she could chat with Connelly and get this thing taken care of as a gross misunderstanding. Donna would be more than willing to move on, as long as the case was officially reopened and set back on the right track of finding the man who had threatened to kill her.

—◦—

Looking back on all this, having come so close to death, I am much more aware of how fragile life is. I used to take things for granted. Every day is a gift, and I want to make the most of it. I want to be a better mother, wife, daughter, sister, Christian, and friend. There is no time to fret about material things or gossip about others. I became more in tune with my moral compass and reflected on how I felt when I behaved or acted in a certain way. I believe it made me a better person, but I have a long way to go. I realize now—but maybe not then, as I contacted Maureen in a state of panic and fear—that this is all part of a greater plan, and I try to turn over the many challenges I face to God. Some days I am better at it than others. Many wonderful things have happened. I know they are part of something much bigger than myself. So I am along for the ride . . . trying to do the best that I can for as many as I can for as long as I can. I have spent too much time in the past trying to please others or not speaking up when in my gut I knew what was going on was wrong. I learned what it was like to be discriminated against. It made me more assertive. I began to spend my time trying to do things that would actually make a difference in the grand scheme of things.

Strange as it sounds, I wouldn't trade anything. I believe you learn most from your greatest challenges. These events, as I went through them, made me stretch and reach farther inside of my soul than I ever thought possible. And sitting there, listening to Maureen talk about contacting the state's attorney and taking control of this thing empowered me. Maureen gave me a breath of life. Somebody believed me. I wasn't alone.

In contacting the SAO, Maureen planned on filing a motion with the court, requesting that an Internal Affairs (IA) investigation be opened immediately based on the harassment and accusations made against Donna, and on the way the case had been handled from the first moment the police arrived at the scene. Maureen explained to Donna that they were going to crack the inner shell of the WPD open and discover what happened. Part of Maureen's strategy included obtaining a copy of the tape recording made by Lieutenant Douglas Moran on October 15, 1993; at the time neither she nor Donna knew that it did not actually exist. Yet everyone else, especially the SAO, knew Moran had allegedly flubbed up the recording and never made the tape in the first place, according to the report Moran had filed back in October.

Involving the SAO shook up the WPD's Vice and Intelligence Division, sending it into a frenzy of playing catch-up. As an example, it wasn't until December 3, 1993, that investigators drew blood from Jeff Martinez to test against the known DNA that had been recovered. This meant that not until the SAO had been contacted did Captain Moran order the test. What's more, Lieutenant Moran did not submit a supplementary report regarding "details of offense [and] progress of [the] investigation" until December 6, a full *three* days after Maureen made an appointment—a meeting set for December 10—for her and Donna to sit with Connelly. In that report, Lieutenant Moran wrote a complete narrative of the events leading up to the investigation's current status. Most interesting was the mention of Donna's children.

Moran wrote: "That the victim states that her two children . . . did not see or hear anything, either during the attack or subsequent police search, and she had persistently refused to allow the police to interview them."

Moran also pointed out that an oil leak inside Donna's home might have been the source for why she thought her attacker had an "oily smell."

The report claimed that Lieutenant Moran and his brother, Captain Moran, interviewed Jeff Martinez on October 19, 1993, the day *after* Donna and John met with Captain Moran and Phil Post. That interview consisted of a few questions for Martinez about his employment. He was asked if he had any psychiatric problems, if he took any psychiatric medication, or if he had been treated for psychiatric issues. Moran's report also confirmed that it wasn't until December 3 that Lieutenant Moran ordered the blood draw from Martinez and also from the security guard who had been caught prank-calling Donna's house the previous year.

Donna refused to be destroyed by this continuous attack on her character. Her only recourse at this juncture had been to hire counsel and meet with the SAO. She had rights and now, after talking with Maureen Norris, understood that those rights had been repeatedly violated by the WPD.

—◆—

This revictimization was beginning to affect my relationship with my children and husband. I was unable to concentrate on anything else but what was happening. It consumed me. The idea of my kids being dragged into the case was disturbing and horrifying. I was alarmed that there was a chance my children would have to be questioned and asked things about their mother that no child should have to even think about. I could not believe that the WPD was not going to let up . . . but it was clear they were preparing to dig in for the long haul. We figured they might admit their mistakes after we contacted the SAO and offer an apology and get back to the business of searching for the man who had raped me. But it was clear when Lieutenant Moran began to backtrack and do what he should have been doing from day one that they were going forward and sticking to their accusations against me.

—◆—

Donna was looking forward to her meeting with state's attorney (SA) John Connelly. Walking into the building, she and Maureen felt confident that they were about to make serious progress.

After formal introductions, they sat down. It didn't take long before Maureen and Donna realized that things were about to get much worse for Donna, and the WPD was not planning on backing down. Yet it was the extramarital affair allegation and the rumor's original source that would set Donna on a mission to reclaim her life and identity, which she felt the WPD was trying to strip from her.

All Connelly would say was that "a citizen in the community" had reported to the WPD that he had "heard" Donna was having an affair.

"Apparently," Connelly explained, looking somberly at the two of them, "somebody gave information to police that they are using as part of the investigation."

"What do you mean?" Maureen asked.

Donna looked on, not saying anything, not quite believing what she was hearing.

"Well," Connelly continued, "this person said, 'With regard to the Palomba case, things may not be as they seem, or as Donna said they were.' This informant heard that perhaps Mrs. Palomba was having an affair and one of her children woke up, and she made this all up to cover up the affair."

—◆—

I was speechless—and quite sickened by this statement. This could not be my reality. Gossip and innuendo were controlling the ebb and flow of the investigation, causing the police to accuse me? Instead of Lieutenant Moran looking into this allegation about me, I realized as I sat listening to the state's attorney that the WPD had relied on a rumor as a fact to go after me.

—◆—

Who was this person? Who was talking to the WPD and giving investigators inaccurate, misleading information about Donna and a supposed affair?

The WPD's source for the information wasn't a "confidential informant," as the SAO had explained to Donna at one point, but a man who knew several of the investigators involved in Donna's case.

"A cop wannabe," Maureen called him.

Al Sullivan* was a forty-one-year-old former acquaintance of John Palomba's who did not know Donna personally. Sullivan had grown up in the same Overlook neighborhood as John; he knew Donna (and John, for that matter) only "casually," he later told police. He had not even met Donna until his high school years and had "been in her company," he admitted, "probably less" than ten times throughout his entire life. Sullivan said later under oath that he had only found out where Donna worked by reading that "Today's Woman" article in the local newspaper weeks before her attack. Previous to that, Sullivan said, he hadn't known much of anything about Donna's life.

Sullivan was not a transient looking to trade information with police for some sort of personal gain or help with a legal problem (motives for most snitches). He had a steady job with good pay. He owned a thirty-three-foot boat. He was married. He went to church. He was a member of the Elks Club. He raised money for charity. He had known the current mayor of Waterbury for twenty years. And he also had friends inside the WPD, including Neil O'Leary and Pudgie Maia, two names that were about to become synonymous with Donna's case. Sullivan had other friends inside the department that he saw occasionally, including the chief and Inspector Jake Griffin, the chief of detectives. What had brought Sullivan to the WPD in 1993, the circumstance that had set this unsubstantiated rumor in motion, was Sullivan's needing a gun permit because of recent problems with break-ins and hoodlums smoking crack near a building he owned. While at the WPD, Sullivan ran into a few of his old buddies, and they got to talking. Some time after that, Sullivan bumped into Detective Neil O'Leary at a social event, where Sullivan mentioned he had some information about Donna's case.

---

* A pseudonym.

When deposed later about his involvement, Sullivan admitted he had heard about Donna being sexually assaulted "a few days" after the incident. When asked who told him, Sullivan claimed he couldn't recall. His reaction to learning about the assault was "shock," he said. "I grew up there [Donna's neighborhood] when I was a little kid. That was a pretty secure place." Sullivan later explained that not long after Donna was assaulted, "rumors," as he put it, began to circulate throughout town. People talked about Donna. Someone had leaked that Donna was the Jane Doe written about in the newspaper, and people in the neighborhood speculated as to what had happened. No one really knew for certain that Donna had been sexually assaulted, just that there had been a break-in and the person had gone up into her bedroom while she was at home alone and John was out of town.

Sullivan routinely spoke to his sick mother about Donna's attack (he went over to his mother's house nearly every day to tend to her medical needs). Several days after the incident, while Sullivan was checking his mother's medication and oxygen level, she asked him if he knew anything more about "the Palomba case." Everyone in Sullivan's family understood that he had contacts within the WPD and was "in the know."

Sullivan told his mother, "Not particularly. I haven't heard much of anything."

"Well," she said, "I have been talking to [Margaret,** a friend and fellow neighbor], and she knew a lot more than I knew. She described a lot of different things, a lot of things that I didn't know and I had no way of knowing. That Johnny was gone for the night—there was no sign of forced entry, and she [Donna] smelled oil."

Sullivan said he listened with half an ear. Every day he went over to his mother's house after that, however, he heard "more and more" about Donna's case. His seventy-two-year-old mother, who had undergone a quadruple bypass and was suffering from a viral infection and, quite

---

** A pseudonym.

frankly, dying, was getting information from somewhere, Sullivan concluded. It seemed to him that secret details of Donna's sexual assault—which only the police should have known—were being passed around the neighborhood quite freely.

One day not long after Donna's attack, Sullivan's mother mentioned that she had heard from her friend, who was calling her every afternoon to keep her company, that there might have been more to the break-in than what at first appeared. "Donna ran out of the house and down the street . . . [that night] and the family had discussed that she was having an affair, possibly with her [business] partner, and that she was using the story to cover it up because maybe the kids walked into the room."

And there it was: the rumor that had added fuel to a fire already burning about Donna inside certain circles of the WPD. Two old ladies, sitting around killing time, talking about a rumor rolling through the neighborhood, were now driving the investigation into what had happened inside Donna's house on September 11, 1993.

Gossip—nothing but speculation—was governing Donna's destiny.

Sullivan knew of this vicious rumor not long after the attack. The question was: What was he going to do with the tale?

"The first few days," Sullivan later said, "I just didn't pay any attention to it. It's kind of rumory garbage. So I just passed it off."

But then his mother talked about what Sullivan described later as "specifics," details about Donna's case that were obviously, to him, coming from inside the family or the WPD.

"They came up with this whole scheme," he said, speaking of his mother and her friend, "of [Donna having] had an affair . . . there was no forced entry . . . it was like the first time ever that Johnny was away . . . this kind of stuff."

Those details, Sullivan recalled, made him take notice. He thought maybe he should turn over what he now knew to the police. It started to "bother" him, he later claimed. But Donna had a blemish-free reputation among neighbors and family members and friends. Yet Sullivan thought, "Anything is possible. Anybody could do anything. So it [was] possible . . ."

Sullivan's mother kept pressing the issue, asking him if it could be true. "I really don't know . . ." he finally answered.

His mother took it one source deeper, claiming that someone in one of the families was saying this same thing.

Not long after Sullivan heard this rumor from his mother, he ran into Detective O'Leary at a social event in town. Sullivan asked the detective to take a walk with him outside.

"Any progress being made in the Donna Palomba case?" Sullivan asked O'Leary.

"We're kind of stuck."

Sullivan never mentioned if O'Leary questioned how he knew Jane Doe's name. He thought about what he knew for a moment, then decided to just come out with it: "Well, I don't know if you're going to believe all this, Neil, but . . ."—and he explained what his mother's friend had told his mother about Donna having an affair and one of Donna's kids maybe catching her in the act and Donna making up this elaborate story of being raped to cover it all up. He told O'Leary that his mother's friend had "formed the conclusion" based on several "clues" she'd figured out.

What were those clues? There were two: John was away, and there was no forced entry into the home.

Concluding, Sullivan told O'Leary, "This is what the family said."

According to Sullivan, O'Leary responded, "I'll put you in touch with someone involved in the investigation."

A few days later, O'Leary phoned Sullivan to tell him he was sending a few detectives to interview him.

"I'll tell them exactly what I told you," Sullivan said. "But you have to keep me out of it—it is all just rumors." Sullivan explained that he was getting the information "fourth hand."

One of the investigators who went to interview Sullivan was Phil Post. Sullivan explained what he had heard, telling Post emphatically, he later claimed, that it was nothing but rumor and speculation and he had no evidence to back it up.

"We'll handle it," Post said.

The supposed genesis of this nasty rumor—Sullivan's mother's friend—turned out to be a relative of John Palomba, a woman who had a well-documented history of medical and psychological problems.

Chapter Eleven

No Two Victims Are Alike

During their December 10, 1993, meeting with state's attorney John Connelly, Donna and Maureen understood that they were up against a machine. Connelly admitted that the tape from Donna's "interview" with Lieutenant Moran on October 15, 1993, did not exist. There was a malfunction of some sort, Connelly explained. The conversation between Moran and Donna had never been recorded.

Was this by design or an honest mistake?

Donna wondered what in the world was going on.

━━━

How could police be so inept and do so much harm to me for simply reporting what had happened? We heard that the tape recorder had malfunctioned. Then we heard that Lieutenant Moran was some sort of technological guru for the WPD. None of it made sense. And I should note here that John and I were together in all of this. He was standing by my side—no matter what. The stress of everything became palpable. I had been judged and condemned. I could not believe this. We still didn't know where the rumor came from—and maybe that was a good thing. I was beginning to feel the anxiety and all sorts of symptoms from the post-traumatic stress of the rape and its aftermath. It was as though I had fallen off a cliff. But then I was able to brush myself off and climb back up. I got near the top again, and I believed that someone was there to rescue me. I was relieved. As I got closer, however, I realized this person was Lieutenant Moran, who slowly peeled my grip away, finger by finger, until I fell again. This time I fell harder, the impact was greater, and I could not get up.

When the police won't believe you, who do you turn to? Nobody was listening to us.

———

Leaving the State's Attorney's Office, Donna and Maureen talked about submitting the paperwork to begin the process of requesting an Internal Affairs investigation. This wasn't an action that a phone call could facilitate. Maureen would have to sketch out the case from Donna's perspective, provide statements, and make good cause for her argument.

While Maureen began that procedure, Donna felt the best thing for her to do was to write John Connelly and thank him.

———

SA John Connelly was the decision maker on where the case would go from that point. During the meeting I got the sense that he was torn as to what to do and he was assessing my credibility. I remember during the meeting, when Maureen or I suggested that Connelly get the tape recording of the interrogation from the police (before he told us something had happened to it), he said something like, "That's my decision!" I got the feeling he had a big ego and wanted to let us know that he was in charge. But I needed to thank him, regardless. Butting heads was not going to get us anywhere.

———

The reason for the letter to Connelly, Donna later said, was to thank Connelly and to let him know how much she appreciated his help. She wanted to motivate Connelly to take action. It seemed Connelly was on the case, asking officers about lab results and a total review of the case file. The other catalyst to Donna's letter was Connelly's remarks during a phone call to Maureen that he would try to get a female investigator assigned to Donna's case, and that he was going to "speak to the informant" himself and judge if the information was credible.

"Your involvement and concern about the case," Donna wrote, "has truly helped me to feel better in a lot of ways. Putting my life back together is an ongoing challenge, but knowing there are those who want to get to the truth . . . really helps. I sincerely thank you for your effort."

Maybe requesting an Internal Affairs investigation could even be avoided. After all, Donna and Maureen felt, wouldn't the SAO and WPD consider the fact that if Donna was willing to take her case all the way to the SAO that she was likely telling the truth? Would she risk everything by taking matters this far? The WPD had offered her a way out, sort of a plea deal, by suggesting to her that she tell them what they wanted to hear to make it all go away. Donna had emphatically said no. By this point Maureen had done a good job of explaining to Connelly exactly what Donna had been through, every detail, every fact. Would Donna go through so much effort if it was all some sort of cover-up for an extramarital affair?

— ⚬—

The opening weeks of 1994 followed a strained Christmas holiday season for Donna and her family. By this time Donna had developed a contact inside the SAO, whom she began calling for information and any progress on her case. Based on what she was told, Donna was under the impression that a new investigator was involved, a woman who had been at the scene on the night of the attack.

Kathy Wilson had been with the WPD since January 16, 1978, promoted to lieutenant in March 1992. One of Kathy's specialties was sexual assaults. At the time of Donna's attack, Kathy was a desk lieutenant, even though she had appeared at the scene that night to advise

Donna and other officers. As March 1994 approached, Kathy was reassigned to Vice and put in charge of sexual assaults, solely because of Connelly's involvement.

Until Kathy Wilson was assigned, there had not been a woman involved in sexual assault investigations for the WPD for years. Kathy's advantage was that she'd had plenty of training in how to handle sexual assaults. She had also been involved with training officers in the very delicate details of investigating sexual assaults, including how to treat victims of sexual assault.

"And how you treat them will go a long way toward their recovery," Kathy said later, during a deposition. "If you treat them well, they will recover from rape trauma syndrome . . ."

One of the points Kathy made clear during that same deposition was that every rape victim acts differently during those crucial moments after the assault.

"Some victims cry," Kathy Wilson explained. "Some victims are hysterical. Some victims take a very long time to answer questions, and you would almost think that they were drunk or high. But they may be in shock." It wasn't unusual, Kathy added as an example, to find a rape victim who was "very detail oriented when reporting her crime," and another victim "very sketchy."

Faced with a traumatic event such as sexual assault, Kathy reiterated, women responded differently. No two people reacted the same way.

When Kathy Wilson talked about Donna's case later on in her deposition, however, she had some rather strong feelings, which ultimately contradicted what she had said only previously: "There [were] a lot of things wrong with this case . . . that would lead an experienced sexual assault investigator to think that things didn't happen exactly as they were reported to the police."

"Kathy Wilson tried to play both side of this," Maureen Norris pointed out later.

The chief evidence for her opinion, the officer insisted, was the way Donna acted after her assault.

Those "things" wrong with Donna's case, Kathy later testified, included what had become common talk of no forced entry into Donna's house; that Donna had left her children alone and fled the scene; that Donna would not allow police to interview her children; that the house wasn't disheveled and everything seemed orderly; that the jewelry taken was "costume jewelry—it wasn't diamonds or gold"; and that Donna wasn't "beat up," because, Kathy added, "Absolutely every sexual assault where it has been a burglar, an unknown person, the women got beat up pretty badly."

Red flags, Kathy suggested, abounded in Donna's case from the moment she arrived at the scene that night. Questions about Donna's claim were increasing inside the WPD. The more they reviewed Donna's explanations of the night, the more certain investigators (including Kathy Wilson) felt that Donna wasn't being completely honest. When Sullivan's rumor came into the WPD, the entire case seemed to make sense.

While at the scene on the night Donna was attacked, Kathy made certain judgments, several of which went *against* what she would later explain (under oath) were often-seen behaviors by rape/sexual assault victims. Some of the things Donna said to Kathy on that night, the investigator later testified, led the WPD to question Donna's story. For one, according to Kathy, when she suggested that Donna go to the hospital, Donna said, "There's no sense in doing that because I didn't see his face—I could never identify him. You're never going to catch him. And besides, he didn't rape me."

But Donna was not of sound mind at this time. Her choice of words had been made under severe duress. What she meant was: *He didn't penetrate me.* How does one explain the details, however, during what is a frantic, traumatic time in her life? Kathy Wilson—the so-called "expert" in this field—should have been more empathetic toward Donna and considered the linguistic challenges she faced under extremely difficult conditions.

While Donna and Kathy were upstairs in Donna's bedroom after Donna had returned to her house, Kathy asked Donna a few questions about the actual rape itself and what had occurred.

Donna said, "He rubbed his penis up against my back."

Kathy thought that to be a strange comment. "Mrs. Palomba," she responded, "you have to go to the hospital because there may be a transfer of body fluids or hair, some fibers that we could collect. We really have to get you to the hospital."

There were other behaviors that Kathy thought were unusual. One involved Kathy telling Donna not to use the restroom at the house after Donna said she needed to urinate. "Because," Kathy told Donna, "if there is any evidence in or on your body, it will wash [it] away. I believe the hospital doesn't like you to urinate until they get to you, where they can collect it."

Donna then picked up her purse, Kathy claimed, "and headed for the bathroom."

"No," Kathy said. "Don't go into the bathroom."

But Donna went anyway.

"It was like talking to someone who wasn't there," Kathy described, solidifying her description of how a rape victim would act. "She was spacey."

These were all behaviors Kathy Wilson would later testify as not being out of the realm of a rape victim's post-assault actions. There was no standard, Kathy said. There was no one particular way a woman was supposed to act. Donna was obviously in a state of shock. In fact, when asked later, Donna did not recollect a lot of what had happened inside the house that night after she went back, confusing even the simplest things.

I will always appreciate the fact that Kathy Wilson urged me to go to the hospital that evening. I had limited interaction with her after Lieutenant Moran took over the case. I remember seeing her at the police department when I went there for a meeting, and she was professional and cordial but I did not know how to read her. It became apparent later on that she was trying to play both sides and never really came to my defense. In fact . . . I remember feeling sick when she said later that I appeared "flippant" the night of the crime. You would think that a female officer may have understood more, but that wasn't the case.

Now, as the spring of 1994 commenced, Kathy Wilson was back on Donna's case and looking at it with lenses similar to those of Lieutenant Douglas Moran. Could Donna have been making up this entire episode? Was she, in fact, caught up in some sort of daze that prevented her from revealing the truth of what actually happened? Had Donna been so traumatized by whatever went on inside her home that night that she had no idea herself what the truth was anymore?

"I didn't make any judgments," Kathy said later. "I didn't treat her any different from anyone that I would have treated if I saw the rapist raping the victim."

Regarding why the WPD did not secure Donna's house on the night of the incident, Kathy said that because it wasn't a murder scene, taping off the house wasn't something that would normally have been done.

"It wasn't a homicide," she said. "And [Donna] said he wore gloves. So there didn't seem to be the chance that we were going to get any fingerprints . . . The house was meticulous . . . So there wasn't like a jumble of stuff and you might miss something."

Another behavior that made Kathy skeptical took place when Donna came to the WPD to give her statement. She "came in and sat cross-legged on the chair . . . you know, like an Indian," Wilson said later. "Kind of nonchalant."

So the way in which Donna sat on a chair turned out to be, for the WPD, some sort of indication that Donna was not telling investigators the truth.

The fact that Donna requested that John be with her when she gave that first statement was another warning sign, according to Kathy, that Donna was acting abnormally. Rape victims rarely want their spouses to be with them when they talk about the rape for the first time.

❧

I'm meeting with these people—Connelly, Wilson, and others—and I am thinking, They're already biased because they have all this other stuff brewing that's not even reality with regard to who I am. They have not arrested me. Yet, on the other hand, the case had been moved out of Vice and was now with the Detective Bureau, which we thought would help us tremendously.

❧

One goal of Maureen Norris's strategy was to get the DNA in Donna's case retested. SA Connelly said he would look into getting famed forensic guru Dr. Henry Lee and his lab to do the testing as soon as possible.

"Originally, they were given a twenty-week deadline," Donna wrote in her notes on the day she heard about this encouraging development. "Connelly supposedly was calling in a couple of favors to Dr. Henry Lee and is trying to speed the whole thing up."

A problem that arose around this same time, which Donna heard about from her contact inside the SAO, was that Detective George Lescadre, Donna and John's one friend at the WPD, who had given them his total support, was being ostracized by his colleague, Lieutenant Moran.

George had been with the WPD for close to fifteen years; he had an untarnished reputation as a dogged investigator who got things done. Sergeant Rinaldi, the cop who had spoken to Donna on the night of the 911 call, had even phoned Lescadre at his house after he hung up with Donna, to tell him what was going on. George later said that Rinaldi told him Donna "had been the victim of a crime." It was well known that Donna was George's brother-in-law's cousin.

"Most people knew of my relationship with [Donna and John]," George said later.

In late January, Donna called George to ask what was going on. From what her SAO contact had said, something serious had happened. George was a respected cop, a guy who had given his life to the department. He hadn't even really been involved in Donna's case.

"Moran asked me to come in and talk to him about your case," George explained to Donna. "I went in on my own time. Phil Post was there. They asked me what I thought was true or false after laying out what *they* believed happened."

George told Post and Moran that he thought Donna was telling the truth. There had been no reason for him not to believe her.

Lieutenant Moran said, "She's lying, George. I don't believe *anything* she's telling us."

When George disagreed, Moran and Post, according to George's recollection, laughed in his face.

"Moran seemed sure of himself, very positive in his words," George said later, testifying about that day. "I don't think he cared what I had to say."

Donna also heard that as soon as SA Connelly got involved and shook things up within the WPD, Lieutenant Moran started acting nervous, running around, collecting things from the case, specifically looking for several "aerial photos" taken of Donna's house, which Donna later claimed had never been taken.

State's attorney John Connelly assigned one of his chief investigators to Donna's case. He was known as Pudgie, but his real name was John Maia, an always-impeccably dressed African American man— "I've never seen him without a suit on"—in his late fifties, with more than thirty years of investigative experience behind him, several of those years with the WPD. Pudgie had contacts on the streets. People respected him.

"I knew Pudgie well and was very glad that he was now involved," Maureen Norris later said. "He was one of those investigators with his ear to the ground; he knew what was going on in Waterbury. He's the type of guy who would listen. In fact, every time I saw him, he would say, 'I'm on it. I never forget about Donna. I'm trying. I'm trying.'"

Pudgie came from a large, well-known family in the region; he knew John Palomba and the Palomba family. Not long after the incident, quite a while before Pudgie became involved in the case, John ran into him downtown one afternoon, and they stopped for a quick chat.

"I heard what happened to your brother," Pudgie said.

"It wasn't my brother," John said. "It was me, Pudgie. Donna was the one who was assaulted."

"That's terrible, man. Listen, I'll do everything I can to help."

Now Pudgie was involved, working on the case for the SAO. Once Donna heard the news of his assignment, she felt things were progressing and there was a good possibility the case was moving in the right direction. The SAO could work in tandem with any law enforcement agency in the jurisdiction. They helped not only with federal cases—drug trafficking, gambling, organized crime, etc.—but also with murders and other types of cases giving the local police department problems.

"Pudgie's the kind of guy who is friends with everyone, streetwise, involved in athletics, and well liked," Donna said. "He knew poor people and homeless and dignitaries alike. He always had many sources for information."

With not much happening as the second week of February arrived, Donna contacted Pudgie, and they had a conversation about what the SAO and the WPD were specifically working on. Maureen had certainly rattled law enforcement's cage. Thus far, however, nothing of any substance had emerged.

＊～＊

Pudgie said he first heard about the case from George Lescadre. I think, truthfully, George wanted Pudgie's help. Pudgie told me that he had gotten permission from John Connelly to get actively involved— to work on the case basically. This opened up a great resource for us; someone who was not judging me, but looking to get to the truth, which is all I ever wanted.

＊～＊

Pudgie bore a striking resemblance to comedian Steve Harvey, with his thick and bushy mustache, athletic build, and carefree, friendly, and endearing spirit and demeanor. He also brought something very important to the table for Donna: Pudgie knew Dr. Henry Lee personally. Lee rose to fame during the infamous "Wood Chipper Murder" case in the late 1980s. He had been part of OJ Simpson's "dream team" defense. According to his bio, over the past four decades, Lee had assisted in the investigations of more than six thousand cases, including war crimes in Bosnia and Croatia; the suicide of President Clinton's former White House attorney, Vince Foster; review of the JFK assassination; the death of JonBenet Ramsey; and scores of other high-profile crime cases. Lee was also chief emeritus of the Connecticut State Police, founder and professor of the Henry C. Lee Institute of Forensic Science at the University of New Haven, editor of seven academic journals, and author/coauthor of forty books and more than three hundred articles.

Pudgie and Donna discussed the possibility that Donna could one day contact the doctor. If she could get Lee to not only retest the

DNA—as Connelly had said he was trying to accomplish—but also to take on her cause, Donna would have a high-profile advocate in her corner, someone who could perhaps take a look at how the crime scene was handled on the night of the assault and make a professional judgment as to if proper procedures were followed. If not, maybe Lee and Donna could make some changes to the system. One of Lee's specialties—probably what he was best known throughout the world for—was crime-scene reconstruction. Donna was also beginning to develop a vision of somehow changing policies and procedures, so that what had happened to her would never happen to another victim of sexual assault.

Right away Pudgie made Donna feel as though the tide was turning. He told Donna, "I've known John forever. I think the world of him."

This made Donna smile.

"I think what happened was that the person [the WPD's informant] was speculating and gossiping about you," Pudgie explained.

"Things spiraled out of control from there. One thing led to another," he added.

Hearing this made Donna feel comfortable.

"We're going to ask this guy to come forward on his own," Pudgie continued, "and tell us why he said those things about you."

"Great."

"I'll give him a few days to do that, and if he doesn't, I'll turn his name over to you and your attorney."

Donna wanted to cry. Someone was finally listening.

There had always been a theory among those who backed Donna that maybe the guy who pulled Neil O'Leary aside that night and told him about that rumor was perhaps the same man who had raped Donna. Or perhaps he had been installed in that rumor-spreading role to protect a cop buddy, or someone higher up. In dispersing the rumor, he was trying to throw off the scent of the investigation.

Donna asked Pudgie what he thought of that theory. Did it hold any water?

"I don't think so. I feel it's unrelated to the suspect. He's probably just some 'busybody' who should have kept his mouth shut."

"What about Jeff Martinez; can you tell us anything about him?" Donna asked, gravely concerned, of course, that the WPD had not investigated Jeff thoroughly enough and were simply blowing smoke about looking at him.

"The reports are thorough, Donna. They did interview Jeff. His wife was with him. He went down to the station willingly. He seemed to impress the investigators. His background checks out. He's had only one breach of peace charge his whole life. Jeff was even willing to take a lie detector test and gave up his blood without argument."

It was easy to trust a guy like Pudgie. Donna felt confident about the information.

Pudgie talked about another WPD detective who had been assigned to the case. Detective Sergeant Neil O'Leary, the same investigator to whom the informant had relayed the rumor at that social event. O'Leary would now be a point man for Donna. Neil had introduced himself to Donna and John on January 19, 1994. Neil said he typically investigated murders, but he was now part of the investigation because Donna's case had been transferred to the Detective Bureau from Vice as part of the SAO's involvement. Neil had been with the WPD since 1980. He had worked his way up the law enforcement chain the old-school way: hard work. What would help Donna's case was that Neil had experience in DNA, having worked in the forensic lab from 1983 to 1988. He had also served in the Criminal Investigation Bureau and investigated all sorts of crimes, before moving on to the Major Crimes unit, with a focus on murder investigation. His best attribute, however, was that from the outset Neil O'Leary had no agenda. There was nothing driving Neil but getting to the truth and solving the case.

Neil already had feelings about the case, according to Pudgie. "He's on your side," Pudgie told Donna. "He listened to the 911 call and said he could hear the pain in your voice."

Donna was impressed. Everything she wanted to happen was beginning to fall into place. Moran and his boys were out, and a new team was taking over.

"If Jeff's not the guy," Pudgie said, explaining that they were waiting on a DNA comparison, "what Neil and I are going to do is start at the beginning. Neil and I are determined to solve the case."

— ~ —

My husband had told me about his encounter with Pudgie and how sincere Pudgie was in his offer to help us. It meant a lot to John and me. We also knew that Pudgie was very connected to the goings on in the city and had established a lot of sources for information. Before we met Neil O'Leary, Pudgie told me Neil was a good guy and he would help us. At that point, I didn't trust anyone within the WPD, including Neil O'Leary. Why should I? They had accused me of being a liar. We decided that the first time I would meet Neil face-to-face, Pudgie would be there.

— ~ —

Donna spoke to her source inside the SAO one day soon after talking with Pudgie and learned that "the Morans," as her source called them, had a history of complaints involving sexual assault cases.

Surprise, surprise.

There were "child sexual abuse cases," Donna wrote in her notes of the conversation, "where the Morans somehow got involved and came at the victims skeptically and acted like they didn't believe them."

To hear this coming from the SAO was stunning. But it did, in some strange way, give Donna some insight into what was going on. There was a pattern. A precedent.

— ~ —

A funny thing began to happen as Donna went about her daily routine, and it scared the hell out of her on more than one occasion. She was driving in the town of Prospect one day on a main roadway. As she stopped for a turn, waiting for traffic to pass, she noticed Jeff Martinez driving toward her in his work truck. Jeff stared at Donna, and she back at him.

A few days later Jeff was sitting at a stoplight in a gray Cadillac when Donna, John, and their two kids crossed the street after attending a play downtown. They happened to walk directly past the front of Jeff's caddy.

Donna looked and realized it was him.

Two weeks went by, and they crossed paths again on the road, making eye contact but not gesturing.

A day after that incident, Donna had an appointment in New Haven, a forty-minute drive from Waterbury. As she headed south on Route 69, a heavily traveled road just outside Waterbury, Donna noticed a yellow school bus behind her. She didn't think anything of it, of course. But after the school bus made a left turn and Donna continued straight, the car in back of the bus moved up behind her and, to her great surprise and shock, Donna found herself staring directly at Jeff in her rearview mirror.

"Jeff was watching me," Donna wrote in her notes.

She was so frightened that she picked up her car phone—at the time a bulky thing akin to a kitchen wall phone—and pretended to call someone. At an intersection ten miles outside town, Donna sped up and parked between two cars, losing Jeff for a moment, only to watch as he slowly drove by, looking in all directions, as if searching for her.

———

I would see Jeff driving around town in his company truck on occasion prior to my attack. I became more aware afterward and looked out for him after he became a suspect. I really felt like he was following me that day on Route 69 . . . my heart was beating out of my chest. I was scared. In my mind, I heard my attacker's words, which seemed to echo every once in a while when fear came up and the anxiety began to take over . . . If you call the pigs . . . Was Jeff Martinez that same person? I was far from home, [with] a car phone that didn't work, and no way of protecting myself. Watching Jeff pass by and not see me was like coming up from underneath the water after holding your breath.

Yes, I could breathe—for a moment, anyway.

CHAPTER TWELVE

Hope

DESPITE A TOUGH EXTERIOR AND A BELIEF THAT HER CASE WAS finally moving in the right direction, Donna still experienced the burden of being twice victimized. All the emotional weight of having survived a sexual assault and then having law enforcement's finger pointed in her face was crushing. Her belief that Jeff Martinez was now following her indicated that perhaps Donna was losing control of her judgment. Yet, when she thought about it, something told Donna that Jeff could be her assailant. After all, he had not been completely ruled out.

In March 1994, six months had passed since Donna's attack. The WPD was no closer to solving the case than they were on the day it happened. One could even argue, notwithstanding Pudgie's and Neil's involvement, that the case had gone backward. In a letter to John Connelly that Donna wrote (but would never ultimately send) after attending a justice system lecture Connelly had given, Donna expressed her profound desire, simply, to get on with her life. She wrote how she had taken "many steps" in that direction, and in "some cases it has worked, in others, I have a long way to go."

Donna's nature was to give 100 percent in whatever she set out to do. "To organize and plan my project and then to go about achieving it the best and fastest way possible," she wrote. This was one way in which Donna dealt with obstacles and challenges. In this particular situation, however, Donna added, "I find myself feeling quite helpless . . ."

A major growing frustration Donna couldn't shake was the DNA. Where was it? When could she expect the results? The common feeling within Donna's camp—Maureen Norris, John, and some of those in law enforcement—was that Jeff Martinez, who had finally been asked to give a sample of his blood in December 1993, was her attacker. It all fit. Now all they had to do was wait for the results of Jeff's blood test against the known DNA.

"I have not been given a date," Donna wrote, "in which to expect the DNA results, and the waiting has been extremely difficult."

Concluding the letter, Donna said she was "truly grateful" to Connelly for personally making several calls to Dr. Henry Lee in hopes of expediting the results.

"But in the meantime, each day is a battle, and I will continue to live in fear until I get some answers."

Maureen felt that, although they were trying, they were not getting anywhere with the WPD, and the SAO, as much as Connelly had said he was facilitating things, couldn't crack that tough blue shell around the department.

"It was a disaster over there," Maureen said, referring to the WPD. "They—the Moran brothers—were steadfast in their determination to say that they hadn't messed up. The police department itself was steadfast in *its* determination to protect them. This is what I believed as we started to head into the spring of 1994."

What became an issue for Maureen early in her law firm's involvement was how discouraging working with the WPD became.

"I felt they were trying to pacify us," Maureen commented. "I almost felt like they had the attitude of, 'Okay, let's just pacify them here with this because Donna is not going to go away. Let's calm them down.'"

During this time, Donna contacted the Sexual Assault Crisis Center (SACS), a service that offered free and confidential intervention, advocacy, and counseling to victims of sexual assault and abuse. With one of the counselors listening on the other end of the line, Donna shared her story of being raped and then interrogated by Lieutenant Moran and accused of making false allegations. The woman she spoke to called what Donna was going through "two-part trauma," the rape and then the assault by the police, and offered to assist her any way she could.

I was distraught when I reached out to SACS and uncertain that they could help me. I wanted to get to a place where I felt safe again. I was having a lot of flashbacks, both of the rape and the interrogation by Moran, but somehow in my mind the interrogation was more frightening, more incredible. The people at SACS were compassionate and caring. I established a relationship with a counselor who would call me at a certain time and we would talk about anything I felt like. It helped—and I would encourage any woman in the same position, or a woman questioning whether she was raped and if she should report it, to reach out. I tried a support group, but it wasn't for me. I did not feel comfortable sharing intimate details to a group of people I didn't know, and at that point the intense feelings I was having had more to do with not being believed than anything else. I also didn't feel right about bashing the police. With SACS, I could speak over the phone to someone anonymously and that person didn't know who I was. I could get advice without having to put myself out there.

SACS could help. But right now Donna had to deal with being believed by law enforcement. The good news was that Donna was developing resources, building a team, preparing to dig in and fight.

A few days after she wrote the unsent letter to Connelly—unsent because it sounded "too patronizing" to Donna—Pudgie called with some welcome news.

"They are trying to push the DNA through."

"How long will it take?" Donna asked.

"Once they begin, it will take three weeks from that date."

"Okay," Donna answered.

"I'm meeting today with Detective O'Leary to talk about that 'informant.' I'll call you back as soon as I know something."

On March 22, 1994, at about four o'clock in the afternoon, Pudgie Maia and Detective Neil O'Leary arrived at Donna's house.

After introductions, Pudgie mentioned that Neil wanted to talk about the so-called informant. Neil explained that he was the investigator who had acted as the liaison between the informant's information and those in charge of her case at the time, Vice and Intelligence—i.e., the Moran brothers. Neil described the events to Donna. He had met the man at a social function one night. Regarding the rumor, Neil explained, "He told me he'd tell me about it but only if his name was kept in the strictest confidence and that his name would never be used."

Neil went on to say that he ran into the informant a few days after the man had met with Robert and Douglas Moran and asked him how it went.

"What did he say?" Donna wondered.

"He said he 'didn't care for those guys . . .' He thought they were kind of strange and cold, and they didn't appear to be helped at all by his information. He said he didn't even know if what he said meant anything to them . . . One of the things he told them was that he had heard you had a boyfriend, Donna."

"Incredible."

It was apparent that Neil was not a fan of the Morans. He told Donna and John that the Moran brothers were "no more qualified to head the Vice Squad than I would be as a nuclear physicist. And the detectives that went to your house on the night of the attack acted improperly. They should have conducted some forensic testing that night."

"I appreciate your honesty and integrity," Donna said.

"Those detectives work for me, and they screwed up. Then what the Morans did is inexcusable. The superintendent and the mayor know about it, and they are appalled by what was done to you."

Donna was still guarded, but felt she had the right guy on the job now.

"Thank you, Neil . . ."

"Things are being done at this moment to rectify this situation. Doug Moran is going to be given a desk job—I think he should be fired. I'm going to work as hard as I can on this, although, I will warn you, it is difficult to pick it up now after so much time has elapsed. I had a three-hour briefing the other day in Connelly's office about the case, and John is extremely upset with regard to how the case has been handled."

Neil and Pudgie stood and asked Donna and John to show them around the house. They wanted to get a closer look at things for themselves and see if anything stood out. Donna realized, while escorting both officers around, that it was the first time since her attack that she had been asked to do this by law enforcement.

After Neil and Pudgie finished looking around, Donna asked about Jeff Martinez and where that end of the investigation stood at this point. Up until now, Jeff was the investigatory white elephant in the room—that person of interest everyone had in the back of his or her mind, but didn't want to come out and talk about with any confidence or accuracy.

With Neil nodding his head in agreement, Pudgie said, "We both feel Jeff is a strong suspect."

"I personally know someone he works with, and my source is going to check Jeff's work record," Neil added.

"We're also investigating the informant," Pudgie said. This also was something that had never been done. The WPD had taken the man at his word.

"If it were up to me, I'd give you his name," Neil said, referring to the informant—also correcting what Pudgie had promised some time ago. "But I cannot break a confidentiality agreement. If it's worth anything, I'd be extremely upset with this guy too."

Donna was reluctant to ask, or maybe a bit overly confident, but she needed to know the answer: "Could I be there when you arrest Jeff if the DNA comes back a match?"

Pudgie and Neil looked at each other.

—◦—

I liked Jeff. I had good memories of all of us growing up in the neighborhood. I did not want to believe that Jeff had anything to do with it, but it was hard to dismiss how he acted toward my sister. Waiting for the DNA was very difficult. There were times when I wondered if I would be better off not knowing. The thought that it could be Jeff sickened me, and I was trying to prepare myself that it could be my reality. If it was him, I wanted to be present at the time of the arrest because I had to know why. Why would he do this to me? I wanted to look him in the eyes and let him know that I was okay and the attack was not going to beat me—that I was a survivor, not a victim.

—◦—

Pudgie and Neil were startled by Donna's request.

"That's Connelly's call," Neil said.

"It's very important to me that I be there when the arrest is made."

"We understand, but . . ."

"Who would arrest Jeff?" Donna wanted to know.

Neil pointed to Pudgie and then back at himself. "The two of us."

After a few moments of goodbyes and promises of staying in touch, Neil and Pudgie said they would do their best to solve the case.

"Thank you," Donna said.

She had tears in her eyes. Her fear of being arrested finally lifted—at least for the time being—and now there were two tenacious investigators on the case who truly cared about her feelings and finding the person responsible for her attack.

—~—

John and I were grateful that Neil and Pudgie met with us at our home. We wanted to divulge as much information as we could and take them back to the night of the crime all those months ago—with the hope of closing the gap as if they could somehow go back in time and recapture what had been lost: the fingerprints and photos never taken, the neighbors never talked to, whatever else they could find. Precious time had slipped away. We were anxious and appreciative, and we wanted them to know how important it was to us that they continue the investigation. We wanted answers. We needed answers. When they left, John and I felt that these were the guys that could get the job done. They believed us. They felt our pain. And they wanted to right a wrong. They filled us with hope and made us dare to believe that we might someday know who the man was behind the mask. All those months had gone by and finally . . . finally, there was a glimmer of light that the investigation would get back on the right track.

—~—

About ninety minutes after Pudgie and Neil left Donna's and went their separate ways, John Palomba took a call from Neil, who admitted he was feeling the gravity of the situation created by the WPD. What Donna had gone through bothered the investigator, he explained. John could sense Neil's sincerity and pain. Neil said he felt the department owed Donna answers.

"I'm in shock that this could have happened the way it did and been mishandled the way it was," Neil said.

"Thanks, Neil. We appreciate that."

"I stopped at the mayor's office and spoke to him."

This got John's attention. "You did?"

"The mayor said he was going to call the head of the FBI in Connecticut and ask him to try to push the DNA through. Both the mayor and the superintendent want to meet with you and Donna, John."

Waterbury's mayor was Edward D. Bergin Jr., and while he shared a name, he had no relation to Edward Bergin Sr., the superintendent of police, who had named his own son Edward.

"They do?"

"I told him, however, that if you were going to be filing a lawsuit against the city, it might not be in your best interest to meet. If you want me to set something up with the mayor," Neil suggested without pushing, "let me know."

"Thanks, Neil."

John told Donna about the call when she returned home from going out. Donna called Maureen right away and relayed the conversation.

Maureen told them not to meet with the mayor, and if they ever wished to, she needed to be present. The mayor's office was on damage control detail now, Maureen explained. They were going to try to pacify Donna, with the hope of sweeping it all under a rug.

Donna was torn. On the one hand, she did want it all to go away. Maybe a sit-down with the mayor was the best resolution. It appeared that Pudgie and Neil were actively and aggressively investigating the case, and Jeff was a good candidate for being her perpetrator. It would all be over soon, and she could move on and wait for the justice end of the case, preparing to face her attacker in court.

If Jeff wasn't her attacker, there was now some new information that might lead to an arrest. As Pudgie and Neil continued sifting through the case, they revisited an event that had taken place in town on the evening of Donna's assault. A stag party. Perhaps someone at the stag party found out John was away and Donna was home alone. John Palomba had known about the party, and it bothered him. He had told the WPD about his feelings long ago, but his theory had not been looked into thoroughly. John wondered why every male at the stag was not being asked to submit a blood sample. John's feeling was that because he had not gone to the stag and his brothers were there (undoubtedly mentioning that John had gone away for the weekend and Donna was alone), someone knew he was out of town and decided it was an opportune time to attack Donna. John had a gut feeling that the perpetrator had attended the stag, overheard someone talking about him being away, and made plans to rape his wife—maybe someone, in fact, who had developed a secret obsession with Donna long ago.

"John had talked about that stag party right from the beginning," Maureen Norris later said, "and that stayed with me. The stag and the missing key from the Palomba family home. John was saying that he did not believe it was a freak coincidence that he had gone away for the first time in his marriage, there was a stag that night with everyone from town, that a key was missing, and Donna was raped."

Maureen and John felt strongly that somehow all those factors fit together.

Meanwhile, Maureen was in the process of filing a Notice of Claim, a prelude, effectively, to a lawsuit. (In most municipalities, you cannot file a lawsuit without first filing a Notice of Claim.) Although they had not decided on filing a lawsuit yet, Maureen was not one to proceed unprepared.

CHAPTER THIRTEEN

An Internal Affair

IF THERE WAS EVER A DOUBT THAT NEIL AND PUDGIE WERE ASSIDU-
ously working Donna's case from many different angles, it was washed
away by a call Donna received on Thursday, March 31, 1994. She was
at the office, trying to go about her day. Life went on, with or without a
resolution. It was near five o'clock. A source (neither Neil nor Pudgie)
from within the WPD called Donna and mentioned "some information," but that Donna was to "keep [it] in the strictest of confidence."

Donna dropped what she was doing, sat down, promised, "Yes, yes.
Of course. What is it?"

"Doug Moran has gone out 'on illness' . . . Also, there is some
sort of high-tech surveillance equipment missing, and the department's new surveillance vehicle, a black Toyota Camry, is also missing.
Nobody is talking about why the stuff is missing or who has it. Doug
has been knocked off of Vice . . ."

"My goodness," Donna said. She had no idea what it all meant,
but the fact that Moran was not officially part of the investigation any
longer had to be a good sign.

"This whole thing about you and your case has the department
rattled." Then a warning: "Listen, since Moran believes that you had
an affair, he may be tailing you."

Was that why the equipment was missing? Moran had taken it?

Donna was perplexed. Would Moran go to such lengths?

"Be aware, Donna. Doug would be wearing black sunglasses."

It seemed to Donna as if she were involved in some sort of Hollywood thriller, not her life. What was she to make of it all?

~

The thought of Lieutenant Moran actually using surveillance equipment to monitor my whereabouts was unnerving. It made me feel vulnerable and scared. It also angered me. What length was this guy willing to go to see his theories proven? Why did he still not believe me? Why was he hell-bent on "catching" me in some sort of nonexistent affair? Did he know the perpetrator? Was there some connection to the department or personally to Moran?

Then part of me thought, Wow, is he ever going to be bored following me going to work, the grocery store, the children's school, and over to my mom and dad's house.

So now there were two enemies I had to look out for: the perp and the lieutenant. I never felt comfortable or at ease. Just stepping into the outdoors opened up all kinds of unsettling feelings—a heightened form of anxiety on top of what I was already experiencing. But it wasn't going to deter me from doing everything I normally did. I was just more cautious.

~

On April 14, 1994, Donna stopped at an intersection in town, looked across the street and spotted Jeff Martinez in a car driving toward her. Jeff seemed to be everywhere Donna went these days.

This time Donna stared Jeff down, but he looked away and never made direct eye contact with her.

A deep breath and Donna was back on her way to a meeting with Pudgie.

John met Donna at the restaurant where Pudgie was already sitting, drinking a cup of coffee. The purpose of the meeting was to catch up on her case's developments. Donna wanted to give Pudgie a copy of notes her sister had made of the ordeal she'd had with Jeff. Maria had written out the entire episode so Pudgie and Neil could get a clearer picture of what had actually happened. There was probably a charge or two in there somewhere, but apparently Maria wasn't interested in prosecuting.

"How are you, Donna?" Pudgie asked in his comforting voice.

"I'm okay."

She then relayed the encounter she'd just had with Jeff.

Pudgie shook his head. "I'll pass these notes on to Kathy Wilson," he said after Donna handed him the narrative Maria had written. "Listen, I wanted to tell you that Moran is back to work."

"What?"

"But he's in uniform now and working behind a desk."

A small sense of relief. At least the WPD was reacting, taking her somewhat seriously.

It's amazing what a meeting with the SAO could do, Donna thought. Pudgie had more.

"I called Dr. Henry Lee. Lee told me he had spoken to a guy by the name of Larry Presley who works out of the FBI's Washington lab. So I called the lab in Washington and Larry confirmed he had spoken to Lee and his lab is pushing your DNA comparison."

This was very promising news; the DNA was moving as fast as it could and the FBI was on it. Donna felt more and more comfortable talking to Neil and Pudgie each time they spoke. Part of this was building a relationship, Neil, Pudgie, and Donna knew, and perhaps even repairing one that had been shattered. There was still a barrier between Donna and anyone involved with the WPD—how could there not be? But slowly, as the days went on and more was done to find her attacker, Donna was willing to pull back on her cynicism about the system.

After a call from Neil, Maria Cappella went down to the WPD on May 3, 1994, to speak about her incident with Jeff. Kathy Wilson had read Maria's narrative. Wilson wanted to meet with Maria downstairs in the lobby. Maria was apprehensive when she arrived and heard that Wilson wanted her to meet with Captain Robert Moran and another investigator, Inspector Jake Griffin, who worked for the WPD's Detective Bureau. Maria told Wilson that she'd feel uncomfortable in their company. But Wilson promised it would be okay; she would be in the room too.

Maria reluctantly agreed.

Inspector Griffin opened the conversation by asking Maria why she never called the police if she felt that Jeff had assaulted her in her home.

Maria had no answer for that. She thought she had given a statement to Detective Lou Cote about the incident, which should have been in Donna's case file. On top of that, she and Donna *had* gone to the WPD with the information, only to be chased out of there by Moran's accusations of Donna lying about everything. Why *would* Maria want to come forward after what her sister had gone through?

"Lou Cote," Wilson piped in, explaining to Griffin and Moran, "took Maria's statement back in October. Then he handed it to Lieutenant Moran—who handed it back to him."

Robert Moran, who was supposedly there on the day Cote handed that report to the lieutenant, looked on without saying anything.

With each new revelation, it seemed that Douglas Moran was prepared to stop at nothing to see his vision of what had happened in this case come to fruition. Cote had taken Maria's statement, but it ultimately wound up in a desk somewhere, collecting dust, and not in Donna's file. According to Cote, he had handed Maria's statement to Lieutenant Moran, but Moran had handed it back to him, making some snide remark about the case and not needing the statement.

"We need to get Jeff back in here," Inspector Griffin said. "Would you like us to arrest him?"

If Maria filed a complaint right there, they could haul Jeff in and charge him.

Maria thought about it. "At this time," she said, "I don't want Jeff arrested."

—❦—

Nagging at John and Donna was the idea that the perpetrator likely knew John had gone away for the weekend. On May 4, 1994, at 10:30 a.m., John, Donna, and Maureen Norris went to the Detective Bureau to meet with Kathy Wilson. Donna and John had discussed things and believed they had an explanation as to how Jeff could have known about John's absence that weekend.

After sitting down and getting comfortable, Donna told a detailed, shocking story. It was back on May 29, 1993, just a year ago, according to Donna's records, that she had called the company Jeff worked for and spoken to his boss about a problem they were having with a glass-covered oak table. The glass had cracked, and they needed a template made and the glass replaced.

Jeff's boss said he would send someone right out.

It was 6:30 p.m. on June 1, 1993, when Jeff showed up to make the template for the Palomba's table. Donna and John recognized Jeff with a friendly hello, and John and Jeff started talking.

"I'm stressed out, John . . . I got into a fight with my brother-in-law. I really need to get away on a vacation."

"That's too bad," John said. "I'm heading out to Colorado in September for a wedding. Family can be tough, Jeff. Maybe a vacation is exactly what you need."

Donna was walking by as the two men chatted, and casually joined the conversation. "I'm probably not going with John, because my business partner is expecting a child right around that same time. I also have a new account at work that is keeping me busy."

After assessing the crack in the glass, Jeff said he'd be back in a few days with the new glass top.

"Can you call first?" Donna said.

"Yes. Sure."

Jeff showed up soon after, but not on the day he said he would. Nor had he called first. Instead, Jeff knocked on the door on Saturday morning, June 5, at 9:30 a.m.

Donna was upset. She was home alone with her two children. She had papers all over the table, which she had been using as a desk.

"You were supposed to call first," Donna told Jeff, clearly irritated that he had not listened to her direction.

"Ah, that's okay," Jeff said, walking in. "I have all day. No need to worry."

As Jeff waited, Donna bent over and cleaned the papers off the table so Jeff could get to work. As she did, Jeff "came up behind her, put his hand on her back, and started to rub her back."

Jeff's touch startled Donna. She turned around quickly and "glared at him," Donna explained. It was not long after the touching incident that Jeff went "out to his truck," Donna further explained, "where he stayed for fifteen to twenty minutes." Donna said she had no idea why or what he was doing.

After he came back in, Donna kept her distance for the remainder of the time Jeff was at her house, never taking her eyes off him and always sitting with "her back against the chair" and her children close.

"I'm so stressed out I could explode," Jeff said at one point.

He eventually left.

That complaint, accompanied by an affidavit outlining Donna's case, written and filed by Maureen Norris, led to an Internal Affairs investigation, which was now well under way. IA investigators had been sniffing around for a few weeks, calling some of the people connected to the case. Within that IA investigation, Donna received bits and pieces of information from various sources. This led to a meeting with Inspector Griffin, Robert Moran, Neil, Maureen, Donna, and John.

Donna and Maureen wanted to know exactly where the investigation stood from the WPD's viewpoint, and more pointedly, what was in, or not in, her file. Every time they turned around, something from that file seemed to be missing.

Donna had learned that there was no sign of the WPD talking to three other people whom she was told had been interviewed (and tape-recorded) by Lieutenant Douglas Moran. Donna had also heard that someone had reported a suspicious vehicle in the neighborhood on the night of her attack; the tipster had given four digits of the license plate and was told the WPD was running a make on the vehicle and looking into it.

"There is nothing in the file about that vehicle," one of the investigators explained to Donna, John, and Maureen.

There was also a question as to where the audiotapes of the transmissions from the night of September 11, 1993, were. The WPD, like many police departments, recorded radio transmissions of police calls coming in and going out. Perhaps an important clue in those tapes that could somehow help Neil and Pudgie had been overlooked.

"That is not available—apparently, that night has been recorded over."

And where were the telephone wires taken from Donna's house—specifically the line that had been cut. Where was that piece of evidence?

"The wires are there in evidence, but the actual telephone line that was cut by your perpetrator is not there."

Donna wanted to scream.

"Donna," Neil said, trying to change the tone of the conversation and focus on moving forward. "We'd like to have a list of all of the males and females you and John know personally, who might have known John was going out of town that weekend."

This was a good sign to Donna; the WPD was looking at her case from a different angle.

"The Morans," Donna added, "said they had ruled out that the locks on the house could have been picked."

Maybe someone had a key?

"We'd like to get Jeff back in here and take a sample of his hair," Inspector Griffin suggested, seemingly ignoring Donna.

The entire discussion seemed rather surreal for Donna. Now they wanted to drag Jeff back in and obtain a hair sample. Why? Didn't they have his blood?

—◆—

I believe this was the first time I entered the police station since October 1993—that day when Lieutenant Moran interrogated me—and then when John and I went back to sit down with Captain Moran and Phil Post. As you enter the station there is a large glass partition separating guests from the front desk officers. As I walked in and saw the officers, I felt all eyes were on me, that they all knew exactly who I was, and it made me self-conscious and uncomfortable. I looked at them and wished somehow I could send a telepathic message relaying who I truly was, erasing all the negative information that they may have heard about me. I had the same feeling as I passed other officers in the hall and as I walked through a busy open area where officers were working at their desks and milling around. It appeared they were trying to be discreet, but I saw them looking up as we marched through to Inspector Griffin's office, where the meeting was held. It was the first time I had met Griffin, and John and I wanted to be sure he knew the kind of people we were. The question of obtaining a sample of Jeff's hair was odd. There would be no need to get Jeff back in for a hair sample since we already had his blood. It led me to believe, after I thought about it, that Inspector Griffin may have said that to let us know they wanted to actively pursue anything they could. They were trying to make us feel comfortable and prove that the investigation was now on the right track.

—◆—

John, Donna, and Maureen discussed Martinez among themselves for a moment.

"We'd like you to hold off on bringing Jeff back in," Donna said, "until the DNA results come back from Washington."

Leaving, Neil said he and Kathy Wilson wanted to meet John and Donna at John's mother's house so they could interview her (John's father had passed away in 1989). For the first time in the investigation, eight months (to the day) after the attack, Neil brought up the missing key John's mother had talked about just days after the attack. Neil was particularly interested in this key. If Mrs. Palomba's story of the key was true and that key went missing before Donna's attack, it meant there had been a way into Donna's house floating around in the world on the night of her attack. This could be significant. It could potentially fit into the theme Neil seemed to be focusing on: people close to Donna and John who knew their schedules, knew a bit about their lives, or had access to their home.

Before they left the WPD, Neil asked Donna about a particular relative. "Does [this person] have a grudge against you?"

Donna was shocked to hear the name, especially in the context of her case and if this person had an ax to grind. "What? Not that I know of."

It was 5:15 p.m. when Neil and Kathy arrived at Donna's mother-in-law's house. For the first time in the now nearly year-old investigation, Donna's mother-in-law sat down for an interview with the police.

Donna listened as Mrs. Palomba was questioned about the missing key and the particular family member. She had no idea why they were focusing on this person.

"She's a nice person who wouldn't harm a soul," Mrs. Palomba explained, referring to the relative. "She's often confused and on medication."

Neil and Kathy shared a glance. Medication?

What they weren't telling Donna, or anyone else, was that this family member was supposedly the person behind that rumor convincing the Moran brothers that Donna's story was "full of holes." This person had told the confidential source's mother about "the affair" and the kids waking up and catching Donna in the act of adultery.

Donna was bewildered by these questions.

The missing key was troubling. I could picture it hanging on a wood plaque with a row of hooks in the back entryway to the kitchen inside my mother-in-law's house. I could see it in my mind as they talked about it. There was a small white label on the face of the key with the word "John" written in my mother-in-law's handwriting.

John's family home was the gathering place at holidays. The house was a traditional two-story colonial with a large living room and a big fireplace that was always roaring on Christmas Eve. The smell of a wood fire and music filling the air were festive and nostalgic. The front foyer was large, and there was a stereo cabinet. John and his family were music buffs and my mother-in-law loved musicals, so there was always some type of music playing. The foyer turned into a dance floor when our kids were little. They were the first grandchildren, and everyone would line up waiting for their turn to dance with them. An abundance of love and warmth filled the air.

Now, suddenly, as I sat there listening to Neil and Kathy Wilson question my mother-in-law, this magical house with its so many wonderful memories was the center of the case. Could someone have taken the key? People were in and out all the time. Sure, someone could have taken it, but who?

I understood the significance of the key and why they were asking about it. As far as that relative they talked about was concerned, we really didn't see her that often. She was a gentle woman, and I remember her sending me a novena card in the mail after the incident. She was quite religious, and I thought it was a nice gesture. I relayed this to Neil and Kathy Wilson.

There was no reason to believe that she held any type of grudge against John or me—so that question Neil posed, as he could not divulge why at that time, had me asking myself more questions.

～～

The following day, Kathy Wilson called Donna.

"Inspector Griffin wanted to know a little bit more about that oil leak in your home, Donna."

There had been an oil leak in the basement of Donna's house at the time of the incident. Griffin thought that maybe when they had the oil tank serviced, the serviceman might have gotten the idea to return, after possibly hearing Donna talk on the phone or to John about him leaving.

"We had the tank serviced, removed, and replaced, actually, a few days after the assault."

"Yeah, I suspected as much," Wilson said, "and don't think it has anything to do with the case, but Griffin wanted me to call anyway."

A day or so after this particular call, John attended a stag party in town. This was one of the problems with knowing everyone from the neighborhood: You got invited to everything. There were lots of people from the old neighborhood at the stag, including several cops John knew, and even a few who had worked on Donna's case. As John stood in line for food, Detective Lou Cote walked up and shook his hand.

"John . . . how's Donna doing? I am so sorry about what happened to her."

"She's good," John said. He could tell Lou was sincere. He had a look in his eyes that John responded to. "Look, Lou, I know you were trying to do a good job. We have a lot of respect for you and have told everyone that you are a good guy."

"Thanks. I appreciate that."

"We know that you had nothing to do with what happened."

"All I can tell you, John, is that they [the Morans] are a couple of fucking assholes!"

John appreciated Cote's candor and honesty.

Another police officer walked up to John after that and said, "If there's ever a trial and I am called, I would nail the Morans, John."

The tide was turning, indeed. John Palomba could feel it.

—◆◆—

There is probably no other job within law enforcement hated more by officers than that of the Internal Affairs investigator. His or her job is to investigate wrongdoing by his or her colleagues, complaints against the department, and other uncomfortable situations that officers find themselves in throughout their working days. Cops, like firefighters and even nurses, often live by a code of silence and vow not to talk about one another's shortcomings, guilt, or innocence. If there was ever a case, however, when IA investigators were needed, it was Donna's. What Donna claimed to have gone through at the hands of two high-ranking officers within the WPD was nothing short of bullying and revictimization. These two cops, both of whom had decades of law enforcement experience between them, had viewed Donna as a liar from the moment she called 911—and nobody had a good reason why she was singled out like this and attacked in such an unprofessional, caustic manner.

The two IA officers assigned to look into whether there had been a conspiracy between the Moran brothers to go after Donna and John met with the Palombas at Maureen Norris's office on May 18, 1994.

"We're taking the case slowly," one of them explained. "We'll be speaking with all of the officers involved, and if you know any of them, please tell them to talk to us and help us to shed more light on what happened here."

"I saw Lou Cote the other night at a stag," John said, explaining what was said. "Lou apologized for what happened."

The meeting was short, more of a formal way to announce that steps were being taken to get to the bottom of what Donna was calling harassment by the department, which had allowed her assailant to remain free and possibly continue to sexually assault other women—a fact that was easy to forget.

On his way out, one of the IA investigators said, "To request a copy of the IA report, just file a Freedom of Information request."

Donna wrote that down in her notes. Maureen said not to worry about it. Of course she was going to do that.

That report, in fact, would steer Donna and Maureen onto the road they would travel next. If the IA investigators did their jobs without bias, a true IA investigation would dig out wrongdoing. It was about justice at this point. The more Donna thought about it, the more she wondered how many other women the Moran brothers had done this to. How many more women would have to endure the trauma she had experienced if she did not stand up and fight?

CHAPTER FOURTEEN

Guilt by Omission

DOUGLAS MORAN WASTED LITTLE TIME IN VOLUNTEERING TO HELP with the IA investigation any way he could, although "help" is probably not the correct way to characterize what the lieutenant did next. Although Donna and Maureen would have no idea what Moran (or anyone else IA investigated) wrote until years later, on May 18, 1994, he sat down and, in his own words, "took the liberty of preparing" a statement of what transpired "in anticipation of your [IA's] request for one." The entire document, which he addressed to the lieutenant in charge of the IA investigation, amounted to a strangely detailed, twelve-page report of the case from Doug Moran's perspective. This statement would be Moran's direct response to the affidavit Maureen had prepared in order to initiate the IA investigation.

She said—and now *he* said.

At best, one could say Moran's document was littered with exaggerations; at worst, untruths. For example, Moran wrote that according to Donna's narrative of what transpired on the night of her attack, her attacker had "threatened" her "with a gun."

This was a true statement on Donna's part. She *believed* her assailant had placed the barrel of a pistol to her lips and to her temple.

Yet Moran then wrote that Donna had "repeatedly stated to numerous investigators that she was unaware of the specifics of any armament . . ." and "felt" her attacker had a "heavy, blunt instrument."

There were several instances—the 911 call, statements, and other pieces of documentation—supporting the fact that Donna clearly stated she thought her attacker had a gun. She had never said anything about a "heavy, blunt instrument" or if she was certain it was a gun—but that she *thought* it might be a firearm.

To find fault in Donna's account of what she believed had happened was alarming.

The subject of where Donna fled when she left her house was where Moran focused his attention next. He took issue with Donna's claiming to have run "to a neighbor's house" and added that the act was inconsistent with what the victim of a brutal assault *should* have done. Moran wrote how, in order "to maintain accuracy necessary for the proper investigation of this case . . ."—an odd choice of words to begin with—"it should be pointed out that, in fact, Ms. Doe ran half a block down the street and around the corner to the home of a friend/ relative . . ." To Moran the red flag was Donna's running to a neighbor's house that was actually not *next door* to her house. The idea that she chose the home of someone she knew was another indicator to Moran that she was setting up her story.

The lieutenant went on to explain that this was a "significant" fact, "because through my training and experience, I know that complainants who falsely report a crime tend to make such reports through friends or relatives from whom they can anticipate a sympathetic, non-challenging response." He called this part of Donna's statement a "flag," according to "texts on investigatory principles."

Further, Moran said Donna was "unarmed, wearing only panties and a tee shirt." Point in fact: Donna wore a bathrobe, corroborated by several officers on the scene that night and by Cliff Warner, the man whose house she fled to—the first house she spotted with the lights on. Donna reasoned that at a house without the lights on, it would take a lot longer to get someone inside to understand what was happening. Donna was in a state of panic and fear, so she was running on pure adrenaline and not making decisions with a clear state of mind.

"Cliff was somebody I did not know all that well," Donna later told Maureen Norris, responding to the report. "He's my husband's *second* cousin."

Was Moran tweaking the facts to fit his side of the argument? Was he leaving out important information that did not support his side of the case?

—~—

As Moran's document continued, it brought a few things out into the open. For one, there had been complete agreement among several officers that Donna had falsified her rape claim. From Moran's perspective, everyone he interviewed—"the first responding officer, the detective on the scene, and the Communications Sergeant"—believed that Donna's claim of being sexually assaulted fell apart on the foundation of her own admissions. Moran found it odd that Donna armed herself with a knife "only after the police had arrived." That she "adamantly refused to go to the hospital to be examined . . ." and kept those restraints on her wrist and neck "like stage props . . ." The sergeant she spoke to on the night of the assault—Rinaldi—told Moran, according to Moran's report, that he "found it odd that, having fled her home in panic, Ms. Doe somehow knew that her phone lines had been 'cut.'"

Moran placed the onus for the WPD not securing the house or taking photographs on none other than Sergeant James Griffin, a cop Moran claimed "was the crime scene supervisor on the night in question . . . I was not working at the time . . ."

Another important point for Moran, upon which he founded much of his suspicion, revolved around what transpired during the sexual acts Donna had described in her statement. Regarding this facet of the crime, it was clear that Moran never once looked at the accusations by Donna as being truthful, but began with prejudice, looking for holes to support a theory he had developed and would not waver from: "Ms. Doe had reported that, despite several attempts, the perpetrator was unable to achieve an erection and that no penile penetration occurred, that digital fondling/penetration were the extent of the sexual assault." Moran went on to say that in speaking to the forensic lab, he learned "a large quantity of sperm/semen had been found on the vaginal swab taken as evidence from Ms. Doe . . . When I asked if the presence of sperm/semen could be accounted for in any other manner, such as premature ejaculation, [the lab tech] stated she did not see how the sample could have been obtained unless penile penetration had occurred."

Every time Moran examined Donna's statement, he claimed in his report, he found another reason not to believe her, based mostly on that "text" law enforcement used to weed out false rape allegations. He wrote that he had asked Donna to undergo hypnosis under direction from his brother, Captain Moran, not because they wanted to find out what had happened, but because they hoped "Ms. Doe's subconscious . . . would serve to clear up some inconsistencies and 'flags' which continued to mount as the investigation progressed."

Moran said he was "puzzled . . . that she instead apparently found the suggestion offensive in some way."

Then Jeff Martinez came up, as Moran explained his role in that end of the investigation, leaving out several specific, significant details. He said he found Jeff to be believable because he did not have a blemish on his record and had worked at the same company and lived in town for a long time. (But apparently Moran did not believe Donna, for whom the same could be said.) In addition, Jeff had been interviewed by Moran over the telephone on the day Donna brought Jeff to the WPD's attention. Then Jeff "used his lunch hour to come to police headquarters," Moran wrote, as if he had inconvenienced Jeff, four days later, on October 19, 1993, where Moran and his brother, the captain, sat down and interviewed him.

"He was later asked for a sample of blood and voluntarily responded to the City Health Department, again on his lunch hour," Moran concluded, "accompanied by his wife. I transported the blood sample to the State of Connecticut Forensic Lab."

What Moran left out of this portion of his statement was that the WPD had not asked Jeff for a blood sample until December 3, 1993, after the SAO became involved and not until Donna and her attorney had lodged a complaint, demanding an IA investigation.

In reading Moran's lofty report, you would have to assume that both Robert and Douglas Moran believed Jeff, essentially, after speaking with him and his wife four days after the assault, even after knowing that Donna's sister had allegedly been the victim herself of Jeff's sexually aggressive advances.

Jeff said he didn't do it. The Moran brothers said okay, great. Donna's a liar. Let's move on.

—◦—

My blood was boiling when I read the report. It was filled with lies, and it sickened me. This wasn't just a strongly worded report; it was an attack on my character, and everything I stood for. I was astounded at the length Moran went to try to discredit me and the incredulous things he wrote. He wasn't there that night, yet he wrote how I ran out into the night with only a T-shirt and panties. How could he get away with that? There were officers that saw me in my bathrobe, which I never took off. The line about me "wearing the nylons like a stage prop" shook me to my core. I was in such a state of shock when I ran for help that I didn't even realize the nylons were still attached. Then I am instructed by the officer on the phone not to wash, not to remove anything, and I obey. And this is what I get for following directions?

—◦—

Donna's frustration would not stop there. As Moran's report continued, so did the insults to Donna's standing and integrity. Next Moran talked about that now-controversial "known, confidential source."

"I interviewed the source," Moran wrote, "at his place of business. He told me he had come forward because he hated to see the police waste their energy and manpower, and that he had 'heard a rumor among family,' to the effect that Ms. Doe had been engaged in an affair and the oldest of her children had interrupted her and her lover; further, that after putting the child back to sleep, Ms. Doe concocted a false rape complaint in the event that the child remembered and repeated what she had seen, that Ms. Doe waited until the children were sleeping soundly, and that she then cut her telephone line, [ran] to a friend's house where she could call the police away from the children. This information could not be corroborated. I advised my supervisor, Capt. Moran, of this new twist."

For Donna this was "a complete lie," as she later wrote as a note along the margin of the report filed by Moran. The wording Moran chose, it should be noted, was interesting in the context of a police report, especially the phrase "this new twist," as if Moran was writing for a cop show audience.

Would any cop who had studied the texts of law enforcement as much as Moran stated he had in this report, relay or use as a final nail a "rumor among family" as gospel to condemn a rape victim—especially without checking with the person who had been the source of the rumor? On top of that, what was standard behavior from a victim of a brutal sexual assault? What were the protocols in place by the WPD to handle such a case? Kathy Wilson had not even been consulted during those important hours immediately after the 911 call. Wilson herself would have told Moran that every rape victim experiences different feelings, has a different way of acting. Why hadn't a female police officer—one who had been at the scene of the alleged crime—been consulted on this immediately?

Further into his report Moran focused on Donna's interrogation, which he referred to as an interview. He claimed to not want to speak to Maria Cappella about Jeff Martinez, the reason Donna and Maria had gone to the station house that day, because he wanted to maintain a sense of anonymity for Donna and protect her confidentiality of being Jane Doe—as if her sister didn't know about the sexual assault.

The reason he tape-recorded the interview, Moran wrote, was because policy dictated that whenever a cop interviewed a sexual assault complainant, he was supposed to either have another officer present during that interview or record it. He claimed Donna could not see the wheels of the tape spinning from her point of view sitting at the table, but that he had seen them turning slowly. He thought the recorder was "functioning properly. It was only later, when I went to play the tape back that I found it had apparently failed."

He blamed himself for the blunder, having placed the microphone switch in the wrong position.

Moran rolled over the fact that he had read Donna her Miranda rights by calling it a stipulation "by the department's standard operating procedures."

What a policy, Donna later thought. She wondered if every potential rape victim was Mirandized whenever she sat down to talk about what had happened.

Then Moran moved on to Donna's children. Moran said Donna had "steadfastly refused to allow any investigator" to interview the kids, a fact that was correct. According to Donna, what came out of the report next was not only a lie but also a piece of fiction that was, for Donna, the most intimidating moment of the interview.

"Following a neural linguistic interview, I attempted to explain to Ms. Doe that in certain cases we have asked the state Department of Children and Families to act as guardian of a child for purposes of an interview when the child may be a witness to a crime in which the parents are involved . . . I further explained that we were reluctant to pursue this as it places both parents and children in an embarrassing position, but there are times when we are left with no other choice."

So this was Moran's explanation for threatening Donna with taking away her children and formal arrest. He had, in Donna's view, not only whitewashed that frightening part of the interrogation, but totally lied about how he had handled it and then wrote about it to IA as if he had done the right thing.

The document continued on and on, Moran giving his version of why he had acted the way he had toward Donna during the early part of the investigation. He had an answer, Donna could see after reviewing the report, for just about everything. Ironically, near the end of the report, when the subject of focusing more on Jeff Martinez as a prime suspect came back up, Moran mentioned how taxpayers deserved more for their money where police complaints were concerned and there was far too much crime in the city to be investigated. Rather than wasting time on Martinez, a suspect, according to Moran, that when "boiled down" was a person of interest based on "a hunch that she had," the WPD owed it to its citizens to move on to more promising leads.

Moran had called a possible suspect brought to him by the victim a hunch. The victim of a sexual assault said she had a suspicion about the identity of the man who had raped her, and Moran blew it off as an instinct of the victim's not worth following. The WPD had DNA available to them to rule the suspect in or out, but he wasn't worth the trouble, according to Moran's investigatory skills.

"In closing," Moran wrote, "I can confirm that I have committed no infraction of Departmental Rules and Regulations, no offense against State Statutes, nor any breach of civility. I did everything in my power to provide a competent and thorough investigation despite various obstacles and influences."

Reading this thing was an incredible lesson in humility for me. I wanted to explode. It was so far away from the truth of what happened. For example, according to Moran, it was somehow my fault that the perp used the word "pigs." I remember distinctly feeling awful about relaying the fact that the perp said, "If you call the pigs, I'll come back and kill you" to Detective Lou Cote. In fact, I thought about not saying it, but then I felt it was important to relay every single piece of information as I had recalled it.

No matter how much time goes by, I will never forget the way this report made me feel. As I think back on it, my stomach tightens, and I feel nauseous.

I believe you learn most from your greatest challenges. I have experienced prejudice and discrimination, and it has taught me to be very cautious about judging others—just one of the many lessons I have learned on this journey that truly started as I began to see how Lieutenant Moran and his brother were viewing the IA investigation and how they were going to fight me on this.

Chapter Fifteen

Speaking of Hunches

As Neil and Pudgie immersed themselves deeper into Donna's life and the investigation, they were not as certain about Jeff Martinez being their guy as they might have shared with Donna and John.

"Look," Neil said, "he was definitely sexually aggressive with Maria, Donna's sister, but you must understand that we didn't know what the foundation was for Maria's relationship with Jeff. That was never discussed. I mean, how would Jeff Martinez find himself in that circumstance with Maria?"

Pudgie and Neil met two to three times a day inside Neil's office at the WPD. Since Pudgie was an investigator for the SAO working on other cases, and a former WPD cop, he often found himself inside the WPD.

"What do you think?" Neil asked Pudgie one day as the trail seemed to be going cold. They truly had no new leads to follow.

"Jeff's been cooperative, Neil."

"Yeah. I know."

In talking with Jeff several times, Neil had come away with the impression of a man who had nothing to hide and was willing to give whatever was asked for. Jeff had consented to a blood test and said he'd be willing to take more. He had consented to a polygraph. He had consented to a total background check of his life. Every time they went to speak with him, he was eager to help. Not once did he ever rub either investigator the wrong way, or even invite a lawyer into the situation.

"He's not our guy," Pudgie said.

"I'm with you."

"Back to square one."

"Yup."

CHAPTER SIXTEEN

The Bad News

DONNA GOT WORD FROM FAMILY AND FRIENDS, COWORKERS, AND others she and John knew personally that the WPD was asking those close to her and John to come in and volunteer a blood sample. The SAO had given its consent to begin the testing. No doubt Donna's case—and any potential lawsuit filed against the city, which she still had not yet decided to file—was becoming an infected sore in the city's political body. If the news media got hold of what was going on behind the scenes, there would be a major meltdown, and Waterbury was a municipality that had already weathered its share of scandal throughout the decades.

For Neil O'Leary and Pudgie Maia, two investigators who were trying to stay neutral within the tumult of the internal investigation going on, the idea was to take a blood sample from anyone who might have known that John had gone away that weekend. One of the problems, of course, was that the person who knew this fact and was guilty of the crime would not come forward and admit he knew John was gone.

"We worried about that," Neil said later. "But this was where we were—it was really all we had to go on. And if we ran into someone who showed us any type of objection, or someone who refused to volunteer a sample, honestly speaking, we would focus on that individual."

Then there was that sticky issue of Jeff Martinez, the name that kept popping up as the go-to person of interest, at least where Donna was concerned. Donna had heard that Jeff's DNA results were coming in any day now from Washington. With word going out requesting friends and family to provide blood samples, what was it that investigators knew about Jeff that Donna and John didn't?

"Donna, it's Pudgie." The call she had been waiting for—and maybe fearing most—came on June 30, 1994.

"Hi, Pudgie."

Pudgie said the results were back. "Jeff's not our guy, Donna. I'm sorry."

In her frustration, the news made Donna think about how deep the conspiracy—a term she now firmly believed fit within her case—ran within the department, and how much control the Moran brothers had over the evidence back when they were in charge of her case. After all, it was Lieutenant Moran who had taken Jeff's blood sample and offered to drive it from Waterbury to the state forensic lab in Meriden, a half hour east.

The questions Donna wrote out on a piece of yellow legal paper after hearing the results of Jeff's blood test tell a story, and offer a glimpse into Donna's mind on that day when she was told Jeff was not her attacker, but still had a suspicion that he might have been.

- Why was the DNA sent to Washington and not done by Dr. Henry Lee?
- Why did Lieutenant Moran have the blood drawn after such a long time and after he (Jeff) had been "ruled out"?
- Why didn't he [Moran] send someone else to do it?
- Why was there a time lapse of two and a half hours from when the blood was drawn on December 3, 1993, at noon, till the time it was delivered at 2:30—what if it wasn't refrigerated?
- How did it track? Where did it go from there? I was told the FBI did not receive it till January 14, 1994?
- What about a profile from the DNA—race . . . age, hair color?
- Get [Jeff] in for questioning?

- Why weren't we alerted that Moran had taken the blood from the beginning—we could have had it drawn again immediately (we knew interviews were missing, notes, etc.)?

Some were legitimate questions. Donna had staked a lot of emotion and pent-up frustration on the results of Jeff's DNA test. After all that she had been through, to have it come back negative with all those questionable variables surrounding it was worth the effort to speak up. If Moran had attacked her the way she had alleged, accusing Donna of lying, and then covered up the incompetence of the investigation and his bullying, why not go so far as to tamper with the DNA evidence?

There was nothing that Donna would not put past Douglas Moran and his supporters.

＜ ～ ＞

It was unnerving to me that Doug Moran was the guy that transported the blood sample. I felt that he knew it would make him look foolish if it came back a match to the DNA in my case, especially when they had "99 percent" ruled Jeff out.

At that point I didn't trust anyone from the WPD completely— least of all Lieutenant Doug Moran.

＜ ～ ＞

Donna's conclusion after sketching out all those questions? Take a new blood sample from Jeff and send one vial to a private lab and one vial to the state lab.

But that was not going to happen. Jeff Martinez had been ruled out. Donna needed to forget about Jeff and move on.

＜ ～ ＞

The anxiety was building as I waited for the DNA results on Jeff to come back. At that point, it was all we had, and I needed answers. I trembled listening to Pudgie tell me there was no match. I was torn.

I . . . was glad it wasn't him, but could the results be trusted? Are we really back to square one? Will the perpetrator ever be found? Will I ever know the truth?

—◦—

Captain Robert Moran weighed in with his report to IA on June 24, 1994. Considerably shorter than his brother's twelve-page explanation, the captain appeared to be standing proudly by the side of his officer, the WPD's investigation up to that point, and the way in which Donna had been treated by the lieutenant. Yet it was how Captain Moran articulated his belief in his officer that hurt Donna most.

Captain Moran highlighted the fact that the Vice Squad did not hear about Donna's assault until September 13 (two days after the assault, that Monday). He made it clear that the officers at the scene "were not members of the Vice and Intelligence Division."

The captain had passed the buck.

Next Moran focused on how Donna had repeatedly asked him to listen to the tape of the interview his brother had conducted with her. His reason for not listening to that tape, which had not existed anyway, was fairly simple: "I felt that Ms. Doe and Lieutenant Moran basically concurred as to what was said during the interview in question, making review of the tape a futile, time-consuming exercise. I feel that it is unfortunate that the tape does not exist, but that it is a moot point."

Donna being victimized for a second time and threatened with jail, as well as having her kids taken away, was now a *moot* point. It didn't matter to the captain.

As far as reprimanding Lieutenant Moran for what he had allegedly done to Donna, Captain Moran said he had never been asked to do anything to the lieutenant and, in fact, "Mr. Doe [requested] that Lieutenant Moran remain on the case . . . indicating that they were not seeking any disciplinary action."

—◦—

This comment from Captain Moran was absurd. It was a clear indication to us that even the captain had no regard for the emotional damage that I may have incurred during the interview by his brother, nor did he, as a leader, have any desire to find out if his brother acted inappropriately. Here was an audio recording of the whole interview, and he could not be bothered to listen to it!

As for John's comment, well, it was taken totally out of context. John didn't want Lieutenant Moran taken off the case simply because he wanted the case solved and the perpetrator found. He wanted Moran to get back to work and get on the right track. This was just one more ridiculous distortion of the truth. They were hiding behind lies.

No matter what Donna, John, or Maureen thought about the Morans, IA was going to have the last word. It would take some time, Maureen was told, for the IA investigation to be completed, but as soon as IA issued a report of its findings, she would be informed.

Maybe Donna could have some closure to one part of her case, which would, by the process of justice, open the door for the most important aspect to move forward.

CHAPTER SEVENTEEN

All Apologies

THE INFAMOUS MISSING KEY TURNED UP. JOHN'S MOTHER, DOROTHY, was reinterviewed on May 11, 1994, after she informed the WPD that she had located the lost key to John and Donna's house.

"I don't think the key ever left my house," Dorothy said.

Apparently the key wound up inside the pocket of a raincoat hanging inside Dorothy's house.

Dorothy explained: "My son [John's brother] said he used the key to get into John's house and then left it inside the rain slicker. He used the key in the beginning of July. It is not unusual for the boys to go into John's house and vice versa to borrow things."

By this time, Neil had tracked down John's friends and family, working on the theory that whoever attacked Donna knew that she would be home alone. It was Neil's only course of action at this point. He had nothing else to go on.

The WPD had taken samples of blood from John Palomba and his brothers, all of whom had been ruled out as suspects.

John's brother James said he had no idea about the key being missing, and on the night of Donna's attack, he was with his fiancée.

Neil figured maybe James had inadvertently told someone that John was going away without Donna.

"I doubt I would have told anyone John was away in Colorado and Donna was home alone," James explained to Neil. "I have no idea who could have committed the crime."

As June turned into July, Neil and Pudgie met with several men who could have had access to the Palomba house and knew that Donna was alone—sheetrock workers, painters, maintenance men, friends, and family—to obtain a blood sample.

Neil was particularly interested in the stag party John had missed on the Friday night of Donna's attack. Neil was confident Donna's assailant had been at the party. The quest then became to track down everyone who had been there and obtain a voluntary blood sample.

"One of the things we learned early on—after Pudgie and I took over—was that John Palomba's mother's house," Neil said later, "was like this place where all their friends and family hung out and came and went. They had big families. This guy had to know Donna. Just by looking at the evidence: her attacker covered his face and her face; he disguised his voice; he threatened to kill her; there was no forced entry. This led us to consider the question: Was the perpetrator familiar with Donna's house? But even beyond all that, it was the very first time John Palomba had ever been away from his wife since they had been married. To me, this was a significant fact that could not be overlooked any longer. So we focused our investigation directly on it."

Stag parties were a staple in Waterbury then, much the same as they are today. You had a stag, and everybody went—even people the groom did not know. It was almost an affront not to go if you knew the groom-to-be. Neil felt strongly that someone at that stag party had heard (while at the party) about Donna being alone simply by keeping his ears open. When Neil looked at the timeline of the night, he realized that Donna had been attacked hours after the stag ended.

"All of John's brothers were there, as well as many of his friends. I could picture people asking, 'Where's John? Have you seen John?' And his brothers and friends saying, without thinking about it because they were among friends, 'Oh, he's out in Colorado . . . he couldn't make it.' The guy we were looking for had definitely heard someone say this— and *knew* Donna was at home by herself."

This type of crime, Neil concluded, was not going to happen with John Palomba around.

"John's a big guy—and he can handle himself. Our guy was well aware of this."

─‿─

In August, Sergeant James Griffin submitted his one-page testimonial to IA. In that handwritten document, Griffin said he was at the scene on the night of the crime and "Upon arrival, I made sure the scene was secure ... and interviewed the victim and secured evidence to be sent to the lab. I made sure that the victim had medical attention. I made an extensive search but could not find a point of entry [forced]. All physical-medical evidence was processed according to standard operating procedure ..."

─‿─

This comment by Sergeant Griffin was extremely disheartening and dishonest. The scene was not secure, as any of the people that were there could testify (and did!). They did remove the bedsheets. I would think that standard operating procedure would be to cordon off the scene, take photographs, fingerprints, canvas the neighborhood, conduct interviews with neighbors—none of which was done. And it was Detective Kathy Wilson that suggested I go to the hospital, not Griffin. He could not even get that right. And to say there was an extensive search ... I was astonished by Griffin's report.

─‿─

At the conclusion of Sergeant Griffin's report, he wrote "... [A] supplemental report [was] submitted [and] the investigation then was turned over to Vice and Intelligence."

Captain Moran had placed the onus on the Detective Bureau, and here was Griffin bouncing it right back to Vice.

─‿─

By the end of the 1994 holiday season, there was still no word from IA regarding its conclusions. Donna and John thought this was a good sign. The longer it took, the more thoroughly, one would assume, the investigation was proceeding.

It was shortly after the New Year. Pudgie and Neil were no closer to identifying a promising suspect. But as Neil O'Leary and Kathy Wilson spoke to more men they learned had been at that stag party, something important emerged. For one, John had asked a friend to "keep an eye" on his house while he was in Colorado. It was obvious from the interview conducted by Kathy (now helping to support Neil and Pudgie's investigation) and Neil that John was nervous about going away for the first time in his marriage and wanted to know that his friends had his back while he was away. But this kind of help-a-buddy-out call could have backfired.

One man Neil and Kathy spoke to said, "Yeah, I was at that stag party." He had gone with a friend. The friend said John had asked him to watch his house because he was going away and Donna was home alone.

The thought was that if John had told one friend, and that friend had told others, just about everybody at that stag probably knew that Donna was home by herself.

Lab results were coming in from everyone Neil and Kathy had tracked down and asked for a voluntary blood sample, and there was no match. Everyone they had tested could be eliminated.

Then the report everyone in Donna's camp had been anticipating finally came in. On May 3, 1995, more than a year after IA had initiated its investigation after Maureen Norris filed her affidavit, her fax machine beeped—and in came all of a page and a half from the superintendent of police, Edward F. Bergin, detailing what IA had found during its thirteen-month investigation.

The department, Bergin's letter to Maureen began, had "concluded its internal investigation of your . . . complaint." Then the letter contained some back-patting for Captain Joseph Cass, the main IA investigator, "for his thoroughness and professionalism in conducting the same." Bergin made no mention of the fact that it was odd for a captain (Cass) to be placed in charge of investigating another captain (Moran) for misconduct. (In fact, such an assignment for an internal investigation almost never produces truth-telling. That blue blood runs deep in any law enforcement department, which was why an outside agency would have been the most objective party to investigate the case.)

"The investigation," began the third paragraph of the superintendent's report, "has found no impropriety on the part of either Captain Robert Moran or Lieutenant Post. It was further determined that Lieutenant Douglas Moran's conduct toward your client was in no way improper. The criminal complaint was extensively investigated and that investigation had to, as a matter of course, investigate any inconsistencies in your client's statements to police."

Maureen was stunned as she sat and read this letter.

"I was devastated by this—because obviously they did *not* do an internal affairs investigation," Maureen said later. "At that point I felt that Donna was up against a wall. It seemed like everybody in the department was trying to protect themselves and they weren't going to do *anything*."

All Donna wanted, she had maintained throughout the IA investigation, was to be acknowledged and to prevent the same thing from happening to anyone else. She demanded the department apologize to her and take responsibility for its personnel. And it wasn't even a public apology Donna wanted, because she was still standing behind her curtain of Jane Doe anonymity.

Apology and accountability weren't going to happen, Maureen now knew.

The report from IA continued, throwing salt on a still open wound.

"Lieutenant Moran was remiss, however, in his handling of the tape-recording equipment and I have spoken to him relative to this finding."

A slap on Moran's wrist for flubbing the recording that could have answered so many questions.

Most of Bergin's argument in his letter centered on the fact that Vice and Intelligence "did not have initial control of the crime scene." Therefore ". . . [A]ny allegation of impropriety relative to the initial handling of the crime scene or evidence cannot be ascribed to them."

Bergin maintained that Donna's initial criminal complaint was "extensively and aggressively investigated by this department [and that] [n]umerous individuals were interviewed and eliminated as suspects."

Where was the response to Donna's main reason for filing the complaint—that she had been revictimized by Moran, bullied, and made out to be a criminal?

"Likewise," Begin concluded, "your client's allegations of police misconduct have been thoroughly investigated and other than the mishandling of the tape-recording device, I find no basis to conclude that any officer acted improperly."

Bergin encouraged Maureen to contact him personally should she have "or acquire any additional information which you wish me to consider in this matter . . ."

Donna had been concerned all along that the IA investigation was being conducted by the WPD and not an outside agency. But she had wanted to give the system one more chance. Now Maureen sat at her desk, wondering how to call Donna and explain to her that the same system that had victimized her was standing by its actions with such a shallow, insulting report by Superintendent Bergin, who was obviously siding with his fellow officers.

Maureen called. "Donna, listen, I received the IA report. I don't think you're going to like what it says."

"Send it."

Donna stood. Maureen faxed it to Donna's office as she waited.

❦

I remember feeling like I had to sit down—and that it was like being stuck with a knife. There was no impropriety on the part of the officers. The idea that the superintendent concluded that my case was "thoroughly investigated," but that he congratulated his officers, was overwhelming to me.

We've pursued every possible channel that we could. We've gotten nowhere. We met with the state's attorney. There were lies. There were all sorts of reasons for me to believe that things needed to change. I could not allow this to end this way.

～

One of the comments that particularly upset Donna was in a supplemental report filed by the IA investigators, who, among other things, concluded that Lieutenant Doug Moran would have been "derelict in his duties" had he not investigated Donna and her allegations of rape the way he had. It almost sounded as though Moran was being praised for the way he had handled the investigation.

Was it all Donna's fault because she had unknowingly given these "red flags" throughout the night of her alleged assault and afterward? According to the IA investigation and the WPD, Donna had not acted in the proper manner after she reported the sexual assault.

～

Every blow became a boost. I was like, "You have got to be kidding me." After the initial blow of that report and the way that the "brethren" of the WPD were sticking together, I wanted to make sure, more than ever now, that this would never happen to another victim put in my position. These guys were bullies. They needed to be confronted. They thought, As long as we keep pounding her, she'll go away— that this IA report would send me running.

I'll be damned. This cannot continue. If it happened to me, it happened to others. It will happen again.

I could not allow for it to continue.

～

Donna was stronger now. Each assault on her character toughened her. She was willing and able to take the WPD head-on—especially the Moran brothers—and fight for what she believed. Her integrity and honor were at stake—not to mention catching the guy who had raped her.

Donna met with Maureen. "I won't take this," she said.

"Yeah . . . it's incredible."

"I want to file a suit against these officers." Donna said, referring to the Moran brothers.

"It's not that simple, Donna. In order to sue them, you need to file a suit against the City of Waterbury."

"So be it. I'm ready."

❧

When Neil O'Leary later looked back at the IA investigation and thought about it, noting how easy "it is to be a Monday morning quarterback," there were several things he wished had been done differently.

"It would have been more appropriate to have an outside agency conduct the IA investigation, but it just wasn't the practice then. I am certainly not being critical of the chief of police back then; he was an extremely honorable man with a reputation beyond belief in the community. But the thing was, he was asked to have an IA investigation conducted and he did it. The outcome was something different."

The chief had no direct involvement during the investigation, but it happened under his watch.

"The chief was going by what his investigators were telling him," Neil said. "And you have to take into consideration that, at that time, there were still a significant number of people within the department who believed there was something wrong with Donna's story—and believed as likely as not that this sexual assault had never taken place. But what happened to Donna became that she was being victimized over and over again."

The unprecedented aspect of Donna's case, something that deeply bothered Neil, was that never before—even with a truly uncooperative victim—had he heard of a lieutenant sitting down with the victim of a crime (a sexual assault, no less) and going after her like Doug Moran had zeroed in on Donna.

"It goes back to lack of training and experience," Neil suggested. "Moran did it based on some information from some non-credible person"—the confidential informant—"who had heard that Donna was having an affair. It was no more substantial than that."

Had Moran listened to the 911 call carefully, walked through the crime scene with Donna, and, most important, spent a significant amount of time with her and gotten to know her personally—the things done by Neil and Pudgie—Neil said, "I think that he, even with very little training in sexual assaults, would have found that there was no *way* that Donna Palomba could have made this up."

Neil went on to explain, "What I did from that first day Pudgie and I got involved was to get to know Donna Palomba and find out what kind of person she was."

Neil said he spent hours just "being around Donna" to find out who she really was, how she reacted to situations, and how she handled herself around cops.

"She may not be the person that she appears to be," Neil said. "But that's not what happened. I spoke to dozens upon dozens of people who knew Donna and asked those hard questions, such as, 'Is there a dark side to Donna Palomba? Is it possible that she was leading some sort of double life?' Maybe she's not the angelic person everyone thinks she is. And the amazing thing I uncovered, after all was said and done, *every . . . single* person I talked to adored this woman, thought she was a magnificent person, a religious person, a family person, a great mother and wife . . . it was incredible how many people adored her."

The more time Neil spent with Donna and the more he got to know her, it became "amazing to me," he said, "that you would *not* believe her."

If only, he concluded, "the Morans would have done the same thing, all of this would have turned out differently."

Or would it have?

CHAPTER EIGHTEEN

The King Can Do No Wrong

SUING A MUNICIPALITY IS NOTHING LIKE CHALLENGING A TRAFFIC violation. Maureen Norris knew from the moment Donna gave her the go-ahead that this would be one of the most challenging cases she had ever tried.

"We had to file this suit," Maureen later explained. "But the lawsuit end of this was very difficult. We knew going in that this was going to be a very difficult, difficult case to win."

The City of Waterbury (like most municipalities) had what's called sovereign immunity from most lawsuits. Immunity didn't protect the city from suits regarding defective sidewalks or building collapses. But when dealing with lawsuits against public officials, the rules were different.

"A suit like this, with sovereign immunity involved, goes back to the idea that the king can do no wrong," Maureen explained. "In order to prove our case, we had to prove that they had violated a ministerial duty, as opposed to something that is discretionary."

"This is extremely tough to do," Maureen told Donna.

But Donna had gone through too much. It was time to get tough.

"You see," Maureen said, "most of the city's rules are written in such a way that you cannot get around immunity. So we had to actually *find* rules that they had broken."

One of the issues in this case was that there was no city policy or procedure that outlined how any and all crimes should be investigated. The fuzzy line of discretion came into play. Cops could use their own judgment. If they said they did no wrong, then the statute was written in a way that backed up their claim of having done no wrong. And their counterparts and colleagues, of course, would stand behind whatever they claimed.

There was no standard protocol for how to respond to a specific crime scene, for example. Sure, there were texts in place *suggesting* what to do. But a cop could make his or her own call on the spot. And whatever that call turned out to be was backed up by the law.

Donna saw the failure of the system here and wanted to not only win this lawsuit, but also change the policies and procedures so that there was a standard way to respond to a sexual assault crime scene.

"Obviously Donna was wronged," Maureen said. "But the question we had to face and answer was, in dealing in the eyes of sovereign immunity, was Donna *still* wronged?"

What became most difficult for Maureen was knowing Donna personally.

"I knew she was going to have to go through hell . . . and that was the toughest part of this."

Not only would she have to endure the emotional torture, but Donna stood a good chance of losing the case against the city.

In her detailed lawsuit, filed against "Douglas Moran, Robert Moran, Philip Post, and the City of Waterbury," Maureen laid out Donna's case within eleven "causes of action" and 119 paragraphs. She broke down Donna's argument point by point, focusing on the improprieties of the WPD and its investigating officers, how they treated Donna after the attack, and how they compromised the investigation and failed to work the case properly from the moment the WPD arrived at Donna's house. That perfect storm of incompetence to which Neil O'Leary alluded swirled around her case as soon as Donna got on the phone with the WPD and started to describe what had happened to her.

As Maureen prepared for what would be a long, tedious process of depositions, Donna voiced her frustrations about the IA report to the one person she had not wanted to reach out to, but who she felt might be able to help her in some way: John Rowland, a family friend. Rowland had just been elected that year as the eighty-sixth governor of Connecticut, an office he would hold until 2004, when he became involved in a corruption and graft scandal that would ultimately land him in federal prison.

—◦—

My husband's parents and John Rowland's parents were very good friends. They lived in the same neighborhood. My father-in-law and Mr. Rowland (the governor's father) had both passed. My mother-in-law was good friends with Mrs. Rowland. My brother-in-law Bill and my husband, John, went to school with John Rowland at Holy Cross. I was desperate to reach out to any-body who could help me . . . once again, with the IA report, I felt as though I was screaming fire in a burning building, but nobody was hearing me. Did this really have to come down to a lawsuit? I mean, not only were the Morans and Phil Post let off the hook, but they were congratulated for doing a great job. I could not allow this to be my legacy. If I didn't speak out, how many more would have to go through what I went through? It disgusted me, and I wanted the governor of the state to understand what was going on in the town where he had grown up and the state in which he governed.

—◦—

Donna addressed the letter personally, "Dear John." After wishing the governor and his family well, she informed Rowland how she had just received a copy of the IA report from her case and was finding it "diffi-cult to explain the anger, frustration, and overall sadness" she felt "with regard to [IA's] response." She said it was "outrageous" that the WPD was "standing united" behind its officers. Donna mentioned how she had desperately hoped the truth would come out and the IA investigation could be conducted "thoroughly and honestly."

"John, I realize this is one family's turmoil in the midst of hundreds of other concerns you deal with on a daily basis; however, it could impact other innocent victims in the future. What has been done here is wrong and it must be addressed. I am tremendously grateful for any advice or direction you could give us in this regard."

One part of this that became important to me as time went on, and would ultimately drive me to see this all to completion, was that through the filing of this lawsuit, I had listed police department policy and procedure changes I wanted executed as part of my settlement, so no other victim would have to endure the nightmare I had been through. I asked for improved sexual assault training to ensure that future victims were treated with respect and compassion, along with an apology and acknowledgment that I had been telling the truth all along.

As Donna waited for a response from the governor, the business of deposing each of the main players started. This lawsuit process, Maureen had warned, was going to take years, not months. The depositions alone would take a year or more. Then there was the chance that the city would want to settle out of court. Yet it all began with those grueling depositions.

The deposition process was long, frustrating, and labor intensive. Most of the depositions were done at Maureen's office, and most of the time John would accompany me. Maureen's partner Bob would join us for some of them. My stomach would do flips when officers would

lie and I had to sit there without being able to speak. Eventually, I
resolved myself to the process and would try my best to focus on what
was being said and take notes to review with Maureen afterward. I
knew that if we were to build a strong case that this was a necessary
evil, and it gave us invaluable insight as to where they were com-
ing from. It truly split the lines and showed for the first time exactly
where everyone involved stood.

The biggest shock to Donna and John during the deposition process
came when Detective Lou Cote stepped into Maureen's office, sat down,
took his oath, and then began talking about his role in the investigation
and his thoughts about how the case had been handled. John remembered his earlier conversation with Lou and how Lou had expressed his
disappointment with the Morans and how things had been handled.

Would Cote stand behind those words?

It was now September 29, 1995, just over two years since Donna's
assault. Cote began by telling the lawyers exactly what Donna had relayed
to him about her attack. Cote's version was pretty much on par with what
Donna had said in her first interview. It was obvious Cote had gone
through the report (or some sort of notes) to prepare for the deposition.

The first surprise for Donna came when Maureen asked Cote,
"After you reviewed the initial report and spoke with [Donna] and
got her statement, and did whatever else that you did . . . was it your
belief that [she] had been sexually assaulted on September 11, 1993?"

Cote seemed stunned by the question, asking, "After I did that?"

"Yes."

"At that time, I had no opinion."

When asked if Cote thought the information provided by Maria
Cappella (at the time) was relevant to Donna's case, Cote answered, "Yes."

Then Maureen raised the question of whether Cote had placed
Maria Cappella's statement into Donna's file. This had been a point

of contention. The "talk" Cote had with Maria—he would not call it a statement—had been missing. No one seemed to know where it went.

"Did you place that statement into [Donna's] file?" Maureen asked.

"No."

"Why not?"

"I did the report, and I laid it on Lieutenant Moran's desk, which is what, you know, is normal procedures, because he reviews the report. And then it is placed in the file. *I* don't place it in the file."

Cote admitted he "had no knowledge" of Moran placing that specific report into Donna's file.

The detective went on to say that there came a time when he disbelieved Donna had been sexually assaulted. It began, Cote testified, when he reread Donna's statement. Her story began to fall apart for Cote there. From the way Donna reacted to an intruder coming down the hallway toward her bedroom, to how she had claimed that, with a pillowcase covering her head, she was still able to discern that the attacker had gone through her drawers, tossing clothes on the floor, looking for money and jewelry and even a set of panty hose to tie her up. This didn't add up for the detective after he thought about it; he couldn't fathom how someone could see well enough through a pillowcase to come to those determinations.

Certainly it would have been easy to figure all this out after going back into the house and seeing the clothing all over the floor. And Donna had gone back up to the bedroom after her attack.

Then, Cote said, it was the gun being placed on the floor. This particular statement by Donna made Cote think that perhaps she had been making up the story as she went along.

"If it was a gun," Cote said, "by laying it on the floor, you are *not* going to know if it is metal. That gun is solid. It is not going to ring. It is not going to make a metal sound if it's a solid item."

Cote never said whether the WPD conducted its own test, placing a gun on Donna's floor to see if it was the least bit possible to recognize, with your eyes closed, as a gun. The WPD, in fact, never reenacted Donna's attack; they merely assumed the metal gun would not "ring" against the wood floor.

Maureen never pressed Cote on the issue, but any seasoned investigator would have done a simple reenactment to see if it was possible.

What truly got Cote to think that Donna was lying turned out to be Donna's behavior.

"And another thing," he said, not making eye contact with Donna or John. "When a victim goes through a very serious trauma, as this would be called, it is known that the brain has a mechanism that shuts down." Donna sat, listening in total disbelief to what this man was saying. She had always considered Cote an ally, someone who believed in her. Cote had even walked up to John at that stag party last year and told him he would testify against the Morans; he said he was backing Donna all the way and didn't agree with the way she had been treated. Now this?

"It is called a release valve," Cote added, describing the part of the brain that shuts down during a traumatic situation. "And it blocks out certain episodes of the crime. You don't remember. You may never remember them. A year later you may. A month later. You don't know. It may never come back."

He was suggesting that Donna had given the WPD *too* many details about her attack; she had recalled *too* much! Donna was being judged on her memory now.

Donna had a hard time controlling her emotions while listening.

❦

Here's the thing about Lou Cote: He [nor Doug Moran] ever bothered to even step foot inside my home. The most Moran did was take photos of the outside of our home. Yes, I did think that if they had had so many questions, why didn't they bother to explore each of them further? During Cote's deposition I felt incredibly betrayed that this detective who looked John and me in the eyes and shook our hands

*and appeared sincere had suddenly turned on us. What kind of person
does that? I felt sorry for him. It was pathetic.*

For perhaps the first time, the following idea was considered: If Donna
had been lying, making up this elaborate story to cover for herself and
her lover, why wouldn't she smash a window, cut a screen, or somehow
make it look like her intruder had forced his way into the house? Why,
if she had given the WPD so many details, so many specifics of that
night that they thought it odd, would she not cover up her crime in
some staged way? Most falsified claims of break-ins, sexual assaults,
and other crimes include some tangible, hard evidence of falsification:
a story that just doesn't line up, a window broken from the inside out,
maybe a timeline discrepancy. There was none of that in Donna's case.

"No," Cote said, he did not find anything Donna did in the beginning unusual.

"Are you aware that [the victim] suffered a scratched cornea as a
result," Maureen said rather bluntly, maintaining her argument that
had Donna made all this up, she would have had to scratch her own
eye—a very serious, potentially blinding injury.

"Yes," Cote said. "I believe that was in her statement."

"How do you think that was inflicted?"

"I would have to see the medical [reports] and talk to her doctor
on that, because I don't know what kind of an injury that was inflicted."

"Don't you think before you made a determination such as this,
you should have talked to the doctor?"

"This case was taken away from me. I am telling you . . . You asked
my opinion. And I am giving you my *opinion*."

Donna looked at John.

Unbelievable.

The Moran brothers had gotten to Cote, they believed. He was
playing it safe. Protecting his job, perhaps.

Further along into Cote's deposition, during what became almost an hour of a back-and-forth between Cote and Donna's attorney, she asked, "Did you ever hear that Lieutenant Moran taped the conversation . . .?"

"I don't know nothing about no tapes," Cote said.

Maureen pressed.

Cote stood his ground, and it was clear where his loyalty remained: "I don't know anything about the tapes. The tapes have never been discussed with me. I have never heard it. I have no knowledge of the tapes. I don't know about tapes . . ."

After several more questions regarding whether Cote had an opinion as to why he was taken off the case, Maureen concluded her questioning.

As he left the room, Donna sat hurt and confused by what she had heard.

━ ～

With regard to Lou Cote's deposition, I could not believe that he had turned against us. Detective Cote took my statement, and he saw me when my eye was still healing. I went down to the WPD that day with John. I tried to be as calm and composed as I could be, relaying as much information as I could about what happened. I wanted to come across as being strong enough to get through this. I didn't want to be an extra burden to the detectives investigating my case. I wanted to show them that I was ready and willing to see this through and was emotionally strong enough to weather it all. Well, Lou appeared to be concerned and sensitive to both John and me as I sat there giving him my statement. Then to find out he thought the way I was acting odd. And the fact that I had remembered details was not in line with how a victim of sexual assault should act. The guy did a complete 180-degree turnaround in his deposition, and it was not the same Lou Cote we met that day.

━ ～

There were no surprises from the Moran brothers during their depositions; they stood firm and strong in solidarity, willing to see the case through to an end they had already established as fact from day one. There was something immutable between these two men, even Neil O'Leary commented later, regarding their stated belief that Donna was lying. Nothing could ever change their minds. It wasn't as though they had set out to conspire against her and frame her; it was that they believed she had lied. With the measly training they'd had with sexual assaults, according to Neil, there was no way they could see between the lines of the case and admit they had made a terrible mistake. In other words, they were too far into this now and were going to stick with their story to the end, no matter what anyone said.

~

As for the Morans' depositions, I braced myself to expect anything and was more prepared. But no matter how prepared I was, it was surreal to sit in the same room across from Doug Moran (knowing what he had done to me), unable to say a word, listening as he spun his web of lies. The Post-Traumatic Stress Disorder (PTSD) I had suffered from already was raging during those days of the depositions. I could feel my heart pounding, ears burning, and this feeling of nerves racing through my body as if I could jump out of my skin. I would rather do physical labor all day than deal with the mental torment that had become part of the norm while we prepared for trial.

~

The depositions dragged on for years. Yes, *years*. Detective Cote's deposition took place in September 1995, but it wasn't until March 12, 1998, more than two years later, that Captain Joseph Cass, IA's chief investigator on Donna's case, sat and talked about how IA went about investigating the WPD.

The slow, grinding wheel of bureaucracy disenchants, disenfranchises, and disheartens the innocent. Think of the people who have spent decades on death row only to later be exonerated. Justice seems to take forever when you fight. But Donna, despite all her frustration and turmoil and disbelief, had weathered the storm quite well. She was in this for the long haul. By the time Cass testified, Donna basically expected him to cover for his counterparts, to continue facilitating what she felt was the big lie.

Certain aspects of Cass's deposition were simply absurd. For instance, Cass admitted he had never spoken to any of the responding officers other than Sergeant James Griffin. It became clear from Cass's testimony that instead of going to the source—let's say Donna, for example, or John—he opted to ask Captain Moran about specific items within the investigation. So Cass's source for investigating misconduct by Douglas Moran was Lieutenant Moran's brother, the captain.

It appeared, from listening to Cass, that he never challenged the Morans regarding anything they did. He just took their word.

This way of handling an IA investigation was inexcusable.

In the end Cass believed the case had come down to a he said–she said dilemma; and in those particular cases, the IA investigator made clear, Internal Affairs always erred on the side of law enforcement. Donna would lose every time.

By the end of 1998, Donna was itching to get the case settled and move on—she knew she would always carry with her this one night of her life, in which she had been brutally assaulted, but it wasn't supposed to take years and years of anguish and discomfort like this. Donna was a forty-two-year-old mother of two growing kids, a career woman, a pillar, really, within her community of friends and family. She had resolved not to allow this one episode to define her. But it was, in many respects, consuming her. She couldn't escape the thoughts of the assault and the revictimization as she went to sleep every night— the darkness itself always being a point of trauma and fear since the attack. Then every morning she woke up to the thoughts again.

An incredible moment came after the depositions concluded, when John's relative, the woman who had supposedly started the rumor that solidified the Moran brothers' already-established belief that Donna was lying, signed an affidavit stating that she was "aware that someone broke into Donna Palomba's house in . . . 1993, however . . . [she] was not aware of any of the details of the crime."

Further, she stated, "I never had, nor do I now have, any reason to suspect that Donna Palomba was or is having an extramarital affair . . . That I never, on any occasion whatsoever, said to [the informant's mother], or any other person, that Donna Palomba was engaging in an extramarital affair or that I suspected that she was."

The substance of the rumor that had initiated the tongue-lashing and threatening interrogation Donna had endured from Lieutenant Moran, the main reason why the WPD had not believed Donna's account of being sexually assaulted, had never taken place, according to its alleged source. Someone had made up a rumor of a rumor, and spread them both. And to think, all the WPD had to do was interview this woman, and investigators—including Cass and his team—would have gotten the same information.

—◦—

This was that rock solid evidence the Moran brothers had against me? This was that supposed 100 percent proof that I purposefully lied to the police—the "countless interviews and photographs," as Moran had said to me during my interrogation, that proved I was lying? This unconfirmed, unsubstantiated, uncorroborated piece of gossip is what they had? And, as it turned out, the "family source" denied she ever said it. How on earth could this have turned the investigators to point a finger at me? It was clear that it didn't matter what I said, they were not going to back down from their theory, even if it meant revictimizing someone who had been traumatized already, not to mention having an armed rapist out there, within the community, running free. Reading this affidavit just inspired me more to go forward and fight these people.

CHAPTER NINETEEN

A New Lease

WITH THE DEPOSITIONS BEHIND HER, BY EARLY SUMMER 2000 Donna Palomba was determined to force change. No matter how her lawsuit against the city turned out, she wanted to fix the way in which sexual assault cases were handled by police departments (starting with the WPD) from the moment police arrived on scene. Donna's lawsuit was aimed toward the implementation of these changes within the WPD. There needed to be a standard policy in place, something like an A to Z instructional manual for the police to follow after arriving on the scene of a sexual assault. Every police officer, Donna knew by firsthand experience, needed to know what to do.

"This was the main reason for the lawsuit," Maureen Norris explained.

The lawsuit outlined what Donna had gone through over the years, including "mental anguish, nervousness, dizziness, nauseating feelings, sleep disturbance, PTSD, paranoia, psychological disorders, phobias, humiliation, depression, headaches, weight loss, anxiety, weakness, trembling, nightmares, loss of appetite . . . a great loss to her marital relationship and . . . psychiatric care."

If she couldn't transform her own case within the parameters of the law, Donna figured she could ensure that her suffering never happened to another sexual assault victim.

Knowing Dr. Henry Lee through an introduction by Pudgie Maia, and with Neil O'Leary having been a student of Lee's some years ago, Donna saw a connection that could help affect positive change. But what if her attacker had been arrested in another state (or elsewhere in Connecticut) and his DNA was sitting somewhere, waiting to be matched up against a known source?

"It is my desire," Donna wrote to Dr. Lee, "to donate the creation of a comprehensive website about DNA and your particular work on the subject."

Donna wanted to publicize and advance the cause of DNA technology and the FBI's national database of DNA samples, where "many assailants can be linked to unsolved crimes from evidence left at a crime scene." She called DNA a "strong weapon" in the fight against rape and sexual assault.

The FBI system and database was formally known as the FBI's Combined DNA Index System (or CODIS). According to the FBI, CODIS began "as a pilot software project in 1990, serving fourteen state and local laboratories." That changed in 1994, when the DNA Identification Act "formalized the FBI's authority to establish a National DNA Index System (NDIS) for law enforcement purposes." Well over 170 public law enforcement laboratories across the United States participated in NDIS as the program moved forward into the late 1990s. "Internationally," the FBI said, "more than forty law enforcement laboratories in over twenty-five countries use the CODIS software for their own database initiatives."

According to the FBI, CODIS (which would eventually become an important factor in Donna's case) "generates investigative leads in cases where biological evidence is recovered from the crime scene. Matches made among profiles in the Forensic Index can link crime scenes together, possibly identifying serial offenders."

Donna described her story in detail to Dr. Lee, capping off the narrative with the good news that there was plenty of DNA evidence left behind by her attacker, but no suspect or person of interest to match it up to. She explained to Lee how several suspects had already been ruled out through DNA testing.

"I continue on with my family and career," Donna concluded sincerely, "but it is unsettling to know that the assailant is out there and could come back, or be attacking others. I have hope that someday he will be found through a DNA match."

Donna had no idea, of course, that this letter truly foreshadowed the years ahead. The project of creating the website, she told Lee, was dear to her heart; it was, effectively, a way for Donna to take back her life and turn a negative into a positive. She had to act. She had to do something constructive. Donna Palomba could not sit around while the legal portion of her case—which now had nothing to do with the assault investigation—moved forward. Changing the way sexual assaults were investigated, locally if not nationally and globally, started right there in Connecticut, and she knew her letter to Dr. Lee was the beginning.

Chapter Twenty

The Evil Mayor

EVENTS THAT LED TO A HUGE BREAK IN DONNA'S CASE WERE SET IN motion back in January 1996, when Waterbury residents elected a new mayor, Philip A. Giordano. Mayor Giordano was thirty-three when he was sworn into office. Born to Italian parents in Caracas, Venezuela, having moved to the United States when he was two years old, Giordano was that seemingly genuine mix of personality and politician that won elections. Charming and good-looking, Giordano had the charisma to talk to the people of Waterbury like he was one of them, the toughness that came from being a former Marine (1981–85), and the experience of a former lawyer who had served as state representative. Although in the end all a smoke screen, Giordano came across as the real deal, an honest-to-goodness city man who knew the streets and understood the needs of Waterbury's residents.

But almost immediately, as Giordano got comfortable behind the mayor's desk, whispers of corruption and misconduct flowed through city political circles. This was still long before bloodhound reporters and angry residents acquired the same information.

One of the officers caught in the wake of the mess Giordano was creating was none other than Phil Post, the investigator who had sided with the Moran brothers, admitting to IA that he thought Donna had been lying. Post was fired for "allegedly offering to dispose of cocaine that turned up at Mayor Giordano's post-inaugural celebration," according to a report of the incident. The newly appointed police superintendent, Edward Flaherty, had recommended Post's firing after an IA investigation and departmental hearing revealed he had violated several policies. This time the system seemed to work.

Giordano was keeping up appearances as the right man for the mayor's job, having brought Post's criminal behavior to the forefront himself. It was Giordano who said Post walked into his office on January 2, 1996, the day after the mayor was sworn in, and held a plastic baggie with a "golf ball–size amount of cocaine" over his desk. A man had brought the cocaine into the WPD, Post explained, when he was manning the front desk. The citizen said he had found it at the mayoral celebration the previous night and knew that it came from someone who worked for the mayor's campaign. According to the mayor, Post told him "twice" during their impromptu meeting that next day how he could "misidentify the drugs so the evidence would be lost." Post was, in other words, trying to show his loyalty to the mayor by covering up a crime.

By the end of 1996, Mayor Giordano had fired three high-ranking law enforcement officials, including the superintendent. It was as if the mayor was coming out of the box cleaning house, shouting to everyone around him that he would not tolerate corruption on *any* level, and would not play favorites. But looks can be deceiving. After four years of Giordano's politics and before an almost certain reelection bid, facts would emerge proving that the mayor was perpetrating one image of himself and his office, while behind closed doors, managing another, utterly vile and sinister evil inside himself.

~

On a Saturday night in July 2000, a few months before the first proposed start date of the trial, Donna and John sat their kids down for a chat. Johnny was twelve; Sarah, fifteen. It was time to tell the kids what had happened. They were certain to have questions and had probably been wondering about the tension in the house and the partial conversations that didn't make much sense to their adolescent ears.

After John and Donna finished explaining what had happened, the kids asked several questions. Sarah said she knew "something had happened" because she had seen a note once, adding, "I heard Daddy talking about it to the doctor one time, and I made noise to let him know I was there because I didn't want to hear something I wasn't supposed to."

Donna wanted to cry. Her children were two more victims of the crimes committed against her.

The next night Sarah sat with Donna on the bed. She wanted to talk.

Johnny was there too. He said, "Mom, thanks for telling us what really happened. It's important for me to know."

Donna knew she had done the right thing.

Sarah took things a little harder. She was older. She understood more. After Johnny had left the room, Donna and Sarah discussed the incident in more detail. Donna felt Sarah deserved answers to her questions. At one point Sarah said, "Mom, I can't stop thinking about him blindfolding you. And he had a gun? I cannot imagine."

"Things are back to normal now," Donna explained. "There is nothing to be worried about."

"Were you scared after it happened?"

"Of course, honey."

"Sometimes I wish I didn't know about it because it's like all I think about now," Sarah said.

Donna thought about how to respond. Then she said, "Look honey, we cannot hide from the fact that bad things happen. We have to try to learn from them and make things better. That's what Mom and Dad are in the process of doing."

"I asked Johnny if he was thinking about it and he said no," Sarah explained. She had a look of worry about her. The situation was weighing heavily on the young girl. "Johnny said we were lucky . . . it happened long ago and now we have an alarm and a new house. Then he asked me if the perpetrator could have been a woman. I asked him why he thought that."

Donna was intrigued, knowing how kids think so out of the box.

"What did he say, Sarah?"

"He said he thought maybe [a cousin of Donna and John's was jealous] . . . and she found out he was getting married to someone else [meaning that wedding John had gone to in Colorado] . . . and she was angry and she robbed us."

It didn't make much sense, but from the mind of a child, it was a reason for the break-in: revenge.

"No," Donna said.

"I won't sleep at Granma's anymore," Sarah said.

"Why not?"

"Because it's in the same neighborhood!"

"Well, you don't have to until you feel comfortable again, honey."

━ ～ ～

It was August 2000. Donna's day in court kept being put off for one reason or another. Now, Donna was told, another month—but it just seemed like forever. So John and Donna decided to get away. The kids needed a vacation, as did the two of them.

━ ～ ～

We knew the trial was coming up and wanted a last getaway while we could break free. Some friends we knew were living in Kill Devil Hills, North Carolina. They invited us out. Jay and Leslie are two free spirits who love nature and people and have traveled the world. They find places they want to see and explore, then find work locally at restaurants or ski slopes and truly enjoy life. Ironically, it was Jay and Leslie's wedding that John was attending in Breckenridge, Colorado, on the day of the attack. Jay and Leslie had a small home in Kill Devil Hills with a vegetable garden and an outdoor shower. Along with some other friends, John and I rented a condo overlooking the ocean. Those friends got there first and insisted that we take the larger, master bedroom. It was a beautiful place with big windows overlooking the ocean. You could actually see dolphins jumping in the water from our condo! There were miles and miles of white sandy beaches and big waves. We spent most days sitting around, enjoying each other's company, and cooling off by surfing the waves. We don't have waves like that in Connecticut, so it was a real treat for all of us. Toward the end of the vacation we decided to do some sightseeing.

By now the thought of facing her accusers was intimidating, and yet comforting in so many different ways, mainly because Donna was embarking on a journey to put this part of her case behind her. It was such a strange twist of fate that she was preparing to face off against the police department (and the cops who were supposed to come to her rescue). In a just world, Donna figured by now she would be moving on with her life, her perpetrator in prison, healing being the only problem she had to deal with. But here she was, seven years after the attack, her children in their teen years, taking a vacation, and getting ready for the fight of her life.

After a fun-filled day of sightseeing toward the end of the vacation, Donna was winding down inside the beach condo she and John had rented with their friends. Donna was rinsing off in the shower. Clean off, freshen up, change clothes. Maybe then a barbecue with the others.

And suddenly, there it was—a lump on her breast.

I felt the lump. I tried to rationalize it. It was small, located at six o'clock on my left breast. My breasts have always been dense and cystic, so I thought, Maybe it's just a cyst. *I tried to shrug it off, but it nagged at me. I told John, who was reassuring, but I knew he was concerned. I decided to call my doctor in the morning and scheduled an appointment for the following Monday morning when we returned from our trip. I kept telling myself not to worry about it until I knew if I had something to be concerned about, but it didn't relieve any of my fear. Our friends owned a Winnebago (RV), and we all piled in later that day to head to Cape Hatteras. We ended up climbing the lighthouse. It was a good distraction. I didn't say anything to anyone else about the lump. Then we went to the Wright Brothers National Memorial and Museum. I remember taking a picture of John and Johnny by the monument. I remember thinking,* How blessed I am to have such a great family and friends.

When Donna got home, she immediately went to see her OB/GYN.

The exam was nerve-racking. Donna's OB/GYN sent her for an ultrasound and advised her to go to a breast doctor. If you believed that your luck hadn't been the best lately, a lump could mean only one thing. How easy it was to think the worst. Donna was strong, yes; but when things are not going your way, the mind tends to favor tragedy over triumph.

"Listen," the doctor said after looking at the preliminary test results. "I'm sure this is a fibroadenoma. Nothing to worry about."

Fibroadenoma is a noncancerous (benign) tumor, a word that might not be a helpful or encouraging way to describe this condition, which is fairly common among females. It's generally fibrous and glandular tissue that is balled up to form a small knob.

Scary, the doctor told Donna, but nothing to be concerned about.

"How sure are you?" Donna asked. She didn't need this now. If it was cancer, she'd be fighting two monstrosities at the same time.

"I am as certain of this as I am of anything in my entire life," the doctor assured Donna.

She walked out of the doctor's office still a little on edge, but relieved about the diagnosis of the lump. She could put it behind her as a cancer scare. Many women have gone through the same thing. It was something to keep an eye on, but nothing to consider alarming.

As Donna's trial date grew closer, word came from the mayor's office that the city wanted to make an offer to avoid an ugly discourse and legal action in open court. Apparently City Hall wanted to settle. The city was willing to negotiate a deal. But Donna was skeptical of the city's desire to enter into a dialogue about settling. Something didn't seem right.

Sure enough, her instincts were spot-on. She'd had a meeting set for July 31, 2000, right before she left for vacation. Then the mayor's office called only hours before to say that "the mayor went out of town suddenly and the meeting would have to be rescheduled." So they agreed on Tuesday, September 12, at 11:00 a.m. The night before that meeting, the mayor's representative called to say there was a scheduling conflict and they would have to, once again, reschedule. They asked if Donna was available on September 18 at two o'clock in the afternoon.

Donna "reluctantly agreed," according to her notes of these conversations.

Then the office called that morning to ask if she could come in later that afternoon, at four o'clock.

"No," Donna said. "I cannot do it."

That day, Mayor Giordano called Maureen Norris himself. "Please, I apologize for this . . . but can your client come in at four?"

"I'll ask her."

It had been more than a year since mediation hearings had begun back in August 1999. To say that Donna was frustrated and running out of patience would not put into perspective how low her confidence level was with the mayor's office, and her trust that the city would listen to her concerns and act on them. The mayor seemed to be running backward, unwilling to commit to anything. Donna wanted changes inside the police department—new policies and procedures. Screw the money—it was about the city doing the right thing. She was not backing down from that fight.

Donna decided that she should take the mayor up on his offer to meet that afternoon. Who knew when she would ever get another chance to sit down and hear what he had to say.

"Let's do it," Donna told Maureen.

By now, surrounding Mayor Giordano and his close staff were rumors of widespread corruption throughout his administration. There was talk that the mayor was involved in organized crime on an undetermined level. It was so common in Connecticut politics during the 1980s and 1990s for certain politicians to receive kickbacks from construction companies in place of city contracts that it was almost expected in some jurisdictions. Giordano was running to unseat Senator Joseph I. Lieberman for a chair in the senate that fall (a long-shot bid he would ultimately lose). What's more, Waterbury was "teetering on the edge of bankruptcy," according to the *New York Times,* even as the mayor considered paying off Donna to avoid yet another pockmark on the face of city officials that a civil trial was sure to create. Things were out of control enough already. And it wasn't the first time a mayor of Waterbury had run into potentially severe legal trouble within the preceding twenty years. Joseph J. Santopietro, elected in 1985, had been convicted the year before Donna's attack (1992) on charges related to a bribery and kickback scheme. There was a common feeling among city (and some state) residents that Waterbury was experiencing the corrupt municipal leadership of the 1950s and 1960s all over again. The seat Giordano occupied while staring at Donna, Maureen Norris, Elena Ricci Palermo, and Cheryl Hricko, the two corporate lawyers representing the city, at 4:00 p.m. on Monday, September 18, 2000, was indeed dirty and well worn.

Donna enjoyed a childhood centered on family and faith. Here she is with her sister, Maria, in 1961.

John and Donna met during their college years in the late 1970s.

Donna's husband, John Palomba, was raised in a large, close-knit family. In this photograph from 1965, the family celebrates the election of Fred Palomba, John's father, as mayor of Waterbury.

Donna and John were married at Blessed Sacrament Church in Waterbury, Connecticut, on October 10, 1981.

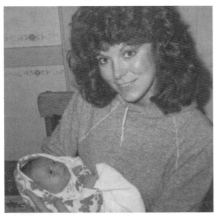

Raising a family came easy for Donna. Here she is with weeks-old Sarah in 1985.

From the moment they were married, Donna and John viewed marriage as a sacred commitment for life.

John and Donna with baby Sarah, two weeks old, October 1985.

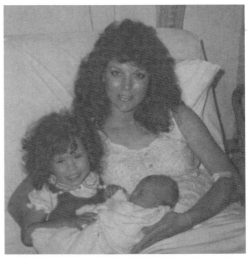

Sarah, Donna, and new addition to the family, Johnny, on August 16, 1988.

John and Donna valued their time together at the family beach house in Clinton, Connecticut (1989).

Before Donna was viciously attacked, life was good. Donna and John loved taking the children on family excursions, such as the Bronx Zoo.

For a family rooted in faith, Sarah's First Communion in 1993 marked a glorious time.

Throughout her entire ordeal, Donna kept the family unit strong and together.

Confiding in family was important to Donna (with her grandfather, Nonno).

Donna's parents, Mary and Louis Cappella, pictured here with Donna, John, and the children in 1995, stood behind her throughout every battle.

The Palomba home in Waterbury, Connecticut—
once filled with wonderful memories—became a
crime scene on September 11, 1993.

Donna's attacker could have walked
through this second floor hallway
leading to the master bedroom inside
the house where Donna was assaulted.

The staircase to the second floor.

The front door showed no signs of forced entry.

Getting famed Dr. Henry Lee involved in her case against the City of Waterbury changed everything for Donna.

John, Sarah, Johnny, and Donna on vacation in Kill Devil Hills, North Carolina, in August 2000 as Donna fought to redeem her reputation while discovering a lump in her chest.

Rocky Regan was an important part of John and Donna Palomba's lives—they shared many memories together. Here, Rocky ran with John in a town road race.

As John "Rocky" Regan faced the iron fist of justice back home, Johnny, Donna, and Sarah spent some time together in Paris (November 2005). It was a welcome break for Donna.

John and Rocky attended parties together and remained close, ever since growing up in the same neighborhood.

Rocky attended John and Donna's wedding and remained friends all those years— including the years after Donna's attack.

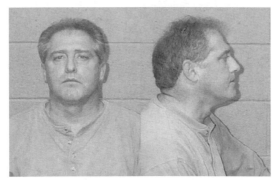

Rocky Regan after being booked in 2004.

Rocky visited John and Donna at the beach house in Clinton during a vacation with family and friends years after Donna was sexually assaulted. (Rocky is on the far right, shirtless, holding a beer bottle.)

Redemption was hers when Donna, flanked by Chief Neal O'Leary, a cop instrumental in solving Donna's case, and Connecticut Governor Jodi Rell, talked about her case evoking a change in Connecticut law.

Donna met lots of people throughout her years of speaking out against sexual assault, including celebrities such as Mariska Hargitay (above) and US Senator Joe Lieberman (below, Chief Neil O'Leary to his right), who fully support Donna's Jane Doe No More initiative.

REPRINTED WITH PERMISSION FROM THE *REPUBLICAN-AMERICAN.*

John "Rocky" Regan's secrets were finally out after he pleaded guilty to several charges stemming from the vicious, evil sexual crimes he had committed. REPRINTED WITH PERMISSION FROM *THE SARATOGIAN.*

No one can break the connection Donna Palomba and Lindsey Ferguson, Regan's last known victim, share—yet both are able to smile and move on with their lives today.

"Sit down, please, Mrs. Palomba," the mayor said, showing Donna and Maureen in. "I apologize for the delays." He seemed wired and shaky. There were other things on his mind.

The rumors of a corrupt mayoral office didn't really matter much to Donna, of course. The mayor was considered innocent until proven guilty in her eyes. Donna knew better than most how it felt to have the brass pointing a finger in your face, or a growing populace calling you a liar. What mattered to Donna and Maureen was the city's terms of a potential settlement. Nothing more. Did city officials want to play ball? Donna was less concerned about a monetary settlement, but would the city agree to the changes Donna wanted implemented within the police department? Those changes were absolutely nonnegotiable.

As the mayor gave Donna his guarded attention, Donna laid out the background of her case before focusing on her policy and procedure recommendations.

"We'd like for you to get back to us by Friday," Maureen said.

The mayor listened intently—as did, unbeknownst to anyone in the room, several law enforcement officers who were eavesdropping on the conversation. The feds had bugged the mayor's office and were also listening to his phone calls. FBI agents were actively investigating Giordano and his office for municipal corruption. Yet that was only half of it. Through the pipeline of that kickback investigation, the feds were about to uncover an unforgivable set of crimes the mayor had been perpetrating, which would bring a new level of hypocrisy, insult, brutality, and inhumanity to that tattered mayor's chair. While Donna sat across from the mayor of Waterbury, describing her attack in graphic detail, Philip Giordano was embroiled in a sexual assault case of his own, only the mayor was the actual perpetrator and children as young as eight years old his victims. In investigating Giordano on suspicion of corruption, listening to his every move and the phone calls he made, the feds had been introduced to a prostitute the mayor was using to get at two children in her life. The mayor might have been giving favors to area mobsters and taking kickbacks, but those crimes paled in comparison to the fact that he was also continually and repeatedly raping two young girls, eight and ten years old, to whom he was given access by that prostitute, who was mother to one and aunt to another.

The special agent in charge of the Giordano investigation, Michael J. Wolf, later put the mayor's crimes into perspective, saying, "The public expects and deserves utmost honesty, integrity, and strong moral fiber from those who serve on their behalf," before adding that the mayor's conduct was "disgraceful."

This was the same man Donna Palomba was negotiating with—a rapist himself (of children, no less).

As Donna met with the mayor, the FBI had yet to uncover that Giordano was involved with the prostitute and her daughter and niece. This would become an issue later, when it was first implied that the FBI had allowed some of the abuse to continue so it could build a case against him.

"When we first determined and believed that Mr. Giordano may have been having inappropriate sex," Agent Wolf told the *New York Times*, "all of the appropriate agencies were notified and performed admirably, first ensuring the safety of the children and then developing the probable cause to charge him . . ."

The evidence was astonishing when later presented in court during Giordano's trial, a case handled by none other than John Connelly, the SA in charge of facilitating the investigation into Donna's sexual assault. Giordano was ultimately charged with six counts each of sexual assault, risk of injury to a minor, and conspiracy to commit sexual assault, all devastating charges that could have put the mayor in prison for life. Giordano came out swinging, calling the prostitute a liar and criminal. But to corroborate her story of supplying her eight-year-old daughter and ten-year-old niece to Giordano for his sexual gratification, the feds provided more than four hours (126 calls total) of taped telephone conversations between Giordano and the prostitute, many of the calls made directly from the mayor's office. The tapes were incredible in their graphic sexual detail, almost unlistenable.

"Who are you going to be with?" Giordano asked the prostitute during one conversation (made just weeks after he met with Donna and Maureen). It was obvious he had known the prostitute for some time and had engaged in this type of behavior with the children already on several occasions.

The prostitute gave the mayor the nickname for her daughter, the child she and the mayor had decided on earlier, an indication that she was bringing the young girl for the mayor's sexual pleasure, to which the mayor replied, "Yup," agreeing that she was the right girl for what he had in mind on that particular day.

But then the mayor, after thinking about it, gave the prostitute a warning: "Make sure! Because if it's the other one, I'll *leave!*"

Apparently, the younger the better for the mayor of Waterbury.

"I did anything he asked me," the prostitute later testified in federal court. She admitted how she had first met the mayor when she was a streetwalker working to support a drug habit. He was a client who simply pulled up and asked her if she was available. Stunning the courtroom as she testified, the prostitute said she had actually "lost count of how many times she had taken the girls to the mayor for sex," adding that his sexual encounters with the children took place inside the mayor's city-issued car, his government office, his old law office, a friend's house, and his own home. He paid the prostitute forty to sixty dollars per visit. The child sexual assaults took place generally between 5:15 and 5:30 p.m., which was after Mayor Giordano's coworkers and staff went home for the night. Sometimes, the woman testified, the mayor would request the children earlier, on school holidays and snow days, when the children were available.

"He wanted *young* girls . . ." she said.

It was four days after that first taped call when the mayor was heard "berating the prostitute for putting both girls in his car [at the same time] before one of their meetings."

"It's awkward for me," the mayor explained, telling the prostitute how he wanted only one child at a time.

Sometime later the mayor can be heard on a call asking the prostitute, "Who's coming with you?"

She named the child.

He didn't approve. The girl she had in mind on that day was, actually, too old.

He said, "I want one of the *little* girls, I told you."

So this was the man—a public official, the mayor of the city, a pedophile and rapist—that Donna and Maureen sat down with to negotiate Donna's case. Donna and Maureen both left the mayor's office that day, September 18, with little confidence that the mayor would be able to facilitate Donna's recommendations of policy and procedure changes.

"I don't know, Maureen," Donna said. "I have a bad feeling."

I did not get a good feeling about him from the meeting. You get a gut feeling the first time you meet someone, and I did not sense that he was sincere in his interest to help. He had blown the meeting off a couple of times, and I only met with him out of courtesy to Maureen. I couldn't believe what I was reading when the story later broke: the mayor had a relationship with a convicted prostitute who was helping him procure young girls for his pleasure? This can't be happening, I thought. And he would entertain these young girls in his private office? I literally shuddered, my whole body trembling. I sat inside that office with him. Did he have sex with these children in the same office where we met? The thought made me sick, and I wondered what he was thinking when I was describing to him the details of my sexual assault.

Chapter Twenty-one

A Breakdown

THE MAYOR'S OFFICE DID NOT SUBMIT A COMPLETE OFFER ON THAT Friday, September 22, as Maureen and Donna had requested. It wasn't until the end of the day, 4:09 p.m., when the fax machine in Maureen's office beeped and the city's proposal scrolled out the bottom. Nothing like the last minute, Donna and Maureen reflected. Jury selection, after all, was set to begin on September 27, just five days away.

The fax was from Elena Palermo and Cheryl Hricko, corporate counsel for the City of Waterbury. The "Doe v. Moran, et als" concerning "Proposals and Regarding Police Proposals," as the offer was now being called, appeared rather detailed in its entirety, yet when one looked at the minutiae, it was a bit more pomp and circumstance than the actual change that Donna had been advocating.

The city had proposed what it called "agreeable" terminology to quantify and assess Donna's recommended policy and procedure changes. The term *agreeable*, according to the city's proposal, "is to be interpreted as meaning that such procedure [of which Donna had recommended being initiated] is already in *use* at the Waterbury Police Department, or that we are willing to implement the concepts of the proposals into existing framework of procedures at the police department."

Whitewash might have been a better way to articulate what was being proposed by the city. Its answer to Donna's demands was nothing more than a transparent apparition of what Donna wanted, a way for the city to favorably appear as perhaps wanting to make changes.

But when one studied the actual language, it was apparent that it was business as usual for the WPD, and nothing was ever going to get done the way Donna believed was essential.

The city's wording within the offer was extremely vague and mysterious. The way Donna read it, the WPD wanted things both ways. Each policy and procedure Donna wanted implemented (Maureen and Donna had spelled out each demand in a corresponding document, numbering them one through thirteen) was considered "agreeable" in the eyes of the city.

Many of Donna's notes in the margins of the city's proposal illustrated her bewilderment: "What's this mean?" and "How?" and "From where?" Counterproposal number nine, for example, read: "There are contractual provisions that apply to the internal procedures to review an officer's conduct at the [WPD]. Such contractual provisions and labor issues would not be conducive to implementing this proposal."

Donna wrote "BS" by what she viewed as an idiotic and confusing statement.

A damn insult.

The city's counteroffer to Donna's proposal number twelve, in which she requested that "The victim in this case should be given an acknowledgement that she was telling the truth and an apology," was this gem: ". . .[I]n other Court case settlements, this would be considered a settlement of a disputed claim wherein the liability would not be admitted."

Nobody was going to be held accountable? Donna asked herself as she read. The city wanted to wash its hands of this case and not even admit its officers had done anything wrong?

Donna felt insulted and patronized. How dare they? This was unacceptable.

"No way," Donna told Maureen.

Days later, it wasn't one of those moves where the mayor wrote a figure down on a piece of paper and slid it silently across the desk for

Maureen and Donna to look at, but it might as well have happened that way. They were notified via telephone that the city was working on a monetary offer. At some point Donna would be faced with a decision: Take the cash and walk away. Yet there was nothing in any of the city's offers and counterproposals that spoke to Donna's wish to see policies and procedures changed. The changes were a moot point to the city, apparently. The mayor's office was talking about buying her out, and then walking away unscathed.

—◦—

The city's offer was muddled with legalese, and I had no confidence my demands would be met. I felt the city was trying to pull the bureaucratic wool over my eyes; trying to, in other words, get out of this without admitting any culpability whatsoever. This was offensive to me. I had been Jane Doe for seven years; it was time for me to come out and tell my own story and effect change! More and more people in our community began to figure out who I was and began to spread vicious rumors and make judgments about me. This case was slowly encompassing every aspect of my life all over again—it was never-ending. Even the WPD's secretary, a woman my family had known forever, was being standoffish and cold to John and me. I was becoming overwhelmed by the process of being forced to hide behind this curtain and not speak about it publicly. I wanted the world to hear about the torment I had to endure at the hands of the WPD— and to me, lifting that curtain began with facing off in a court of law against those officers who accused me of lying.

—◦—

On Monday, September 25, 2000, Maureen Norris called the city's corporate attorneys' office handling the case and told them that her client had made a decision.

"She's going to trial. There will be no more negotiations."

With that, Donna's trial, which had been set to begin in days, was postponed to January 2001.

﹏

The following month, October, as the leaves burst into the East's startling fall colors of orange and yellow and red, both good and bad news arrived from Dr. Henry Lee. As part of Donna and Maureen's preparation for trial, Maureen had asked Lee to testify on Donna's behalf. Lee's testimony, they knew, would be invaluable. Lee wrote: "I am willing to supply expert opinion and testimony related to crime scene and forensic issues"; however, ". . . issues relating to police procedures and practices are beyond my area of expertise." Lee said Maureen was going to have to find "another expert" to comment on those matters.

Lee could certainly testify about something having to do with crime scenes and how officers responded, having once said that the most important part (or moment) of any crime-scene investigation was when the first responders arrived and what they did. The patrol officers who showed up first, Lee had said, could make or break a case.

Weeks before her rescheduled trial, with Christmas approaching, Donna went in for a routine yearly examination with her gynecologist. Routine, Donna should have known by then, was not part of her life anymore.

After the exam Donna's OB/GYN, sounding cautiously optimistic, said, "Not for nothing, but that lump feels like it has gotten bigger. I don't think we should leave this alone. We need to do something about it."

The lump that was supposed to have been nothing to be concerned about had grown since the end of summer. Donna's doctor encouraged her not to waste any time. "Go in and see your breast doctor."

Donna went immediately.

"I'll get you right in to remove the lump and ease your mind," he explained. "But it is nothing, Donna. I'm telling you."

"I have a trial coming up. I cannot have any surprises right now, doctor."

"I understand. Let's get it out and you'll see that it's nothing."

Hours later Donna went under a local anesthetic, and her doctor removed the lump. After the operation her doctor came back in to see her, reiterating, "I want to reconfirm for you, Donna, this is nothing." He said he'd send a sample down to the lab for a biopsy to ease her mind and prove that it was a noncancerous growth. "I'll call you tomorrow. I don't want you to worry about this."

Donna couldn't sleep that night, which should have been an indication that her instincts were speaking to her.

<center>~~~</center>

The thought that the lump could be more than a cyst was frightening, and the first thing I did that night as I lay awake was ask God to help me. This was not the first time I had to deal with cancer. In January 1984 I went to the dermatologist for the very first time for a mark on my stomach that had a small halo around it. The young doctor said that it was nothing to be concerned with, but noticed a dark mole on the underside of my upper left arm. He asked how long it had been there, and I told him I didn't recall, since it was in an area I could not really see. His face turned ashen, and he said I needed to get the mole removed that day and called a nurse in to assist. Within forty-eight hours after testing the mole, I was in for more surgery to excise the area further. It was melanoma.

We did a lot of praying over those scary few days, and we were all incredibly relieved to find that the surrounding tissue was clean and that I didn't need any further treatment. So there it was: the realization that had the mole not been discovered in time, I may not have lived past my twenties.

When I pray, I always ask for God to help me deal with what's ahead. I know it is part of His greater plan and not my will but Thy will be done. I did the same when I found the lump while we were in the Outer Banks. I prayed that whatever obstacles lay ahead of me, God would give me the strength to deal with them. If it was His will that it not be cancer, so be it. I also used the opportunity to strengthen my relationship with God. To think about all that He had done for me and my family and how often when things are good I do not thank Him as much as I should. The situation humbled me. This new predicament strengthened my commitment to give thanks to God always—but maybe more important, prepared me for what was ahead.

Donna's doctor called the next day. She had been anticipating this news all night long. She didn't really need to hear him say it. She knew.

"Donna, Donna, Donna, I am *so* sorry," he said. "Listen, I want you to come in here so I can look in your eyes and tell you how sorry I am and that it is going to be okay. But you have breast cancer. The tumor came back positive."

Chapter Twenty-two

A Battle Begins

Donna Palomba was fighting two cancers at the same time. She'd waited seven years for her day in court against what had become a growing cadre of police officers and civic leaders who had accused her of lying, and now she had a second, internal cancer to fight as well.

If I am going to die from cancer, I want the truth known before I breathe my last. It is my only recourse and hope for redemption—that secondary condition we rely on when our truth has been stripped from us.

Donna's family grew concerned for her mental and physical well-being. Was she sacrificing her health by moving forward with the suit? Was she taking her cancer diagnosis seriously? Stress was not the best remedy for fighting cancer.

Donna, however, believed that putting the brakes on the legal process now would be even more detrimental to her health, and extremely so to her state of mind. She needed to face down whatever crisis came her way, find a solution to it, or deal with the ramifications of failure. To quit now and begin a full-on battle with cancer would destroy any momentum she had built up in her case, and the lack of resolution would fester inside her.

Cancer treatment, Donna and her doctors decided, would have to wait until the trial was over.

The city made an eleventh-hour offer of a financial settlement. Within that offer was the claim that city officials would "work with" Donna regarding her demands for changes in policy and procedure.

❦

Sitting, listening to the offer, however, I realized that it was a half-hearted attempt once again to buy me off. I got a sense the money was a way to purchase my silence. How easy would it have been for me, I considered, to take this money and begin my fight against cancer. The money, nearly a quarter of a million dollars, would certainly help in that regard. Everyone told me to take it. But I thought, This is my life! My reputation had been irreversibly damaged. I would never be the same person in this community. Some people would always doubt my story and view me as a liar. If I accepted a payout, it would have given those who don't believe me more reason not to. More important, how would other rape victims hiding in the community, afraid to come forward, feel? The city had pushed me around for over seven years. I needed to go to trial as much to set the record straight—and publicize this fiasco—as to bring Jane Doe out from behind the curtain and into the spotlight, simply so she could speak for women victimized and re-victimized by the system. After all, I felt, I probably was not the WPD's only victim. How many more victims were being mistreated?

❦

Donna was now forty-four years old. It was January 5, 2001, when opening arguments in *Jane Doe v. Douglas Moran, et al.*, began. Donna and John should have been celebrating John's birthday; instead, they were heading into court.

Each side took its respective role and laid its case out for the jury. After both unassuming opening statements were made and the 911 call from the night of the crime was played, the most important person involved in the case took the stand.

Donna appeared strong despite shaking a little and feeling on the verge of tears. But she had no trouble talking jurors through every last aspect of being the victim of a brutal sexual assault inside her home during the only time her husband had been away in all the years of their marriage. And then the tale of betrayal unfolded, as Donna spoke of how, when she needed the police the most, they had turned their backs on her and made her feel as though she should question herself.

As she sat for what turned out to be nearly three days on the witness stand, Donna talked about hearing those footsteps that changed her life.

The sound of the attacker's voice.

How he smelled.

That she believed he had a gun.

How he covered her face and tied her up.

Threatened to kill her.

And then, without warning, disappeared into the night.

But that was only the half of it, she explained.

Raped once, she turned to the WPD for help but, within a few weeks, felt as though she had been assaulted all over again, this time by Douglas and Robert Moran.

"Here he is," Donna told jurors at one point, "threatening me . . . I left there believing I was going to be arrested. I have never been unfaithful to my husband. I was a victim. Now, I was being attacked by the police. It was too much for me to bear."

As she answered questions on the witness stand, it did not take long for the local press to begin what Donna later called "their biased reporting" of the case. Instead of allowing the testimony to speak for itself, one local newspaper account seemed to editorialize the cross-examination Donna endured by the city's attorneys. Those lawyers, Cheryl Hricko and Jayne Welch, according to Donna, were relentless in their attack on her character, and the local press never questioned that strong-armed tactic of trying to beat down the alleged victim of a rape until she cracked. In her questioning of Donna, Hricko "maintained that police did a thorough investigation that revealed some oddities and inconsistences in the case . . ."

Hricko's argument banged the "no forced entry" drum the WPD had been beating for years. It cited inconsistencies in lab reports, and the idea that the "evidence" left at the scene did not support what Donna had told police. That rumormonger, the "confidential informant" Moran had used as the main source for his accusation of an extramarital affair, was now being called "an outside source," as he was introduced (anonymously) by Hricko.

Not to Donna's surprise, because she and John had already found out during the evidence phase leading up to trial, Hricko produced a tape recording of that day when Donna and John sat with Captain Robert Moran and Phil Post. The WPD had secretly recorded the interview so many years ago when Donna and John had made their complaint about Douglas Moran and his finger-in-the-chest accusations against Donna.

On top of the fold of the local newspaper following the first day's testimony, the headline read: TRIAL: Woman sticks to story that she was raped.

"Sticks to story." The phrase struck Donna as catering to the WPD, as though there was still a question about Donna being sexually assaulted. It was Donna who had brought the suit against the city, not the other way around. For Donna and John, the way the article was written told a story unto itself—to some, she was guilty by walking into the courtroom.

On Wednesday, January 10, 2001, Kathy Wilson took the stand and verified that Donna "fit the rape category." In one contradictory breath, however, Wilson then explained that Donna's crime-scene reactions weren't distraught enough. And then she switched back to another description, saying Donna was wandering the scene like a "lost soul." Wilson ultimately used language like "flippant" to describe how Donna acted after she had claimed to have been sexually assaulted. To listen to Wilson, a woman who had been trained in how to manage, speak to, and deal with a sexual assault victim, one might get the idea that Donna's irregular and inconsistent behavior was a red flag. The problem with this testimony, though, was that Donna's behavior, the way in which Wilson described it, was actually textbook. It was completely in line with what any rape victim might do moments after being attacked.

Finally, Wilson agreed when asked by Donna's attorney, Robert Kolesnick, Maureen Norris's colleague, that she would definitely include Donna "in the category of sexual assault victims."

Throughout the next three days, a series of witnesses testified without surprise. George Lescadre, Neil O'Leary, Donna's father, her sister, and IA investigator Joe Cass all stuck to their original deposition testimony. While Donna's family members and O'Leary and Lescadre defended Donna's position, Cass sided with the department.

The next major hurdle that Donna's attorneys had to overcome came from Lieutenant James Griffin, the (at that time) detective sergeant who happened to arrive at the scene that night and thought, almost immediately, that Donna's story was questionable.

Griffin's biggest problem with the crime scene upstairs in Donna's bedroom turned out to be the bedcovers, which were, Griffin explained, "turned down." The contents of Donna's pocketbook, which she claimed her attacker had gone through looking for money, were there on the bed in what Griffin called a "tidy pile . . . I thought it might have been inconsistent with a struggle," the detective added. "It [the bed] was slept in," he claimed, "but it wasn't torn apart."

From there Griffin stayed firm in his desire to paint Donna as a victim who was acting erratically yet often with composure, not like a woman who had been brutally raped. Griffin called Donna "calm and lucid, but upset, don't get me wrong . . ."

Late into that same day, January 18, Robert Moran took the stand and defended his brother and the way the case was handled by the WPD, playing off anything and everything that was done to Donna as part of the process of getting to the truth. Remarkably, Moran admitted that he did not listen to the 911 call before ordering his little brother to reinterview Donna under a new, threatening hard line of questioning. The way he testified, one would believe that Moran took his brother's word for fact, without looking into matters himself or even talking to other investigators working the same case. These were incredible statements, truly, by then-Captain Moran. It was the "inconsistencies in the case," Robert Moran testified. Doug's overbearing behavior and accusatory attitude toward Donna were needed in order to get to the truth after that "information" came in that she might have been lying about the assault to cover up an affair. Moran called his brother's bullying a "very direct" line of questioning, "which might have made her feel abused." Nonetheless, it was authorized because there were so many questions surrounding Donna's story—questions that needed to be answered in order for the investigation to move forward.

Dr. Henry Lee was the most well known of the witnesses to testify. His theories had been tested and retested and proven to be the best in the business of crime-scene reconstruction and analysis. Lee talked about the importance of "securing the crime scene and the necessary use for fingerprints, photographs, sketches, measurements, and detailed notes," none of which were implemented in Donna's case during those important moments after the call came in.

"Assume there has been an assault in the master bedroom of a house and the outside phone lines have been cut, there was no sign of forced entry, and the victim had to flee for help," Maureen explained.

"Yes, I understand," Lee answered.

"What would be the perimeter that would need to be secured?"

"In that particular case you describe, it would be the entire house on the outside. No one other than authorized personnel should be allowed in the house until it is processed entirely. You would secure the perimeter with the use of yellow crime-scene tape, or by positioning officers to be sure that no one could get through."

After Lee finished, Donna followed him out of the courtroom, catching up to the doctor in the hallway as he was heading for the door.

"Thank you, Dr. Lee," she said. Lee stood with Dr. Jerry Labriola, a longtime friend, colleague, and writing partner. Labriola had written several books on his own, but also a half-dozen books as Lee's collaborator. "Congratulations on the new book," Donna told them both. Two weeks prior, Labriola and Lee's *Famous Crimes Revisited: From Sacco-Vanzetti to O.J. Simpson* had been published.

"I appreciate that," Labriola said.

"Listen, Donna, if you need me for rebuttal testimony," Lee explained, "I'll be happy to come back. If I am not available, I can send a very qualified lab person in my place."

Donna was grateful. Lee's heart, she knew, was in the place of justice based on the evidence. And that was all she had ever asked for.

CHAPTER TWENTY-THREE

Oddities

SEVERAL MORE WITNESSES TESTIFIED OVER THE NEXT TWO DAYS, and the trial went into a weekend break. On the following Tuesday, January 23, Maureen Norris called David Johnson, a psychologist from Yale who had treated Donna for PTSD. The local newspaper covering the case from gavel to verdict called Johnson a "paid witness," not missing an opportunity to try to diminish his—and possibly Donna's—credibility. Yet by the time Johnson finished outlining his nine-page résumé, there were few inside the courtroom who could say that the man was not an expert in his chosen field and extraordinarily qualified to comment on what Donna had been through, whether he was being paid for his testimony or not.

Johnson said there was no doubt in his professional opinion that Donna had been traumatized twice—once by the rape and a second time by the WPD, adding, "It completely turned her upside down. The sense of betrayal went very deep."

Concluding his testimony, Johnson reiterated a point that Maureen Norris had been leaning on as one of her main themes throughout the trial: that the "treatment Donna received by the police was more damaging to her emotional/mental state than the rape itself."

This concept was something Maureen and her team felt they needed to keep repeating.

The following day, Doug Moran (now, quite incredibly, a captain in the WPD) casually walked into the courtroom, his head held high, an unmistakable smirk on his face. As the proceedings began, he would, Donna later said, "Bring a book every day and . . . sit there reading as if he was in a library instead of a courtroom, unfazed by what was happening around him."

Donna felt sick watching Moran stroll in as if it was just another day in the life of a cop. She had already listened to one lie after the next told about her by a series of witnesses paraded into the courtroom to bolster the WPD's position and protect the Moran brothers. The good ol' boys club was alive and well, in action in the courtroom, pointing fingers at Donna, now making her out to be a money-hungry adulteress who would stop at nothing to win a lawsuit and protect her community standing from an affair's scarring effects.

Moran continued to ring a bell that had become a familiar sound during the trial for many of the city's witnesses—the "oddities" surrounding Donna's demeanor after the rape. The way Donna acted was front and center in this trial, and Moran was there to explain how nothing Donna did after her alleged attack made sense to him. In fact, he recalled, when he looked at her behavior closer, the more it seemed obvious to him that she *was* lying.

Moran talked again about there being no forced entry. He found it "odd" that Donna had left her sleeping children home alone with a supposedly armed rapist running around the neighborhood. He also said it would be, in his professional opinion, "unusual for a burglar to be armed," as Donna had claimed. An additional mitigating factor for Moran, something that for him did not add up, was that Donna's "panties were cut off . . ." In most rape crimes, Moran stated, the victim's underwear was "ripped off," or the victim was "forced to undress."

There had been a standard, apparently, for rape scenes that Moran had followed at the time.

Then Moran talked about the "tip" he had received from his "confidential informant." Because that tip included information about the children waking up and catching Donna in the act, and because

Donna was constantly opposed to her children being interviewed by the police, Moran was utterly convinced of her guilt, he said.

When Maureen questioned Moran about the tape recording from September 1993, he said he did not destroy the tape intentionally and denied adding documents to Donna's case file in the hope of covering up mistakes he had made.

I was disgraced and fighting for my dignity and emotional security, as well as my integrity. This, mind you, while a cancer grew inside me and my rapist sat on the sidelines and watched all of this. For all I knew, he could have been inside the courtroom watching the proceedings. One of the biggest factors fueling the spread of cancer is stress. That's no secret. I was at my limit as Doug Moran testified. One by one, Lieutenant Moran and his boys turned out to ridicule me. They proceeded to tell one lie after another. At one point, the city's lawyer, obviously shooting for histrionics, screamed, "Without a rape ... there cannot be any damages!"

One of the things helping Donna get through it all was the writing she was doing during the trial: sometimes in the courtroom, sometimes at home in the quiet of the calm, cold winter darkness. It was comforting for Donna to think about what she wanted to say and put her thoughts together on paper. Throughout the trial, as each witness testified, Donna took notes and worked on ideas for Maureen's closing argument. Part of what Donna wrote was not only cathartic for her, but inspiring and potentially life-changing as far as reaching jurors who might have been, while sitting and listening to the city's witnesses, on the fence.

So finally we are here—you the jury have a unique opportunity to make a statement about the wrongdoing by finding these officers and the Waterbury Police Department guilty. No one is above the law. People, including police officers, must be held accountable for their actions. This abuse of power on an innocent victim inflicted by the people we pay to protect us was especially and egregiously evil. You can't put a price on what they have done to Jane and John Doe. Their lives are forever changed. Please do the right thing and find the police department negligent and find Douglas Moran guilty of abusing this victim. We have proven guilt. Come back and rule in a significant way.

Then Donna boiled the case down to why it was so important to her to receive absolute justice. It was clear that Donna Palomba's fight was not going to end here in this courtroom, regardless of the verdict.

Nothing will make the night of September 11, 1993, go away. But you have the power to stand up for what is right and just. You can help John and Jane Doe retrieve their dignity, and you can allow them a new start in the long road that lies ahead. The incident was tragic. The investigation was pathetic. But the integrity and honesty of Jane Doe can be publicly restored and, in fact, it should be. Please, in the name of justice, do the right thing and find in favor of Jane Doe. Send a message that investigating a violent crime is serious and policies and procedures need to be followed. Send a message that abusing an innocent victim of rape is not only wrong, but inexcusable.

As the lawyers rolled out their closing arguments, the local newspaper reported that the "ALLEGED RAPE VICTIM WANTS $2.5M." The headline made Donna seem like a woman looking for a payday. It mentioned nothing about Donna wanting, more than anything else, changes in policy and procedure within the WPD. She was being portrayed as someone looking to capitalize on a claim of being sexually assaulted—exactly what the WPD had been saying for the past seven-plus years.

Donna wondered, after following the newspaper accounts of her trial, if there was some sort of conspiracy to protect her attacker, as if everyone knew who this person was, but did not want to come forward and identify him. Or perhaps there was simple arrogance and ignorance when it came to treating victims of sexual assault, which was one more reason Donna felt she needed to see this through. It seemed preposterous, sure, that a conspiracy could be unfolding in front of her; but Donna had been victimized twice, and many troubling things continually ran through her mind.

In her closing argument, Maureen set her well-proven claims against the police department into one amazing, revealing, and startling metaphor, depicting Doug Moran as "a man [who] sat there picking the wings off a grasshopper."

The image was remarkable: A bully pushing around a defenseless woman half as strong, who had been traumatized to the point of, Donna once wrote, "depression, overwhelming feelings of sadness, tension, nightmares and interrupted sleep, a growing rage and bitterness toward people in town and my accusers, a constant feeling of worry and dread." Donna had written out the differences in her life pre- and post-rape on a sheet of paper. Before her ordeal, Donna had "enjoyed being alone, could relax easily and quickly, [she was] more carefree and friendly, less apprehensive, trusting, more social, able to spend quality time with her children, energized and excited to do new things." Post-rape became the polar opposite—an endless well of dealing with "anguish and trust issues, feeling unsafe all the time, stomach cramps from nerves, nausea and digestive problems."

Additional notes Donna wrote in her trial steno pad summed up the toll the post-rape trauma caused by the WPD had taken on her:

"I'd give anything to go back the seven years—my children will never be five and seven years old again—they are now fifteen and twelve and I wonder about all I have missed."

In looking back on it all, Donna ruminated, "Why [would] anyone put herself through this if she was not telling the truth? . . . What I wish is that I could go back seven years—I would give anything to go back . . ."

Donna and John held each other as Maureen spoke to the jurors, the passionate lawyer making the argument that a victim of rape—at the scene of that crime—should be treated with the utmost sincerity and compassion, regardless of what a cop *thinks* took place. To accuse a woman of lying about what was done to her, weeks after she was allegedly raped at gunpoint, while she was ostensibly and progressively handling the post-attack trauma well and making progress toward healing, was to stomp on her emotional security for the rest of her life. Donna would never be the same—no matter what happened in court. Doug Moran had intimidated and terrorized Donna, Maureen suggested. He had made up his mind and went after her for no apparent reason, finding only the pieces of the evidence puzzle that fit conveniently into *his* claims, no matter where that evidence came from. Because of this, as the psychologist who had evaluated Donna had testified, Donna would be scarred for life.

"Their lives have value," Maureen stated emphatically, speaking about victims of rape in general. "Please let your verdict *reflect* that."

Cheryl Hricko was unabashed in her closing comments to the jury. She went straight at Donna's reaction after the crime: what Donna said, how she said it, and the way in which she presented herself. All of Donna's behavior, Hricko opined, pointed to a woman who had made up a story to cover up an affair.

One of the points Hricko keyed in on early was the idea that because Maria Cappella, Donna's sister, let Jeff Martinez into her apartment, he could not have been all that intimidating or threatening.

"Why would you let this gentleman in your home at that particular point in time? And if he is proven to already be sexually aggressive at the front door, then why is he invited in and asked if he'd like [something to drink]?"

This might have been a good point had it been the least bit relevant to Donna's rape allegations. On top of that, what did Jeff Martinez have to do with Doug Moran's hostile, slanderous interrogation of Donna?

Hricko hammered Donna's behavior during the minutes, hours, and days after the assault, right down to when Donna called her attacker a "gentleman" on the 911 call. "Endearing terms such as 'gentleman' . . . are just *not* associated with a brutal attacker such as this man . . ."

How could this be significant to an investigation, Maureen asked herself while listening to her adversarial counterpart, if these people had no idea how Donna customarily spoke? What if Donna used the word "gentleman" as common, everyday practice? The city was taking literally a term used in the heat of the moment—when *any* human would be searching for words in a terrified, scrambled mind. That one point infuriated Maureen and Donna.

Meanwhile the notion that this was the first weekend John Palomba had gone away by himself in twelve years of marriage was now considered an indication of Donna's guilt, according to Hricko, who suggested that because John was away, it was the perfect opportunity for Donna to have an affair.

"If you look at the children's room from the point of view of Donna's bedroom," Detective Neil O'Leary explained later, talking as an experienced investigator, making an important point that not one investigator looking at Donna's case had ever considered, "you could see down the hallway and just about into the kids' rooms. So the children had an almost straight eye line into Donna's bedroom from their rooms. If the theory is that she had an affair and one of the kids caught her, you'd have to ask yourself as an investigator— which no one did—why in the heck would she leave her door open, for one, and unlocked, for another? It would be unthinkable to have your lover in your room, your children there down the hall, and your bedroom door open and unlocked!"

And because Donna had gone back to work within a week's time, Hricko said, the WPD believed that behavior was inconsistent with someone suffering from a brutal rape.

Hricko went on so long that at one point the judge said, "Miss Hricko, you are going to have to wrap it up."

Given all the evidence the WPD had uncovered, Hricko concluded, it was absolutely reasonable for Doug Moran to question Donna's account. He would have been negligent if he had not.

❦

Days passed. The jury seemed to be deadlocked. In actuality, however, several interesting scenarios were being played out in the jury room as the jurors discussed Donna's case. Immediately, everyone believed that Donna had been raped and that she had not lied about her attack. There was no question about Donna's story, or her character. The problems for the jury began with the actual jury verdict form itself. The form made it difficult and confusing for jurors to choose individual counts associated with the case.

"If it was a matter of guilt or innocence, like on TV," one juror later said, "it would have been all over. Deciding on damages made us all not want to be there . . . it felt like we were in prison."

On Wednesday, January 31, 2001, nearly five days after the jury was given the case, John and Donna Palomba stood and hugged each other tightly as the jury found the city, Doug Moran, Robert Moran, and Phil Post responsible, ruling against the WPD. The jury awarded Donna $190,000 in damages, a far cry from the $2.5 million dollars Maureen Norris had asked for during the proceedings.

"We had no doubt," that same juror added, "that Doug Moran was a liar. There was a difference of opinion on the experts . . ."

As a whole, according to one juror who later spoke about the deliberation process, the jury "was offended by the $2.5 million-dollar amount. It was way too high."

Some of the jurors did not want to give Donna any money at all.

Still, Donna won. Ultimately, within its verdict, the jury of two men and four women agreed that Douglas Moran and his brother, Robert, the former captain (who had by now retired from the WPD), were "negligent for injuring Donna and traumatizing her [and] not properly investigating her 1993 rape claim."

Outside the courtroom Donna told reporters: "We tried very hard to settle this without going to trial. The case was really not about money—it was about change!"

Donna also said she wasn't done with the WPD. She was going to do everything in her power to see that the department made changes in the way it dusted for fingerprints and photographed rape scenes in the future. In addition, she felt there should be a qualified, specially trained police officer in sexual assaults at every scene and available to handle all rape complaints.

"It's a disgrace what happened," John Palomba said bitterly as he walked with Donna out of the building and reporters crowded around them.

"Today is a victory for all victims who have been abused by police," Donna said.

Maureen made one of the last press comments, and put Donna's case into perspective as she said, "Look, if you're raped, you're raped! No one asks for that."

The question for Donna now was: Where to go from here?

Chapter Twenty-four

Still Jane after All These Years

Donna had demanded an apology and change in policy from the WPD. In the short term she ended up with neither. The WPD flat out refused to acknowledge that Donna had won her case. The city paid the damages, and Donna received her share after expenses and fees for the lawyers and experts. But she was still reeling from the realization that it was business as usual for the WPD. Nothing had changed.

In April 2001, Donna decided to go public with her story—in her own way, that is. She reached out to John Murray, the editor of the *Waterbury Observer*, a monthly paper Donna respected. As they talked, Murray encouraged Donna to tell her version of the events and get her agenda out there for the people to read and decide upon for themselves.

That front-page story, simply and appropriately titled "Survivor," said it all, with the subtitle putting Donna's struggle into perspective: "One woman's eight year triumph to overcome rape, and a confrontation with Waterbury Police . . ."

Now it was Donna's turn.

"She was crushed at the [other local newspaper's] trial coverage," Murray wrote in the opening of his article, "which rehashed rumor, and overlooked key facts that won the case."

———

My trial had lasted about a month. There were twists and turns, but toward the end it became apparent that I was winning. The court reporter from our [local paper] covered the police beat, and she came to the trial sporadically and sat with the defense. Her reporting was skewed toward the defense, and she didn't bother to cover the trial on the day Neil O'Leary testified. I would come home from court knowing that we had a good day and read the paper the next morning and become sick to my stomach. Here I was, trying to clear my name and set the record straight, and the biased reporting just added to the swirl of misinformation and innuendo in our community. Anyone following the story would have to scratch their heads when the verdict came back that the officers were found negligent based on the printed word. It was maddening. I had my surgery and six-plus weeks of radiation facing me, but it nagged at me. Then I thought, wait, there is a monthly alternative paper in town. I called John Murray, the publisher of the Waterbury Observer, *and asked for a confidential meeting, and he obliged. I met with John, and we worked together for the next two months. This was my opportunity to tell the world the unadulterated truth of what had happened.*

Donna remained Jane Doe in the article, but Murray explained for his readers who Donna was within the community. John and Donna were given the names Rachael and Bob for the story.

The nine-page article about Donna's ordeal left no stone unturned. Murray wrote about the entire case, from a moment-by-moment account of Donna's rape to the trial against the city seven years later. For the first time, Waterbury citizens had an idea of the toll the case had taken on Donna and her family. Her story—still without the ending of her attacker being brought to justice—was finally out in the public domain in its entirety.

Probably more important to Donna than the story being published was that the *Observer,* to its credit, published the changes Donna wanted within the WPD in a sidebar space taking up about three-quarters of the page. The boldface-type accompaniment to the main article outlined those thirteen pivotal points of change in policy and procedure Donna had wanted implemented based on her research and personal experience.

Regarding the local newspaper's coverage of the trial, Maureen Norris's colleague, Robert Kolesnick, had one of the more controversial quotes of the piece, saying, "We don't try our cases in the press. But the [local] paper's coverage raped her all over again."

Equally important to Donna was a column Murray published in the same edition of the paper in which her story ran. Murray titled it "RAPE" and outlined the many misconceptions and facts surrounding the ubiquitous crime. The main theme of the column was that many victims of rape are often afraid to come forward and report the crime—and a case such as Donna's doesn't help that.

"Silence is killing us," Murray wrote, quite appropriately, near the end of his column. "It's time to talk." He quoted a survivor of rape who had said that when a victim of rape comes forward to tell her story, "It helps take away the power of this experience, and its subsequent shame . . ."

～•～

What appalled Donna most was the fact that Doug Moran was still on the job as the year 2001 ended. More than that, Robert Moran had retired years before and had been appointed by Governor John Rowland, a friend of the family, to a cushy job as vice chairman and chief of operations for the Connecticut Board of Parole. Sure, Donna had won her civil court case. She had come out and told her story. But when one looked at the results, the fact remained that the same situation could still happen under the current WPD regime.

～•～

The anxiety of my attacker being someone in the community that knew me became overwhelming as time passed after my civil trial.

Neil O'Leary and Pudgie Maia, still investigating my case, were still convinced the crime was premeditated and my attacker knew John was away for the weekend.

Everywhere I went, now that my case had become public, I was still Jane Doe. However, around town many people knew exactly who I was post-trial. This became a test for me to deal with. I didn't know if my rapist was someone from my business world, or my personal or social life. I was convinced that he was someone close—and, as time went on, that was the most terrifying part of it all.

Neil O'Leary was still with the WPD and certainly qualified to solve the case. He went up against his fellow officers during my trial, and I knew he wanted a resolution. Neil cared about John and me deeply. He was being ostracized at work. But then you had others inside the WPD, many of whom were still unqualified, essentially, to solve my case—and I had to ask myself: Besides Neil and a few others, since winning the lawsuit, was the WPD even interested in solving it?

❧

Donna's instincts about her attacker were accurate. Yet neither she nor John had any idea just how close the assailant was.

Pivotal in identifying the man who raped Donna was Neil O'Leary, who became a captain within the WPD near the end of 2001 and, by 2003, the chief of the Waterbury Police Department.

Regardless of what anybody else inside the department thought of Donna's win in court, the chief of police was now on her side and determined to solve the case.

Neil had never forgotten about Donna.

One of the first initiatives Neil implemented as the new chief was an overhaul of the policy and procedure manual for the WPD, much of which was based on Donna's case and the recommendations she had wanted to make all along. Donna offered her assistance on the sexual assault portion of the manual, and Neil allowed Donna to consult with his staff and make suggestions.

I feel a bit of redemption sneaking back into my life. A sergeant from the WPD I had been working with on the manual asked me to come into the WPD one day in November 2003. Something remarkable happened. Something I will never forget as long as I live. Something that changed my outlook and feelings. When I arrived at the WPD, the officer said, "Although you have never received an apology from the officers who were negligent, I want to, on behalf of the entire Waterbury Police Department, apologize for what happened to you."

I was brought to tears. I felt as if nothing could bring me down from the high I was on heading into the mid-2000s. My world was coming back together.

During the spring of 2001, as Donna prepared to go under the knife and then receive radiation therapy to eradicate the cancer growing inside her, the never-ending drama, corrupt practices, and controversy surrounding the city of Waterbury once again exploded as Mayor Giordano's secrets of sexually assaulting two young girls were finally exposed.

Waterbury was known then as one of the worst places in America to live, according to several surveys done by popular magazines. The city did not need any more bad press. This largely blue-collar town, situated in the western hills of a rather exclusive portion of the state, had enough boarded-up buildings, closed businesses, and jobless claims to blemish its face already. But as news came in that the mayor was not only possibly involved in corruption by receiving kickbacks for favors, but also implicated in the most horrendous crime a human being could commit—raping a child—a new low entered the political arena in Waterbury. When these allegations rose to the surface, articles began to circulate around the country trashing a city that seemed to be steeped in garbage already.

When Giordano was brought in and charged with sex crimes against children, the city was suffering from a seventy-five million dollar budget deficit. Broke didn't even begin to describe the city's financial status.

Waterbury alderman John Sarlo had worked for three mayors, all of whom had been indicted for various crimes against the city and/or its people. Sarlo was devastated, like most everyone else, by Giordano's unforgivable crimes.

"We might elect crooked people," Sarlo told the *New York Times* in half-jest. "But one thing we do in Waterbury is find the guilty people and we convict them."

Indeed, Giordano was convicted in 2003 of sexually abusing those two young girls provided to him by the prostitute he knew. He was sentenced to thirty-seven years in prison. There were hours of tape-recorded calls made between the ex-mayor and the prostitute, many of which contained conversations of Giordano setting up the assaults on the girls. When the prostitute (who received a ten-year sentence for providing the girls) testified about her bringing the girls to the mayor, Giordano screamed from his table in front of the witness bench, "Fucking liar!"

But the Giordano scandal was a disruption, essentially, for Donna, and especially for WPD Chief Neil O'Leary. For years Donna's case had more or less sat idle while Donna spent her time putting her life back together and thinking where she could make the most difference and effect the most change. Neil was always cognizant of the fact that to make progress there would have to be a major break in the case. These types of cold cases were generally solved by a tip or a DNA hit. Technology sometimes caught up with cold rape cases and brought a suspect to the surface without anybody trying and when nobody was expecting it.

As the summer of 2004 came in with a bout of hot and hazy weather, Neil and Donna had no idea just how much their lives were about to change—and it all began with a morning habit Neil had developed as chief.

CHAPTER TWENTY-FIVE

If the Shoe Fits

It was Monday, August 2, 2004. WPD Chief Neil O'Leary was in his office after a relaxing weekend, doing what he did every morning: going through the reports of major cases that occurred the previous night/weekend to see if anything jumped out and needed his direct attention. First and foremost, Neil was a cop's cop; he took his job as administrator seriously, but he was nothing if not a police officer, the same as the men and women he supervised. Of course, Neil had no idea yet that on this day, the seeds of solving Donna's case were germinating within those reports sitting on his desk.

Scanning through various breaking-and-enterings, fights, domestic violence charges, drug arrests, DUIs, and other crimes, Neil came across an alleged sexual assault reported by a woman that past Saturday, two days ago. The report mentioned a twenty-one-year-old woman who had claimed a man she knew and worked with had been sexually aggressive and ultimately attacked her that afternoon.

The report piqued Neil's interest. Not with regard to Donna's case (which was not even on his mind), but the accusation itself and the man against whom the woman had made the accusation.

Neil knew the guy—John "Rocky" Regan.

I cannot believe this, Neil thought to himself. *John Regan?*

"I knew the family," Neil said later. "They owned and operated a [roofing] company in town, and everybody knew them. Everybody *liked* them."

215

Indeed, the Regans were a "prominent" family in Waterbury. Rocky Regan's wife was a schoolteacher, his father was a dentist, his grandfather had a local school named after him.

Neil dialed the Detective Bureau. A female detective who knew the case answered. "I took the statement from the woman," she explained.

"Really." Neil was still blown away by the idea that Rocky Regan, a happily married, churchgoing, hardworking father of three boys, well-known and especially well-liked in the community, could have done such a thing.

"Chief, I have to be honest with you," the detective said. "She's very credible. I believe everything that she's saying. I believe that she was victimized here."

Neil was stunned. "Thanks," he said and hung up.

As he sat at his desk, Neil stared at the report then read it more closely.

John Regan was about to turn forty-eight that November. He lived in a rather exclusive section of Waterbury with his wife and kids. Regan's parents owned a nice home on Cape Cod, Massachusetts. Regan's parents liked to spend their summers on the Cape, and their children looked after their house while they were gone. So Regan told the woman he worked with, "Listen, I need to go check on my parents' home . . . we can look at a couple of jobs we're working on along the way and stop in at the house and have a quick look around." Regan wanted to be sure the house was secure.

The woman had no reason not to trust him. She had been with the company for a few years and knew his family. She'd spent plenty of time with Rocky alone. He'd never been anything other than a gentleman.

Once inside his parents' house, Rocky took a quick look around the home to make sure the windows and doors were still locked up. Nothing seemed to have been tampered with.

"Why don't you sit down," Rocky told the woman. They were in the rear sunporch area of the house. He pointed to the couch.

Then, out of the blue: "I want to make love to you."

This statement startled the woman. "No, Rocky," she said, thinking maybe he was joking around.

So Rocky lunged at the woman, according to the incident report, and "pulled her onto his lap, pushing her down, forcing himself on her." He tried to kiss her, groping at her breasts and vaginal area, saying that he wanted her.

"Come on," Rocky said. "I want to lick you."

The woman fought with him, screaming, "No . . . no . . . stop it. No! What're you doing?"

She tried to get away from his grip, but he "would not allow her," added the report.

Rocky continued the attack, aggressively and violently trying to "put his hands down her pants." Now she was on her back, Rocky on top of her.

"Let me go . . . I want to leave."

Rocky was growing increasingly forceful and impatient as she fought him off, but within a few moments, the woman was able to break free. She ran out of the house and down the street.

Near the end of the block, shielded from view of the street (the woman was hiding now), she called her boyfriend and told him what had just happened.

"Stay there," he said. "Hide."

He then called the police.

Shortly after, the boyfriend picked her up a few blocks away from the Regan family home. She was cowering behind a house. Her boyfriend brought her directly to the police department.

Incredible, Neil said to himself as he finished reading the report.

The woman was able to tell police the man's name, of course. She also said she had proof that she had been inside the house and ran out. One of her shoes had fallen off as she struggled to break free. She was certain Rocky didn't see it. The shoe should still be inside the home.

Throughout that day—Saturday—the WPD tried to locate Rocky Regan.

He was nowhere to be found.

On Monday morning, after Neil finished reading the reports of the incident and talking to those officers involved in the case, he notified the state's attorney and then told his detectives to keep working on it. Track the suspect down and interview him.

"See what he has to say."

Still, none of this had Neil thinking about Donna—that is, until he started driving away from the WPD for an appointment. Neil later remembered the exact cross section of streets (West Main and Thomaston Avenue) where he was sitting when the epiphany relating to Donna's eleven-year-old sexual assault case hit him like a sucker punch. He had been driving and saying to himself over and over, *Regan, Regan, Regan . . . how do I know that name?* There was more to it than just knowing the Regan name from being a Waterbury native. Something else spoke to Neil.

Oh my goodness . . . the connection flashed through Neil's memory. *The stag party! That night Donna was assaulted there was a stag party for a guy named Regan! Darn it all. There it is.*

Neil turned his car around and drove back to the WPD. The first thing he did was examine Donna's case file and the reports from all the DNA samples (by then there were close to fifty) taken over the years. He searched through the names once.

No John Regan.

Then again—just in case.

Nothing.

John Regan had *to be at that stag party,* Neil thought. *The groom-to-be shared his last name.*

Back in his office, Neil called a friend who knew John Regan's cousin to get the cousin's phone number. This was the same Regan whose stag party had been at the forefront of Neil's thoughts so early on in Donna's investigation when he and Pudgie had taken over.

"Hey," Neil said over the phone, finally getting Rocky Regan's cousin on the line. "Like to ask you a few questions about something." It was casual, as if Neil was calling a buddy about something. "This is Neil O'Leary."

"Hi, Neil," Rocky Regan's cousin said. "What can I do for you?"

The chief of police calls, you want to help him out as best you can.

"Let me ask you a question. Are you related to John Regan?" Neil wanted to be sure this was not some sort of coincidence that would wind up a dead end, sucking the air out of any excitement momentarily pumped back into the investigation.

"Sure, Neil . . . John's my first cousin."

"Really . . .?" Neil said.

"Yeah."

"Well, listen . . . I'm going to test your memory here. Going back to September 10, 1993"—it had been almost eleven years—"I was wondering if you recall if John Regan was at your stag party?"

"Yes."

"How are you so sure?"

"Because Rocky worked the door collecting money."

～✦～

Neil was overwhelmed—yet guardedly optimistic that he had found the man who had attacked Donna—after more than a decade of searching.

"Donna, I'd like to meet with you and John this afternoon," Neil said on the phone with the Palombas. It was the same day of his conversation with Regan's cousin.

Donna could feel the urgency and excitement in Neil's voice. She'd never heard him sound like this before. She sensed he wasn't calling to catch up.

"Neil, what is it?"

"Let's talk about it at the restaurant."

They met in the town where John and Donna had moved after selling their house in Waterbury, at an upscale restaurant downtown, private and quiet. It would not have been smart to meet in Waterbury.

After they sat down and ordered, Neil wasted little time. "Look, I'm just going to come out with it . . . Do either of you know John Regan?"

"Of course we do," Donna said. She looked at Neil, then at John. "Rocky's one of John's best friends from the old neighborhood."

Overlook. So many years ago. The old gang.

"I've known Rocky since kindergarten," John Palomba said. "We went to high school . . . we played football together."

The fact that John and Rocky were friends clinched it for Neil, but he maintained his composure. Not only was his gut telling him that Rocky Regan had attacked Donna, but the entire scenario now fit together so perfectly.

"Has John Regan ever been over to your house?" Neil asked.

"Oh, yeah," Donna said. "Of course. Neil, what's going on?"

"Are you kidding me?" John said. "Rocky put a roof on our garage."

"When was that?"

"Oh, I don't know . . . maybe right before I was attacked," Donna said.

"Really?" Neil responded.

John seemed a little taken aback by all the questions. Finally, he said, "Look, Neil. I know you're doing your job. I understand. But listen, John Regan would *never* do this to us! It's impossible." John looked Neil directly in his eyes. He was more serious than Neil had ever seen or heard him in quite some time. The tone in his voice clearly evoked a core, inherent belief that Neil was going after the wrong guy here.

"Well, John, I'm just trying to cover all the bases."

"Not him, Neil," John said. "No way. Not Rocky."

"Donna," Neil said, "has John Regan ever made any untoward advances toward you or anything like that—ever?" Neil then explained about the accusations Rocky's coworker had made, first asking them both for their confidentiality about the case.

"No, no . . ." Donna said.

—◦—

For me, this idea that Rocky was my attacker came completely out of the blue. Rocky wasn't someone I interacted with regularly, and he had never crossed my mind. Neil certainly got my attention, and I was troubled by what he was telling us. For one, why would Rocky attack his coworker? I knew there were two sides to every story, and I wondered what had happened. I tried to recall any past encounters with Rocky through the years that would raise concern, but there was nothing I could think of while sitting there talking with Neil. John was adamant that there was no way it could be Rocky. I wasn't so sure, and it continued to nag at me. The more I thought about it, the more I began to think about Rocky differently. No one could be ruled out completely, and we told Neil to do whatever he had to do to find out if there was a connection.

—◦—

There was a lull in the conversation. John got up and excused himself to use the restroom.

As Donna and Neil sat waiting for John to return, Donna said something to Neil that the WPD chief later said he'd never forget.

"You know, Neil, I don't really want to say this in front of my husband," Donna looked toward the bathroom to make sure John wasn't coming back, "but sometimes, when Rocky looked at me, the way he did it, he gave me the creeps."

Donna said she'd never told anyone about her feelings, especially John.

"I understand, Donna."

When John sat back down, Neil explained that his officers were in the process of bringing Rocky in to question him about the incident with his coworker. And they were going to ask Rocky to consent to a DNA sample. That would prove or disprove his involvement in Donna's case.

"I'll call you guys as soon as I know anything."

Neil left and radioed in to his people to serve the arrest warrant on John Regan.

After the meeting with Neil, John and Donna discussed what the chief had said. Neil wasn't certain about Regan yet because they had not checked the DNA. As the Palombas waited to hear from Neil, John Palomba grew considerably agitated and impatient. He was certain that Neil, as much as John liked him and respected his law enforcement experience, was wrong.

"There was no way," John said, "that Rocky could have done this to us."

Rocky was a likable, social, "working man's" man, friends said. He worked for a roofing company. He traveled a lot for work, which made Neil think that perhaps there were additional victims in other cities across New England, but anybody who knew the guy claimed he was a family man and "hands-on, dedicated" father, who took his role as a parent seriously. Is that the same type of person who could be a serial sexual offender?

That new roof Rocky had put on the Palombas' old garage in their former neighborhood not long before Donna was raped had been more or less a friendly favor. John helped Rocky with the work. Soon after, John went down to Rocky's house and helped him with the roof on his house. When they were finished, Donna and John had Rocky, his wife, and their kids over to the house for dinner to thank him.

After her attack, and especially after Donna and John had moved out of the neighborhood, Rocky and John didn't see each other as often or talk on the phone as they used to. But John didn't walk away without making attempts to carry on the friendship.

"I called him many times and wanted to go out for a walk one night or something. And I'd leave a message with his wife and he'd never call me back. I'd ask around, 'What's going on with Rocky?'"

For some reason, Rocky had stopped connecting with John, severing the friendship.

Donna thought about it. Her mind was telling her not to rule Rocky out. She also recalled one time, long after the rape, when Rocky had visited at her parents' cottage along the Connecticut shoreline. When he arrived, Donna walked out to greet him, giving Rocky one of her customary hugs she gave all her close friends. Rocky had lunch with them, enjoyed a few beers, and took a swim in Long Island Sound. John asked him where he had been lately and why he was being such a snob about returning phone calls, but he never really responded.

Can you imagine, Donna now considered, *if this is the same man who attacked me?*

She felt sick.

The days went by slowly for Donna. Rocky was brought in, charged with attempted assault on his female coworker, and bonded out. The community rallied around him, saying there was *no way* this family man, a hardworking husband and local son of a prominent dentist, could be responsible for what this woman had accused him of. Almost everyone in town believed she was making it up, probably hoping to file a lawsuit against the company and walk away with a payday.

The woman was then fired from the company for which she and Rocky worked.

When Neil's officers had processed Rocky on the charges made by his coworker, they asked him if he'd be willing to hand over a voluntary DNA sample.

Rocky never flinched. He gave it up unconditionally.

This was not a good sign. If Rocky was Donna's rapist, there was no doubt he would have paid attention to the newspapers and Donna's story and would know that there was DNA available. If he was guilty, why give up the sample without a fight? Furthermore, with the money his family had, Rocky had hired one of the most expensive lawyers in the state. Why volunteer a sample if you had committed the crime?

It was the only time since that August day when Rocky allegedly attacked his female coworker that Neil O'Leary began to think Rocky Regan might not be his man.

Neil was personally keeping an eye on things. He called the lab and told them to put a rush on the DNA sample from Rocky. Donna had waited long enough. There was no sense, if it was negative, that she should be put through any additional agony.

"It was odd for me to be involved in this case," Neil later said, "so inherently, yes, because I was chief of police; but, on the other hand, no, it was not so surprising because this had been my case since 1994."

In early October 2004, a few months after Regan's DNA sample had been submitted, Neil took a call from the lab.

Chapter Twenty-six

Reality Check

Neil contacted Donna at her office on October 20, 2004, a Wednesday.

Donna was busy. She had a lot on her mind. After being on the board of the Business Women's Forum for a few years, Donna had taken on the position of chairwoman. When Neil called, Donna was rereading a speech she had written for a conference the following day. It was slated to be a large-scale event, with famed money woman Suzy Orman scheduled to give the keynote address. Donna explained to Neil that now was probably not the best time to talk.

Neil sounded passive on the phone. It was a surreal feeling for the seasoned investigator: here he was delivering good news and bad news at the same time.

"I have some news I need to share with you and John."

Donna's "head started to spin," she later recalled.

"Neil, could it wait another day? Like can we meet on Friday?"

Neil hesitated. He thought about it.

"Sure, Donna."

I couldn't go there, not then. We made arrangements for John and me to meet Neil in his office on Friday morning. I got through the conference. It was a busy, exciting day, and I had a lot to do. Still, I had flashes of what was ahead. It was as if my two worlds were colliding.

Chairing this annual conference with hundreds of attendees was now competing with the news I had been waiting for all these years. The business executive in me had to hold it together for one more day. I knew that Neil wouldn't be calling me into his office, telling me to bring John, if he did not have new information. Those DNA results, we both knew without saying, had come in.

Friends and family had given John Regan the nickname "Rocky" because he broke a lot of windows at Kingsbury Grammar School in Waterbury, where he had what a former friend called "a bit of a disciplinary problem, but nothing major." Regan was a kid who liked to cause mischief, like scores of kids that age who toss rocks or instigate problems on school grounds.

Rocky Regan was a powerfully built man, wiry, agile, with a somewhat devious appearance that people always thought to be compassion. Rocky was scrappy. John Palomba and Rocky went all the way back to kindergarten. Along with other neighborhood kids, they grew up playing stickball and punchball in the school yard and spent most of their youth in the Overlook area of Waterbury. They attended each other's birthday parties. They played baseball in the spring and, both being bigger than other kids, went on to play football.

"It was mostly a Catholic neighborhood, and everybody knew everybody," John Palomba later said. "I used to go to the New York Giants game every year with Rocky's dad and my dad—and Rocky."

When it came time for high school, John and Rocky went to Holy Cross, a rather renowned Connecticut school, especially when you're talking about football. Both made the varsity team. Rocky was "an average" outside linebacker who had a tough time excelling in a more competitive arena with kids his own size. Former teammates called Rocky a "good athlete ... very talented ... a tough kid." John stood out as an outstanding defensive back, among a litany of other positions, including punter and kicker; he was named all-state and most valuable player of the Naugatuck Valley League. The connections between John and Rocky were such that not only were their fathers good friends, but John's godmother's husband and Rocky's father—both dentists—also covered for each other during family vacations.

The divide came when John went to the University of Connecticut and Rocky went to Norwich Academy. They stayed in close touch and visited each other on their respective campuses, keeping the friendship alive, but they were now apart for the first time. After college John asked Rocky to play softball with him in a men's league, and they played together on a slow-pitch team for years. Rocky, John, and a bunch of old friends even got together and rented a neighborhood gym to play basketball once a week. These were guys who helped each other out, covered for one another.

John and Rocky both got married in 1981, right around the same time, and went to each other's weddings. After they started families, they played poker together at a different house each month—before and even *after* Donna was sexually assaulted. John used to like taking walks around the neighborhood with Rocky, especially when it snowed. After Donna was raped, the walks became a place for John to sort out his thoughts and emotions. After the assault, John would call Rocky repeatedly but not get a response, and ended up walking alone or with another friend.

"Other guys told me that Rocky wasn't returning their calls either," John said.

Regan had distanced himself from the entire group.

Donna now had a sinking feeling, as she thought about why Neil wanted to see them, as to why Rocky had become so standoffish.

Chapter Twenty-seven

Betrayal

Donna Palomba had been functioning on very little sleep prior to the meeting with Neil. Her adrenaline, from simply thinking about the possibilities Neil had to share, pumped hot and fast, feeding an already ramped-up well of anxiety. The conference with Suzy Orman had gone off without a hitch; everything turned out the way Donna had envisioned. But now it was time to see Neil and face the fact that after all this time, the big break in the case had arrived.

Donna had agreed to meet with Neil on Friday (October 22, 2004), but she waited to tell John about it until Thursday night, which was just after the conference. She hadn't wanted to talk or think about John's reaction or the meeting before then.

The elevator ride up to Neil's second-story office inside the WPD was incredibly tense. Donna's nerves were shot. She trembled as though out in the cold without a jacket. The most nerve-racking question was: How was John going to react?

"I have a feeling Neil is going to tell us that Rocky has been ruled out, but they're onto something else," John said, just as the elevator arrived at Neil's floor.

Donna looked at her husband, confident that wasn't the case, but she didn't say anything.

As they walked through the door into Neil's office, John said, "No way. It cannot be Rocky. Don't worry, Donna, Neil is going to tell us that it's *not* Rocky. That they have another suspect."

Donna kept quiet.

Neil's spacious office was split into two rooms—a front reception area and a back interior office space. There was a door—now closed—separating the two.

"Come in, sit down," Neil said, walking up to them.

"What is it, Neil?" Donna asked pointedly.

"Well," Neil said, "I have something to tell you. We got a hit on the DNA in your case. John Regan's DNA matches that of the man who raped you, Donna. I'm so very sorry."

Donna looked at John. The color in his face, she recalled later, drained out, rage and disbelief wrapped up in John's expression. A life-long friend had betrayed him. It was as though they had all been living in some sort of alternate reality. Had he heard Neil right?

"We finally know!" Donna said excitedly, crying, staring at John, trying to bring the best to what could be a dangerous situation. "Oh, my goodness. We know, Neil!"

John sat shell-shocked.

"John, listen, we're going to take care of this," Neil said. "You gotta promise me that you won't go after this guy." There had always been that underlying possibility of John taking matters into his own hands.

John looked as though he might explode right there.

"John, listen," Donna said comfortingly. She put her arm around her husband's shoulders. "You have to listen to Neil. You're a spiritual person. Think about the outcome. What good is it going to do if you take this into your own hands? You'll be behind bars. It'll be a nightmare for us."

While staring at her husband of more than two decades, Donna said later, "My heart broke."

—◦—

I quivered uncontrollably, crying, as my emotions went from shock to gratitude, betrayal to anger, relief to fear. Then the melancholy set in.

I am about to be vindicated. After eleven years, we now know—unquestionably—who committed the crime. It was an incredible feeling. It proved Moran and his boys were wrong about me. My husband, obviously, was devastated. John sat and thought, How could I have brought this animal into our lives? *He immediately felt guilty and angry and blamed himself. He felt betrayed, obviously. An enormous betrayal. A friend. A best friend. Someone from the neighborhood. Someone he trusted and cared about had done the unthinkable. I knew then that John would want to kill John Regan—for not only tormenting and raping me, but allowing this to go on for so long.*

The door separating Neil's two office spaces was behind Donna and John. Neil got up from behind his desk and sat down next to the two of them. He said, "I know this is emotional for you two, and I wanted to tell you first. But I have some people in the next room waiting for you."

Donna and John walked into the adjacent room and saw SA John Connelly with Maureen Norris and Pudgie Maia, along with a few other investigators.

Neil opened the door to the second section of his office. Maureen Norris stepped forward, nearly in tears. Then the state's attorney and several others followed. Here were all these people involved in solving my case over the years waiting to comfort us. Neil knew what I had been through. He understood how I felt. His compassion was a grace, a blessing. Maureen hugged me. My husband stayed standing next to me, shaken to his core; he was overcome with emotion.

"Eleven years of trauma washed away from Donna on that day," Maureen said later, "and this marvelous peace came over her."

Donna could celebrate a triumph. Her life was coming back into focus.

Neil explained that John Regan, who was awaiting trial on the "unlawful restraint" case involving his twenty-one-year-old coworker, would be arrested at his place of employment that day on kidnapping charges.

Kidnapping?

Disappointingly to Donna and John, the statute of limitations on sexual assault had run out in Donna's case; Regan could not be charged with raping Donna.

Once news broke that Regan had been arrested in Donna's case, a community already in disbelief again rallied around the man. There was no way, those who knew Regan best were saying, that he could have broken into the Palomba house and assaulted Donna. And then, just like that, gossip and rumor reared their heads again, with "whispers," as one newspaper reporter later put it, "of an affair" between Donna and Rocky. It was the only answer for some people: Donna was covering up an affair with Regan by claiming he had assaulted her.

Regan pleaded not guilty during his arraignment a few days later and was set free after posting a $350,000 bond. This move—allowing his bond to be low enough to meet—would prove to be a costly and dangerous decision, because, despite what friends and family said of the man, Regan was not yet finished committing violent sexual crimes.

Chapter Twenty-eight

Face-to-face

OVER THE NEXT YEAR, JOHN REGAN WAS IN AND OUT OF COURT, attending pretrial hearings related to his attack of Donna Palomba. Numerous legal specifications had to be sorted out before the state could actually try Regan—chiefly, what the specific charges would be. Could they get him on stalking, first- and second-degree kidnapping, and/or sexual assault under some sort of grandfather clause? It was a legal mess. Nobody in law enforcement wanted to see Regan walk with only a few years.

It was during Regan's fifth pretrial hearing that Donna and John showed up in the courtroom for the first time. It was time for Donna, she knew, to face her attacker, her husband's former best friend. She needed to send Rocky Regan a message that she wasn't going away. John, too, wanted to face this man who had claimed to be a friend all these years.

It was Monday, April 25, 2005, a typical spring day in New England. John and Donna entered the courthouse at 10:30 a.m. John's office was only a few blocks away, so Donna had met him there and they walked up together.

"John and I had given it a lot of thought beforehand," Donna said later. "We both wanted to be there. It was time I faced Rocky."

John Palomba remained composed. He was ready for this. Those images of finding Rocky and ending his life had somewhat faded. That rage had been, apparently, part of the healing process—although, Donna said later, "John still dreams of killing Rocky nearly every day."

"I'm kind of looking forward to this," John told Donna as they walked into the courthouse. "It's about time to make Rocky squirm."

After going through security, they waited for Maureen Norris to arrive, sitting on a bench near the courtroom entrance. It was interesting to watch different people walk by, Donna thought, as she interlocked her arm with John's, holding him close.

Maureen arrived and got busy figuring out which courtroom—there were several—Regan's pretrial would be held in.

"It's there," she said, pointing to a room to the left of where they sat. "Wait here, though, until you guys are called."

Maureen walked away. As she did, Donna spied a man walking quickly by the front of the courtroom doors. He had just exited from the courtroom on their right.

That's Rocky, Donna realized. He must have seen them before John and Donna noticed him.

Rocky appeared nervous and anxious to get out of their line of vision. He entered the second courtroom, but within a few minutes came back out, walked quickly to the exit door, and actually left the courthouse.

—◆—

I think he was scared to death. I had heard he had always been with someone at the other pretrials (wife, sister, friend). This time he was all alone, and I think he freaked out when he saw us.

—◆—

As they stood waiting, a tall woman with long, straight, strawberry blonde hair walked by. John and Donna didn't know it then, but she was Hope Seeley, Rocky's high-powered, high-priced attorney from the office of (Hubert) Santos and Seeley, in Hartford, Connecticut. Santos and Seeley had been the defense attorneys on record for some of Connecticut's most notorious and famous cases, including the appeal portion for Michael Skakel, who, nearly thirty years after the fact, was convicted in the 1975 murder of Martha Moxley, one of his Greenwich, Connecticut, neighbors.

Seeley recognized Maureen Norris immediately as everyone got situated to go into the courtroom. According to Donna, Seeley "gave John and I the once-over."

Before they went in, SA John Connelly came out and said hello. "Is there something you wanted to say to the judge, Donna?"

"Sure," Donna said. "Something along the lines of, 'Your honor, the reason why my case was solved after over eleven years is because of the actions of the defendant this past summer with regard to another case. I ask that you strongly consider allowing the evidence from each case into the other. It is pertinent and valid information for the juries to hear, and it is important to help establish the character of the defendant.'"

"That's okay to say, but now is not the appropriate time. The judge today is just moving the cases along, and it wouldn't be the same judge hearing the case."

Donna understood. She was more or less merely voicing a concern. "What about the DNA?" Donna asked Connelly. There had been some talk of the DNA being tossed out of the case.

Connelly said everything would be done by the book, adding, "But I should tell you that the defense is going to try to get it knocked out just the same. And, although you're not going to speak today, Donna, I will let the judge know that you are here."

They walked into the courtroom together. After sitting through a few cases, John and Donna watched as Hope Seeley walked in with Rocky and pointed toward the back of the room, where she wanted him to sit and wait for his case to be called.

After some time, the judge called Rocky's case.

Neither John nor Donna had seen Rocky in years. As he walked toward the front of the room, Donna noticed how different he looked from the way she remembered him. The all-star wrestler, football player, genuinely healthy-looking man with an always-friendly disposition now had a large bald spot in the back of his graying head, glasses, noticeable weight gain, and a bit of a beer belly. As Rocky walked up to the defendant's table, he was greeted by Seeley and another of his attorneys, Marty Minnella, who stood and put his arm around Rocky in a gesture that disgusted Donna and John.

The judge asked if everyone had had a chance to review the case thoroughly and if everything was in order.

After the matter of a missing document was settled, the judge said, "I understand that you are trying this case personally, Mr. Connelly, is that right?"

"That is correct," Connelly said. "Your honor, I mentioned to you before that the victim may have some questions today. I want to let you know that I have spoken with her and answered those questions, so she will not be speaking. But I do want to let you know that she *is* present in the courtroom here today."

"Thank you," the judge said. "I am putting this case on the trial list."

They discussed schedules for a few moments and then the judge dismissed everyone. It was over before it ever got going.

Rocky turned and immediately exited the courtroom in an anxious dash to get away. Donna noticed that his face was "all red." As he left the room, Donna stood in a stance of "I'm not going away" and stared at him.

Maureen, Donna, and John met outside the courtroom. Maureen said she wanted to introduce Donna to someone.

"John, Donna, this is [the twenty-one-year-old coworker Rocky had attacked]." She stood calmly with her fiancé.

Donna had had no idea the woman had been sitting in the courtroom the entire time. Donna hugged her. "What a pleasure to meet you, finally. Thank you for being so brave. And thank you for coming forward . . . my case was solved because of you! I'm so glad you were able to escape."

As they talked, John spoke to the young woman's fiancé; they both agreed that "Rocky is scum."

"He'll get his in prison," the fiancé said.

Walking away from the courthouse, John and Donna talked about how glad they were that they had decided to go. It would be a great help in the healing process.

"We can only pray now," Donna said to her husband, "that there won't be any problems with that DNA evidence."

Chapter Twenty-nine

A Picture's Worth ...

ON THURSDAY, OCTOBER 20, 2005, DONNA CALLED JOHN CONNELLY. She probably didn't need to remind the SA that in two days, October 22, it would be the one-year anniversary of Rocky's arrest.

"Yeah, I know," Connelly said. He seemed a little frustrated himself by the snail's pace at which the court case was moving. The court had been pondering a trial date, but nothing had been set.

"Have you heard *anything?*" Donna wondered.

"Have you spoken to Neil recently?"

"No."

"You should give him a call and tell him that you spoke to me." There was something in Connelly's voice; he had information he obviously wanted Neil to share with Donna.

"They're involved with investigating Mr. Regan," Connelly said.

Was this a hint? Why wasn't he forthcoming with the information?

"Has he been involved with something else?" Donna asked anxiously.

"He might have been. Call Neil, Donna."

Indeed, Neil had something to share. An observant Wal-Mart employee, a man who worked in the film department, had recently called the WPD.

"Rocky had been going in to get film developed," Neil explained to Donna, "and the employee recognized him from his picture in the paper. The roll of film he brought in to be developed most recently had all sorts of women who didn't know they were being photographed. They are all pretty women in shorts, short skirts, and tight tops."

"What?"

"Yeah, apparently, Regan has been averaging two rolls of film per month. They are all pictures of pretty girls who didn't know they were being photographed."

"You've got to be kidding me, Neil?"

"No, Donna, sorry. Through records we've determined that he started going to Wal-Mart about a few months ago to have film developed. Based on the records Wal-Mart keeps, Regan has developed fifteen rolls of film, twelve of which I believe are now in our hands. I need to be careful with this and handle it right."

"Have you identified any of the women?" Donna asked, wondering deep down if she had been one of Rocky's photographic targets.

"There is one girl that they have identified that works at one of the banks in Cheshire. She's been on two rolls. We haven't said anything to her." Neil explained that Donna needed to keep this conversation between them. No one could find out about this during the investigation. Then he explained that Rocky had been driving his father's minivan lately. "And we believe he is driving the van so he can take the photos from the back of the van without anyone noticing."

Donna was floored by this new revelation. Rocky had never stopped his behavior, and it was possible that his behavior (and his desire to stalk women) was escalating.

"I'm taking my time with this," Neil said. "We want to see if Rocky's pattern changes now that the weather is turning colder."

Donna thought, *He'll just hang out at a health club where girls wear less clothing!*

"Look, Donna, tell John about this, but please, no one else."

"Yes, yes . . . of course, Neil."

"We're working to get a search warrant. I think we will have enough to arrest him on a charge of stalking or something similar."

This was great news to Donna.

The van that Rocky was driving *was* the perfect vehicle for stalking and photographing women without their knowledge. Borrowed from Rocky's father, the van would also become the perfect vehicle for something else Rocky had mind—something more evil that he was planning as he packed for a trip to upstate New York.

CHAPTER THIRTY

Fright Night

LINDSEY FERGUSON WAS ENJOYING THE FRUITS OF HER HARD WORK during nearly four years of high school in Saratoga Springs, New York. Running was Lindsey's love and forte. She excelled in both track and cross-country. Heading into the fall of 2005 as a senior, Lindsey was thinking about where she was going to attend college the following year. She was considering a career as a schoolteacher or in some branch of psychology, but like a lot of kids, Lindsey had not yet decided on her major. In the best shape of her life, the blond-haired, blue-eyed student-athlete was being courted by several colleges. The University of Virginia and the University of Michigan, along with Notre Dame and several others, had tried to recruit her. She had her choice, essentially.

Saratoga Springs, New York, is twenty-eight square miles with about 28,000 residents. That's small-town America in the Northeast by today's standards, but when summer comes and horse racing fans, tourists, and summer residents flock to this gorgeous piece of real estate in west-central New York, the population swells to almost 100,000.

Coincidentally, since 2003 Sarah Palomba, Donna and John's daughter, had been attending Skidmore College in Saratoga Springs, only 2.4 miles north of where Lindsey Ferguson was running through her final year of high school. Before Sarah had made her college decision, Donna, John, and the kids visited the school and took a look around the town to make sure it was safe enough for their daughter.

We liked Saratoga. North Broadway, the road that Skidmore is on, is lined with gorgeous estates, and the town itself has an upscale yet friendly feel. Of course, the town of Saratoga is probably best known for the horse track. That whole summer before Sarah went away was difficult. I kept trying to get my mind around the fact that my baby girl had grown up and she was not going to be sleeping under our roof anymore. Sarah was valedictorian of her high school class, incredibly bright and independent, but I would often catch glimpses of the little girl inside. John and I were incredibly overprotective, so when we took Sarah up to New York, we spent a few days there. Boatloads of parents would come and go, and John and I were still there. We walked the campus, talked with security. Checked out the dorms. Finally, the campus security officer who patrolled the grounds daily came up to John and me and asked if we were going to enroll. I guess that was our signal to leave. I left Sarah with a bunch of books, some spiritual, some inspirational, and reminded her that she was never alone and that we loved her more than she would ever know. The ride home was rough. I went through a box of tissue, and anyone that knows me knows that I do not cry easily. It just so happened a bunch of our friends had their firstborn going off to college as well, so we threw ourselves a "Sip and Sob" party to have some wine and console one another.

Amid the chaos of life with Rocky Regan roaming free, some uplifting news came to Donna as she, John, and Johnny prepared to leave for a much-needed trip to Paris. On October 26, 2005, Dr. Henry Lee contacted Donna about a press conference he said he was planning for that November regarding the recent "great success" of the CODIS convicted felon database program. First instituted in 1994, Lee said, the program had been upgraded, and there had been "400 hits since that time on cold cases." For the state of Connecticut, Donna's case was becoming the poster child of cold case hits, demonstrating that tenacity and resolve were advantageous in helping to crack cases using CODIS.

"Would you be willing to speak at the press conference?" Lee asked Donna over the phone.

"We'll be in Paris," Donna said with a touch of trepidation in her voice. After all, Donna had not gone public with her story. She was still widely known only as Jane Doe. "More than that, Dr. Lee," she added, "I have not come out in public yet—nobody knows me by name."

"You were public during your trial when I testified," Lee said.

"Yes, but my name has never been published."

"Could you write a letter for me that I can read at the press conference," Lee suggested. "I won't use your name."

"Yes, I can do that."

While these developments were unfolding, and especially while trying to cope with the idea that a family friend had committed such an evil act, Sarah Palomba wanted to talk about what had happened long ago to her mother. After all these years, Donna didn't want her daughter to have any questions left unanswered, and she felt the need to tell Sarah *everything*. Sarah was home visiting during a break from school. They sat down in the kitchen to have an early lunch before heading out shopping.

"Do you want to know the details?" Donna asked as she and Sarah finished their lunch.

"Yes," Sarah said.

Donna talked her daughter through the assault as best as she could. As Sarah cried, Donna tried to console her. "There were some incredible people that worked hard for me." She explained who they were. "I believe God has a plan and things happen for a reason, honey. He can turn something evil into something good—and He has helped me to heal greatly."

She listened intently, sometimes shaking, but I was calm and strong and explained why we hadn't told her the details before (when we had that chat when Sarah was just a teen). She said years ago she had put two and two together and knew (I was raped). She had seen a book I kept by my bed about rape and noticed mail that had come in from the Connecticut Sexual Assault Crisis Service. John had been the one to tell her it was Rocky who assaulted me and she couldn't believe it. She liked Rocky and remembered clearly that he was a good friend of John's. She remembered him working on our roof. She remembered Rocky coming down to the beach and staying for lunch.

They talked a little bit about the road ahead, regarding where the prosecution of John Regan was going. No one seemed to have a clear idea.

"We don't know," Donna said, referring to the outcome of it all.

"I'd be willing to testify if it goes to trial," Sarah said. "If you need anything, Mom, I'll be here."

They stood and hugged.

"I'm very proud of you, Mom."

On Halloween day, October 31, 2005, Lindsey Ferguson finished her cross-country training at Saratoga Springs High School, 140 miles north of Waterbury, and headed into the school building to talk with friends and make plans for the evening. It was Lindsey's last chance to spend a high school Halloween with friends. The gang she hung out with would all be splitting up and heading off to college next year. So Lindsey and her two best friends decided to go out trick-or-treating one last time together. They agreed to meet at one friend's house after going home to shower and change into their costumes.

Lindsey grabbed her gym bag and headed outside. It was just about dark out, the sky still showing some dusk color. Saratoga Springs High School had a large parking lot north of the track-and-field training area, with several tennis courts on the east side next to a baseball diamond. Outside the school, Lindsey and her two friends split up in different directions. The parking lot, since school had gotten out hours ago, was empty save for several of the coaches' vehicles and those belonging to students staying after school to practice sports or participate in extracurricular activities. It was right around 5:30 p.m.

"See you tonight," Lindsey yelled, waving to her friends.

"Okay."

As they walked their separate ways, a teacher, Ray Harrington, headed for his car as well. One of Lindsey's coaches, Art Kranick, stepped out the door at the same time.

Walking toward her car, Lindsey noticed a van parked directly next to her vehicle, facing the same way. There appeared to be someone sitting in the passenger's side, closest to her driver's door. The person looked to be waiting for someone.

Lindsey hadn't noticed the van when she had parked earlier. There had been no other cars in the immediate area.

Still walking, Lindsey got her keys ready so she could unlock her doors quickly. As she moved closer to the van, she realized it was parked so near to her car that she would have to shimmy her way between the vehicles, almost touching the sides of each at the same time.

When she got close enough, Lindsey could make out the person sitting in the vehicle. It was a man, maybe close to fifty years old. Gray hair. Scruffy five o'clock shadow. He was staring toward the school building, not paying any attention to Lindsey.

"I didn't think anything of it," Lindsey said later. "I could see the person sitting there. A lot of students drive home from school with their parents. So I assumed this man was waiting for his child so they could practice driving."

Lindsey squeezed in between the two vehicles, wiggling her way toward her car door to get in.

She unlocked the front driver's side door, reached in while still standing outside the car, and unlocked the back driver's side door. She pulled her upper body back out of the car, opened the back door, and threw in her bags.

As she shut the back door and moved toward the front, Lindsey heard a noise—the creak and whine of the van's side (sliding) door opening up.

Thinking that the driver wanted to get by, Lindsey moved closer to her car door. But within a breath, she felt the man's hands grab her.

"I had so many thoughts going through my head at that time," Lindsey recalled later. "I initially thought, *Is this a Halloween prank? A joke?*"

Whatever she might have believed was happening, Lindsey screamed as loudly as she could out of pure instinct.

That scream alerted Ray Harrington and Art Kranick, both of whom had just reached their vehicles. It was such a deep, guttural cry for help, so naturally terrifying, that both men knew it was no prank.

"In fact," Harrington later said, "something was badly wrong."

Lindsey began to fight, squirming and trying desperately to get out of the man's hold. He had one arm around her shoulder, the other arm around her waist, and was aggressively trying to pull Lindsey into his van. At the same time, he was trying to cover her mouth and grab at her breasts.

Lindsey, because she was bigger and stronger than most kids her age, having worked out and run all her life, was able to wiggle out of his grasp. She fell into the driver's seat of her car, butt first.

Now she was in the perfect position to use her powerful legs as a defense.

The man, disturbed by Lindsey's sudden break from his grasp, lunged after her. Smartly, Lindsey used her feet to kick him away—as she continued to scream for help.

For now, Lindsey had won the battle with what had turned out to be a real monster emerging from the dusk of Halloween night.

CHAPTER THIRTY-ONE

Festering Anger

THE MONTHS FOLLOWING CHIEF OF POLICE NEIL O'LEARY'S REVELA-
tion that John Regan had snuck into the Palombas home and sexually
assaulted Donna, she later explained, were filled with "anxiety, stress,
and an immense sense of fear that he would come after me, my husband, or one of my children. Moreover, I also worried that John would
go after Rocky and do something we would all regret. John was so
angry with his former friend."

Seeing Regan inside the courtroom during the pretrial hearing
had convinced John that hurting Rocky probably wasn't the smartest
thing to do. But that feeling of vindication seeing him begin to answer
for his crimes in a court of law did not last long.

As the weeks passed after the pretrial proceedings, Donna had
never seen her husband so distressed and consumed with anger.

---

*I no longer had to wonder who had raped me, but at the same
time, I dreaded what would happen if Regan decided to come after
me. Meanwhile, my daughter was away at college in that quaint
upstate town of Saratoga Springs, New York. Our belief was that
she had been far enough away from the mess back home and thus
free from any of the concerns we faced back in the Waterbury region
with Regan free on bond. Even better, she'd headed off to Paris
to study abroad during the fall 2005. During that entire time*

while Regan awaited trial (it had been just about a year since the DNA had hit on Regan), he continued to proclaim his innocence. Neighbors reported seeing him tossing a football with his kids. He attended local sporting events and dined out at local restaurants with his family. He was going about his life as if he was an innocent man being wrongly accused.

⌒⌒

For the past year, Donna and John had gone over it so many times. There was irrefutable DNA evidence against Rocky that he had committed one rape and charges pending that he had attacked a coworker. Yet, in Donna's opinion, because the Regan family "had money, he had been released on that $350,000 *cash* bond and allowed to roam free."

As the rage in John ebbed and flowed, Donna prayed "every night and every morning" that he would not take matters into his own hands, but wondered sometimes what he was thinking.

"I have dreams of killing Rocky," John confided in Donna one day.

"Your faith, John," Donna kept reminding him. "If you do anything, all you would be doing is making things worse for all of us." All those years they had waited for justice would be for naught. Wasted.

What John didn't tell Donna was that he *had* made a choice to kill Rocky. He had thought about it seriously, long, and hard. It was time. John had even disclosed this to his best friend.

"You know, I *have* to kill him," John said one night while out walking.

"Johnny, you cannot do that."

"I don't have a choice," John said.

John's friend looked at him. "Well, look, if that's your decision, I'm gonna tell the police that I was in on it too."

"No, no . . ." John said. "You cannot do that."

John walked away from that conversation beginning to think that killing Rocky would only "hurt those I really care about."

Was it the right thing to do?

As John weighed the ramifications on his life and soul that a decision to kill a man would cause, Rocky was making matters easier for John to finally let go.

Chapter Thirty-two

Caught in the Act

Several people heading out to their cars in the parking lot of Saratoga Springs High School—students, teachers, and coaches—heard seventeen-year-old Lindsey Ferguson screaming for her life.

And then the most bizarre thing happened. He let her go. And Lindsey was now sitting in her car, scared, shaking, crying, not knowing what had just taken place.

"My adrenaline was absolutely pumping and pumping . . ." Lindsey recalled later.

Lindsey's attacker started to shut her car door on her leg, which she didn't even realize was still sticking out of the car. Staring at her, not having much luck closing the door, he spoke what were, although Lindsey did not know then, familiar words to the women he had attacked previously: "Don't tell anyone about this!"

By this time Ray Harrington was running toward Lindsey's car, yelling at John Regan to stop what he was doing.

"You . . . hey . . . what are you doing?"

This startled Regan. He looked at Harrington.

"Who are you?" Harrington yelled as he made it to the van and Lindsey's car.

"It doesn't matter," Regan shouted angrily.

"The hell it doesn't," Harrington said.

Harrington flipped out his cell and called 911 just as Regan ran around to the front of his vehicle, hopped in, and took off.

As he did, Harrington read the license plate number to the 911 dispatcher on the other end of the line.

Lindsey was now in total shock, surrounded by several friends who had jumped inside the car to console and protect her.

"Lindsey, are you okay?" asked a friend.

Lindsey realized for the first time that she had escaped the clutches of a madman who had tried to take her away from family and friends.

"I had a hard time believing that this had just happened to me."

Now Harrington was running after Regan's van—at one time right alongside it—as Regan slowly drove out of the parking lot, hoping, obviously, that he would blend in with any traffic and not bring further attention to himself. Although Regan was a twice-accused sexual deviant, he acted as if he had done nothing wrong.

"As if he might be able to drive out of the parking lot slowly so nobody would notice him," Harrington later said.

Coach Art Kranick was in his car as Regan drove out of the parking lot and onto the street. Kranick followed close behind Regan, talking on his cell phone to the local Saratoga Springs Police Department (SSPD).

Those around Lindsey asked what had happened.

"I don't know . . ." was all Lindsey could say.

As teachers and students tended to Lindsey, Kranick chased Regan and eventually caught up to him, at one time even exchanging words with Regan as they drove.

This time, John "Rocky" Regan was caught in the act of trying to abduct a woman for his twisted sexual pleasure. But the sexually driven abduction attempt, as the rest of the evening would reveal, was only half of it. What Regan had in mind for Lindsey was far different from what he had done to Donna or his coworker. Apparently, rape and kidnapping were not the only crimes Regan was thinking about committing on this night.

CHAPTER THIRTY-THREE

No Escape

THE CHASE CAME TO AN END. COACH ART KRANICK HAD CAUSED SO much commotion and disruption in Regan's getaway plan that Regan actually pulled over to the side of the road not far from the school and got out of his van.

"What the hell do *you* want?" Regan screamed at Kranick.

"What do you mean, what do *I* want? You just attacked a girl in the high school parking lot!"

"You're crazy," Regan shouted, tossing his hands in the air as if to shoo Kranick away.

Without saying anything more, Regan hopped back into his van and sped off.

Kranick followed close behind, not allowing Regan out of his sight.

About a mile down the road, Regan pulled over again and got out of his vehicle. This time, however, Saratoga Springs police also arrived on the scene, following Kranick's lead from his continued connection via cell phone.

Police immediately approached Regan, who became "hostile, combative and very angry," said the prosecutor who would soon be involved in the case.

"How *dare* any of you question me about what I was doing?" Regan snapped.

"What were you doing in the parking lot?" a cop asked.

"I was making cell phone calls. I startled the girl. Nothing more."

At the same time, police had arrived at the school parking lot and began questioning Lindsey Ferguson. After hearing her story, it was decided that she would be taken to where Regan was being detained to see if she could identify him. From there, she could go down to the police station and file a formal report. This way Regan could be held in custody.

Lindsey was driven by the area where Regan was being questioned by police officers. She sat in the backseat of a nondescript car with tinted windows. There was no way he could have seen her as they drove by.

Looking at him, "I felt nauseous and sick to my stomach. Immediately, I felt so disgusted looking at him. I knew for certain—right away—it was him."

Regan told police he was in the area—so far away from home—working on a house, and that he worked for a roofing/construction company back in Connecticut and had traveled to the region for a job and additional sales-related projects.

Meanwhile, the impact of the situation had hit Lindsey. She was sitting inside the SSPD station, trying to collect herself as best she could, thinking . . . *This is not a joke. This guy was seriously trying to abduct me. This is something that you hear about on television.*

Everyone was at the police station: Lindsey, her friends, her parents, coaches, teachers. Everyone who had been there in the parking lot identified Regan as the guy who had tried to abduct Lindsey.

Lindsey noticed that her eye bothered her. She thought it might have been her contacts, but didn't say anything about it.

"Lindsey," someone from school, a teacher, said, pointing to Lindsey's thigh.

She looked down.

In the struggle, Regan had—as he had with Donna—gone after Lindsey's eyes and scratched one of her contacts out. It was now stuck to her leg.

"I don't even remember him touching my eyes."

As District Attorney Jim Murphy became involved, a new part of John Regan's criminal life became apparent, proving just how lucky Lindsey was to have fought for her life and escaped.

As police searched Regan's van, they uncovered a horrifying collection of tools. He had a brand-new tarp. A length of rope that had been tied with slipknots into a noose. Photography equipment. A pitchfork. A rake. And topping it all off, an empty syringe, accompanied by what was a large dose of antihistamine in a separate container. It appeared, from the evidence in Regan's van, that he had schemed to abduct Lindsey, do whatever it was he had planned to her, and this time make sure there was no DNA or a witness left behind to testify against him. Even more disturbing, once the police went to that empty house Regan said he was working on, they found all the windows with the shades down and the curtains drawn.

Prosecutor Murphy later said, "My conclusion was that he was going to tie her up in that van in an instant because he had those pre-tied slipknots. Then he was going to inject her with that antihistamine to knock her out. And then take her to this house that he was working on that he had the shades pulled and the curtains drawn."

From there, many of those connected with the case later agreed, Regan was going to kill Lindsey Ferguson.

The SSPD popped Regan's name into the computer system to see what came up, and there it was, staring back at the officer: Regan was out on bond awaiting trial on charges of kidnapping and unlawful restraint in Connecticut.

And yet, there was still one more discovery to be unearthed inside Regan's van and back at his home in Waterbury—a find that would spark police all over the Northeast to take another look at cold rape (and murder) cases.

CHAPTER THIRTY-FOUR

Suicide Is Painless

NOT UNUSUAL FOR CHIEF NEIL O'LEARY, ON OCTOBER 31, 2005, HE was working late into the night after most of his officers had gone home when news from New York State arrived. Reflecting later, the news did not necessarily shock the seasoned investigator, but then again, this night it made Neil sit up, shake his head, and feel a bit sick, as well as greatly relieved.

After a knock on his office door, one of Neil's detectives poked his head in.

"Come in . . ." Neil said. "What is it?"

"Chief, you're not going to believe this, but we just took a call. John Regan was taken into custody in Saratoga Springs, New York."

What the hell was Regan doing way up there?

Waterbury to Saratoga was a 140-mile trip, almost three hours north, Neil thought, as his officer explained what Regan had been picked up for.

"Saratoga?" Neil asked his detective. "What?"

The detective gave Neil all the details.

He was going to murder and bury Lindsey Ferguson, Neil told himself, shaking his head, while back in Waterbury, half the town was behind Regan, painting him as the all-American boy being railroaded by two women who had affairs with him and didn't want to admit it.

Incredible.

"I really believe that in Regan's mind there wasn't going to be any chance of DNA to be uncovered up in New York," Neil commented later. "We had several women come forward later and accuse Regan of attacking them going back to as far as the late 1970s and early '80s, but the statute of limitations had run. This proved he has been a sexual predator for a very long time."

Ultimately, Saratoga Springs' chief of police Ed Moore's team of investigators uncovered hundreds of photographs inside Regan's van. They were a stalker's stash, a collection of images you'd see some deranged character in a Hollywood thriller film snapping: women on bike paths, jogging, walking, in shopping malls, and just being themselves out in public, unaware that a madman was secretly following them and taking pictures. Some of the photos, investigators learned through time codes on the camera, had been snapped only hours before he attacked Lindsey. This man, who had committed several sexual assaults (attempted or otherwise) and had been apprehended while out on bond in a case with a DNA match, was picked up trying to kidnap and possibly assault a seventeen-year-old girl. This latest case—along with the discovery of the photographs and other "items" found in Regan's van—demonstrated Regan's hubris and the escalation of a serial sex offender who was perhaps planning on graduating to something more sinister. Regan showed the classic signs of a sociopath who believed, even when the heat was on, that he was capable of beating the police and the system. Only this time—thank goodness—Regan was caught in the act.

"I am convinced," Neil concluded, "there is DNA sitting in an evidence collection room, up on a shelf somewhere, in some police department within the Northeast that has John Regan's DNA as a match, but has just not been submitted."

Neil called Donna that night.

She was devastated. Immediately, Donna wanted to reach out to Lindsey and console her, tell her it would be okay. Tell her she was a survivor, not a victim. Tell her she would get through this.

On Tuesday, November 1, 2005, John Regan was arraigned and charged with attempted first- and second-degree kidnapping, along with attempted unlawful restraint. This time, there would be no bond for Rocky Regan.

When Saratoga Springs police chief Ed Moore spoke to the press, he called Regan an "organized offender, who was planning on taking [Lindsey] to another location."

Any armchair criminal profiler will agree that, for women, it is that *second* location where they end up dead. Women are told to never, ever relent and go to a second location with someone who is trying to abduct you—because that second location is where death generally occurs. Fight for your life, even if it means dying at that first location.

Saratoga County district attorney Jim Murphy told news reporters that Regan had "planned the crime," but the "'to whom' was random . . . There was no indication, at this point, he knew who [Lindsey] was. There is no indication that [Lindsey] was stalked."

The community of Saratoga was shocked about the news that a man, in near broad daylight, had tried to abduct a teenage girl from what was considered a safe zone, a school parking lot. It did not take long for news of Rocky's arrest and the serial nature of his crimes to be reported back home to the Waterbury citizenry. His supporters could no longer deny that Rocky was likely a serial predator hiding in plain sight.

During the brief court proceeding, Regan hobbled around the courtroom, shackles on both ankles. He stood before the judge with his head bowed, chin nudged up against his chest—a familiar pose this serial offender would take whenever in court. At times, one news report noted, Regan picked at his cuticles as if the court was wasting his time. He never once made eye contact with anyone in the courtroom besides his attorneys.

During the investigation, four search warrants were issued for Regan's van, home, his parents' home, and his place of business.

Newspapers on November 2, 2005, reported that Regan was a suspect in two additional sexual assault/kidnapping cases in Connecticut, commenting that not only was Regan reared in a "prominent Waterbury family," the son of a dentist, the husband of a second-grade schoolteacher, but also that a school had been named after Regan's grandfather. This Waterbury golden boy, however, was looking down the barrel of forty or more years in prison, depending on how many additional women came forward and how many additional charges could be tacked on. A teletype had gone out to police departments throughout New York and New England. More film of Rocky's had been uncovered in Connecticut under a search warrant—and there, police found more disturbing photographs of women's legs, women biking, sitting, shopping, and going about their lives. But the photos that interested Neil O'Leary most, when he was called in to have a look, were of the former coworker Regan had tried to sexually assault—the woman whose case had led Neil down the road of making Regan a major suspect in Donna's attack. Regan had been stalking his coworker—and other women—for some time, obviously obsessing about her. Neil began to consider another question as he went through the new evidence: Was Donna among the women Regan had photographed?

With the new charges Regan faced, having been literally caught in the act, he must have realized the jig was up. He couldn't talk his way out of this one, relying on the fact that his family was respected and had money and he had never been in trouble. And when cowards like Rocky Regan, who prey on women, finally realize there are far too many witnesses saying the same things about them, and far too much evidence to contradict their lies, they tend to opt for the easy way out. No, not a plea bargain deal. Something more permanent. Something gutless.

After his court appearance on November 1, 2005, Regan went back to his cell and went to sleep. The next morning, November 3, which just happened to be Rocky's forty-ninth birthday, he got up, took his bedsheet, tied one end around his neck in a noose and the other to the top of his bedpost, then sank the weight of his two-hundred-pound, five-foot ten-inch frame down on itself, apparently hoping to reach that white light and put an end to his misery.

— ⌒ —

Neil O'Leary called and told me that Rocky had been taken by ambulance to the hospital and that he had tried to kill himself. I felt sick. Part of me wished he would die, but then we would never know what else he had done and who his other victims might be. There were so many unanswered questions. As I thought about it more, waiting to hear if he would make it, I wanted him to live.

— ⌒ —

Regan's suicide attempt didn't work.

After guards discovered Regan had passed out (he had been unconscious for ten minutes, according to one report), he was transported to Saratoga Hospital's intensive care unit, where he was treated for a few days and released back to the jail's medical unit under close supervision and guard. Regan would be okay—no irreversible damage had been done. He had escaped final judgment—at least for now.

Meanwhile Regan's lawyer came out swinging, claiming his client was being painted with "a broad brush [to] characterize things in ways they are not." The impetus behind those photos Rocky had taken, for example, was not the sinister plot of a serial sexual offender, counsel suggested, but "There is a completely innocent explanation."

Of course, everyone was eager to hear why a man accused in two sexual assaults and an attempted kidnapping was taking hundreds of photographs of women's legs and body parts without their knowledge, not to mention traveling with what appeared to be a serial killer's tool kit.

But those answers never came.

A fifty-year-old Waterbury woman, after reading about John Regan's latest crimes, stepped forward to say Regan had kidnapped and attempted to sexually assault her twenty-four years earlier. Waterbury Police told the press they were investigating whether Regan may have committed other crimes, including the murders of two Waterbury prostitutes during the 1980s. Both girls had last been seen not far from Rocky's home.

There was no telling, honestly, the extent to which Regan's crimes stretched, how many women had been the victims of this man's twisted, deviant sexual appetite.

On November 10, 2005, Regan was admitted to a psychiatric hospital in central New York "for evaluation"—which was perhaps his plan all along. Later, a report would detail Regan's physical and mental health, along with his educational background and social, family, and personal history. According to the report, after college he had gone to work for the roofing company bearing his family name, as a salesman and crew leader. Six years later he started a job at a wholesale building supply company, where he worked until 1992. He bounced around after that, working for various construction companies, a roofing company, finally settling down with a manager's job at a construction supply house, bringing home a nice $95,000 annual salary. He was fired, said that same report, after he was arrested for attempting to sexually assault a coworker.

The health report was more interesting. In 1988, after a routine exam, Regan tested positive for hepatitis C. After receiving treatment, he told the interviewer, his hepatitis condition "leveled off." Since his suicide attempt, Regan had been taking the antidepressants Selatex and Tranzdone. Regan also said he had been drinking "a quart of whiskey a day" since 2004.

As he sat in the hospital (and later, while in jail), Regan stayed in touch with his wife of twenty-five years and his three sons, all of whom lived at home and sent letters, accepted Regan's phone calls, and visited him.

Weeks after entering the psychiatric hospital, Regan was indicted by a Saratoga Springs grand jury on charges of attempted second-degree kidnapping.

Lindsey came forward and said she was ready and willing to testify against Regan in court anytime the prosecutor needed her to. She wasn't some sort of weak young girl who was going to cower in a corner somewhere and hide from her attacker, allowing this maniac to get away. Lindsey was going to do her part to put Regan in prison for as long as the law would allow.

The media picked up on the story of John Regan and took it national—CNN, MSNBC, ABC, and many of the major cable talking-head crime shows, including the outspoken Nancy Grace. Soon Regan was being discussed as a potential suspect in several high-profile cases of young girls who had vanished and were found murdered throughout New England, including Molly Bish, a sixteen-year-old Warren, Massachusetts, lifeguard who had disappeared after her shift one day at a Warren swimming/fishing pond on June 27, 2000. Molly bore a striking resemblance to Lindsey. Authorities could prove that Rocky was in the general area of where Molly had disappeared while working her lifeguard job. Sadly, Molly's remains were recovered some time later in nearby woods.

These developments sparked interest in Donna's case once again and got her thinking about her next move. The one constant in Donna's life, besides trying to protect her identity at all costs, had been her desire to see that laws were changed with regard to the statute of limitations on sexual assault cases (where DNA was present) and what those first responders did after arriving at an alleged sexual assault and/or rape crime scene. This fight drove Donna. Inspired her. It was her goal to one day effect great change not only in the state of Connecticut, but the entire nation.

As fate would have it, Donna received an important piece of news as the 2005 Christmas season approached. Nancy Cushins, the executive director of the Connecticut Sexual Assault Crisis Service (ConnSACS), called. Donna had earlier expressed a desire to help ConnSACS. ConnSACS planned to introduce legislation that would make the statute of limitations for sexual assault retroactive. They were working on finalizing a bill for the next legislative session. It would allow for victims such as Donna, regardless of how many years had passed before a suspect and crime were matched by DNA, to see their attackers prosecuted for the crime of sexual assault and rape.

"I've been reading all the publicity about John Regan," Nancy said, "and we thought it'd be great if you could testify in front of the house legislators when the bill is introduced."

This was Donna's chance to help effect the changes she wanted so desperately. On the other hand, however, she realized it was becoming harder to achieve her goals and remain anonymous.

~~~

I was torn. I knew that by coming forward I could make a greater impact. I also knew that my family was very concerned about me coming forward. My husband in particular did not want us to be in the public eye. He did not even want me to tell my story to the Waterbury Observer *when I did. We were healing very differently: my husband John wanted to move on with our lives and leave the past behind. I could not do that. I became more educated about sexual assault. It is the most misunderstood and underreported crime and affects so many young people. I could no longer remain silent.*

~~~

Nancy Cushins explained that similar legislation had been introduced by two people back in 2001–2, but it had not met with any success. With a woman such as Donna, in her position, having faced the remarkable fact that Regan could only be charged with kidnapping in her case, Nancy believed a tremendous emotional impact could be applied with the house legislators. The bottom line was: If DNA had specifically matched John Regan as the man who had allegedly sexually assaulted Donna, why did it matter how many years had passed since the attack took place?

"It's illogical," Donna said, "where there is DNA involved, and I think a strong case can be made to make it retroactive."

Nancy and Donna agreed to stay in touch while Donna considered testifying.

At Dr. Henry Lee's press conference in November 2005, held at the state capitol in downtown Hartford, Connecticut, he read Donna's letter outlining her case and what had happened to Lindsey. He discussed how DNA had, after eleven years, a major impact on Donna's case, essentially introducing a viable suspect, and had brought a tremendous amount of publicity to Donna's "Jane Doe" story and the need for change in these types of cases. Lee had built the conference around the idea of updating the media, mainly, on Connecticut's role in the DNA database/CODIS. Connecticut Governor Jodi Rell, who had taken over for embattled Governor John Rowland (who had resigned in early 2004 after a fraud investigation that ultimately landed the governor in federal prison), stood by Dr. Lee. Alongside the two of them were several law enforcement officials, state prosecutors, and state representatives. Lee had the attention of the house and the public.

Addressing the crowd, Governor Rell said, "There is no greater responsibility of government than public safety. No more important task than solving cold cases."

Dr. Lee explained how the DNA project CODIS began in the early 1990s, claiming that Connecticut was "the first state in the country to create a database," and adding enthusiastically, "We have a very good record in Connecticut. Very few states can match our record. Every day this DNA is working and lots of cases are being resolved."

Then Dr. Lee pulled out Donna's letter and read it, after which he concluded, "This letter shows how everybody worked together to solve the crime. John Regan fits the profile of a serial rapist. We think there are many other kidnapping cases he was involved in."

Donna's old friend John Murray, from the *Waterbury Observer*, probably put this portion of the story in context best in an article that winter, writing, "Although [John Regan] has yet to be convicted of a single crime, the mounting evidence against Regan in the last 13 months has transformed from a 'he said–she said,' into an avalanche rumbling furiously down a craggy mountain pass."

By the middle of December 2005, a judge had signed a warrant to arrest Regan on charges stemming from an incident in 1981, the oldest sexual assault accusation on record for Regan. The case involved Regan allegedly trying to force a woman to give him oral sex.

This was great news to Donna. She had been doing so much lately behind the scenes. But the media was not letting go, and they were in this, Donna knew, for the long haul. *Good Morning America* was interested and willing to interview Donna in silhouette so she could remain anonymous. In consulting with Neil about this, Donna told him, "I am considering coming out in the open and giving *GMA* an exclusive under the right set of circumstances."

"Really?" Neil said, surprised.

Donna had spoken to everyone in her family about it, she said, along with her doctor. She had even mentioned it to her parents.

"The key," she told Neil, "is to have it done on *my* terms. I would not want it taped and I would want the angle to be a message of hope; the fact that an individual can overcome a trauma with her life very much intact. I also want to let women who are suffering in silence know that there are resources out there. I persevered through a great deal of evil, and the outcome is one of hope."

It was here, as Donna began to consult with friends, family, and even a media consultant, that the seeds of what would become Donna Palomba's new passion in life were planted. She decided, after talking to Neil, that "a website would be the most logical resource" to accomplish the short-term goals she desired. Donna had already bought crimevictim.com and victimrights.com, along with a few other URL addresses. But these names hadn't entirely captured for Donna what she was feeling, or what she wanted to present to victims and survivors of sexual assault and rape. There was another name out there, she was convinced, but it just hadn't come to her yet.

Then John Murray called about another interested media source. He had taken a voice message from a reporter at NBC's *Dateline* who was looking for information about John Regan. *Dateline* was in the beginning stages of gathering information, the reporter said.

So now there were *Geraldo*, *GMA*, CNN, NBC, and scores of other media outlets vying for Donna's attention. Certainly, if one looked hard enough, it wasn't difficult to figure out that Donna was the "Rachael" in John Murray's ten-thousand-word story he had written about her case, but to most of the world Rachael was just another Jane Doe. Yet, Donna wondered, how could she participate in any of this media exposure—getting her all-important message out to the public so that it would stick—and still remain under that anonymous umbrella of Jane Doe? It just didn't seem possible anymore.

She'd have to make a choice.

CHAPTER THIRTY-FIVE

Pleading

As Donna began to think seriously about removing her Jane Doe mask while working doggedly on getting legislation passed to support retroactive sexual assault charges, John Regan was released from the psychiatric hospital in upstate New York and arraigned again in Saratoga on January 6, 2006.

During his first official arraignment on charges of attempting to kidnap Lindsey Ferguson, John Regan casually pleaded "not guilty."

He wanted to go to trial. Prosecutor Jim Murphy claimed outside the courtroom that he and his team were absolutely ready.

"She is eager to testify," Murphy said of Lindsey. "She's willing to tell her story." No prosecutor wants to subject a youth to the ordeal of facing her attacker in court, but Lindsey was prepared.

Regan was placed back in lockup inside Saratoga County Jail. His stay at the hospital was over.

On this same day, Donna met with Selim Noujaim, the Connecticut state representative from the 47th District, and expressed her desire to advocate changing the law as it pertained to sexual assault and the charge's time expiration. That sort of law made no sense to Donna. It flew in the face of DNA technological advancements. The law by itself would often cancel any progress investigators might make within an investigation over any number of years. Wouldn't this particular law—the statute of limitations—stop investigators from going back in time to investigate cold cases?

Donna sure thought so.

"I'd like to see Mr. Regan charged," Donna said. She was firm. She wanted Regan to pay for what he had done to her—she wanted her day in court with this monster.

"I understand," Noujaim said. "But if you proceed with something like this, be prepared that you would have to testify." It was well-known by then that Donna had been steadfast in her desire to remain an anonymous rape survivor and victim of John Regan.

"I could," Donna said, "and am willing, as long as I won't have to get into specifics with regard to John Regan [because his case had not yet gone to trial]."

"Chief O'Leary would have to be willing to testify too," Noujaim added. "Neil's a good friend of mine—you know that?"

"He will," Donna responded.

Noujaim then got House Republican attorney Chris Adams on the phone and asked him to look into the statutes surrounding Donna's fight to change the law.

Adams said he would.

Another big question for Donna was whether Regan, if convicted of kidnapping in New York, would have to register as a sex offender and become part of that database.

The answer, she was disturbed to find out, was no.

So Donna decided to speak with the attorneys involved in prosecuting Regan to find out why he was not being charged with attempted sexual assault in New York, and if there was a chance he ever could be.

The first thing she did was call Jim Murphy. It was February when Donna contacted the prosecutor. Donna mentioned how attorneys from Connecticut were probably going to contact him about getting Regan extradited back to Connecticut to face those charges filed for attempting to sexually assault his coworker, not to mention her pending case against Regan.

"If Connecticut begins making noises to get him back, I will tell them," Murphy said pointedly, "to kindly wait their turn." Murphy wanted to see Regan prosecuted in New York to the fullest extent, as soon as possible.

Donna believed Murphy was sincere and determined to see that Regan paid for his crimes. She felt good about Murphy being on the job, even if it involved another case. She also found out that Regan's attorney was an "expensive guy," somewhere in the neighborhood, she learned, of "hundreds of thousands of dollars."

Regan's attorneys had already contacted Murphy, the prosecutor explained, to begin talking plea deal, but Murphy said he wanted to think seriously about it and, of course, first talk to all the victims involved.

"Regan will claim," Murphy explained, "that this is his first offense." He had not been convicted of any crimes in Connecticut yet. That would work to his advantage, the prosecutor told Donna (who was, of course, appalled by this notion). "He currently has *no* convictions."

Donna didn't like hearing that. "This is ludicrous since there's a DNA match."

"I'm sorry, Mrs. Palomba, but that's the law."

"I'd like to reach out to the Ferguson family," Donna mentioned.

"That'd be fine," he said, but explained that now was probably not the right time.

They talked some more about the law and how Donna could effect change using her case as an example, and Murphy applauded her for all she had done thus far to help sexual assault victims, warning, "It will be an uphill battle."

Donna knew all about uphill battles. She was ready.

"I'm thinking of developing a website for young girls and victims nationally."

"That's a good idea."

"NBC's *Dateline* has reached out to me through a third party," Donna said.

Murphy said the popular NBC news magazine show had contacted his office too, along with SA John Connelly. "You can do whatever you want," Murphy said, but regarding a potential appearance by him on *Dateline*, "John Connelly and I take the same stance and we cannot do anything to jeopardize our cases against Mr. Regan."

Donna took that into consideration.

"I congratulate you and what you've done, Mrs. Palomba, and for getting through what was many years of not knowing. You can call me anytime."

Donna hung up and thought: *How refreshing to speak with someone who is an intelligent advocate for victims and wants to do the right thing.*

❧

In March 2006, John and Donna drove to Saratoga to pick up Sarah for spring break. Donna had contacted Saratoga police chief Ed Moore, and he met them at a local Starbucks while they were in town. It was the beginning of what would become a long-term friendship. Donna and Ed would go on to do great work together with regard to victims' rights and sexual assault crime-scene first responders.

Ed assured Donna and John how "seriously" they were taking Regan's case in Saratoga. He explained that they could not have asked for a better, more dedicated and determined prosecutor to try these brutal, severe crimes.

Donna immediately felt encouraged talking to Ed. He had a way of making her believe that they were all in this together, and that everyone wanted to see Regan put behind bars for as long as possible.

After they spoke for a while, Ed handed Donna his card and gave one to Sarah, telling her, "If you ever need to reach me, please do. Contact me anytime."

Donna knew he meant it. She and John could feel safe when Sarah went back to Skidmore, knowing that their daughter had an ally in Saratoga she could turn to at any time.

Donna indicated a desire to meet with Lindsey Ferguson.

"Look," Ed explained sincerely and respectfully, understanding Donna was only trying to help, "it's not a good idea right now. We need to conclude the New York cases against Mr. Regan before you meet with her. We need to be very cautious in that regard. We don't want to do anything that his attorneys could use against us."

Ed said that the next hearing in Regan's New York case was scheduled for about a month away, April 13, 2006. Then Ed told Donna and John that Regan had been ruled out in a case in Warren, Massachusetts, involving a teenage lifeguard, Molly Bish, who went to work one morning and vanished (and was ultimately murdered). Regan was indeed in the area at the time, and he looked extremely good as a suspect, but an investigation into his exact whereabouts proved he could not have committed the crime.

Donna said she appreciated the information. They said their goodbyes and agreed to stay in touch.

When the April 13 Saratoga hearing date arrived, it was deferred to May 8 because of scheduling conflicts claimed by Regan's attorneys. The reason for the hearing was to decide whether to preclude a potential jury from hearing about the items Regan had in his van at the time he tried to abduct Lindsey. His attorneys were arguing that the items were nothing more than tools Regan needed for his job—everyday utensils someone in Regan's line of work required to conduct routine business.

Shortly before Regan's May 8 court date, Neil O'Leary called Donna and left a message: "I've been talking with the Saratoga police, and there is something I need to get with you about . . ."

Upon returning home and hearing the recording, Donna was anxious.

Neil called back and said, "Listen, Donna . . . we found something in Regan's van I need to tell you about."

Her stomach tightened. "What is it, Neil?"

"Are you at your computer?"

"Yes."

Neil said he'd e-mail it.

"I immediately got a sick feeling," Donna said later, "not knowing what I was about to see."

It was a photo. Regan had digitally photographed a picture of Donna from an article that had been in a local newspaper in September 2005. Donna had received the Woman of the Year Award from the Business Women's Forum and made the front page of a Waterbury newspaper. Apparently, all signs indicated that Regan was still fixated on Donna Palomba after all these years.

"I don't think he was following or still stalking you, Donna," Neil said, trying to reassure her. "It was the only photo they found of you inside his van."

One was enough, Donna knew.

"Have you found out anything else?" Donna asked.

"The DNA on the dead prostitutes [who were last seen on the streets near Regan's house] was not a match to Regan," Neil confirmed. Rocky could be ruled out of those horrible crimes, even though he lived down the street from where both girls had walked their beats.

"Everyone feels Rocky has done more crimes, Neil."

"Yeah, I know. Fact is, though, those crimes dating back to the 1980s and '90s will most likely remain unsolved. Most of the detectives on those old cases have retired, and in many of these cases it was *before* DNA was ever collected or used."

Donna mentioned that she was thinking seriously about meeting with producers from NBC's *Dateline*.

Neil said they had reached out to him too, and he said he'd do the show only if Donna was involved.

Ed Moore contacted Donna soon after she spoke to Neil and explained that his investigators had taken a successful trip to Waterbury, meeting with Neil and his team, and the case building against Regan was stronger than it had ever been.

"What we were hoping to find," Ed said, "we found."

Still, the main worry at this point was that a jury would not be allowed to hear about those "items" found inside Regan's vehicle at the time of the thwarted abduction. Ed explained that the judge presiding over the case in New York often erred on the side of caution regarding the type of evidence that could lead to a convicted defendant winning an appeal. The judge, in other words, did not want anything in his trial that would come back later on appeal and offer the chance for the defendant to walk. He would toss it out beforehand if there was a question.

"I'd be shocked, however, if he suppressed this evidence," Ed said.

Donna was concerned that Rocky was going to skate on this New York charge with a slap and a few years in jail.

A few days before the hearing, prosecutor Jim Murphy called Donna to bring her up to speed on what was happening.

"The hearing is still on," Murphy said, "as far as I know. And we're prepared."

"What about media coverage?" Donna asked. She was interested in this for many reasons. She also figured that *Dateline* would likely be covering the case in New York. Producers would be at the proceeding.

"There are no cameras allowed in the courtroom," he said. "You'd have to fill out an application with the judge and get it approved."

"What about a decision?"

"That will take some time. The judge won't have it right away. This judge usually takes, oh, two to three weeks."

Donna wondered about the charges.

"I am not so sure we'll be successful with a kidnapping charge, seeing that Lindsey was not *physically* transported anywhere."

This worried Donna. It would mean far fewer years behind bars for Regan. Also, Donna was concerned about the charges in her case being affected by this same issue. She had not been transported anywhere either. Could a suspect be charged with kidnapping if he broke into a house but then left without the victim?

Later that day Donna received word of another development from the SAO handling her case. Regan's attorneys in Connecticut were on their way north to speak with his attorneys in New York. One of Regan's New York attorneys was apparently pushing Regan to make a plea deal so he could escape any serious time that might come with a conviction by jury.

"They're going to advise him to take twelve years," Donna's contact at the SAO told her.

There certainly seemed to be a lot going on behind the scenes with regard to John Regan and lawyers and deals. But Donna was being kept in the loop. That was a good sign.

"The prosecutor up there won't budge," Donna said. "They want the full fifteen of a five- to fifteen-year sentence."

"The talk is on."

"Will there be any *chance* of parole with something like that?" Donna wondered.

"Parole is determined by the Department of Corrections up there and is based on good behavior. A good way to look at it is about 85 percent of the actual sentence."

Donna and John, listening on speakerphone, looked at each other. *Why is it that the bad guys always catch a break?*

"What would you and John be comfortable with, Donna?"

She didn't hesitate: "Twenty years! *No* parole."

"That would mean he'd have to plead to twenty-five years . . . and we're not sure that Regan would do that."

It was clear to Donna and John that although Regan was indicating a desire to plead, it would be only under certain conditions. There wouldn't be a hearing on May 8—that much was clear. Moreover, Regan was playing things as if *he* held the cards. And depending on where you sat, in certain respects he did.

"We also want him to register as a sexual offender," Donna added.

"Not sure about that. I'll look into it. You may be able to make that a condition of your plea."

John Palomba mentioned that he had read an article about a case in New York where a perpetrator had not been charged (because authorities did not yet know who he was), but his DNA profile (left at the scene of the crime) had been charged with rape before the statute ran out. Thus, when they finally apprehended him (if ever), they could go back and charge the man with the crime—basically charge the DNA profile as if it was a person and put a face on it later.

"We'll look into that."

"Tell me about that picture of you Neil found? It's old, right?"

"No, no," Donna said. "It was 2005."

"John [Connelly] or myself will call you back when we have some news, Donna. Hang in there."

They hung up. A few hours later, Donna's contact inside the SAO called back.

"The hearing has been postponed for two weeks."

"Why?" Donna asked.

"It appears the attorneys are working hard toward a plea."

John and Donna set up a meeting with John Connelly for the following afternoon.

When they arrived at three o'clock, Pudgie and Neil were there, as well as Maureen Norris. Donna felt as though Connelly wanted to speak to her about considering a plea in her case too.

According to Donna's notes, Connelly immediately started talking about "bundling" the cases together, which was what Regan's attorneys from Waterbury had traveled north to discuss. They wanted to see if, within one plea bargain, they could package all of Regan's cases (in Connecticut) together and come to some sort of agreement on Donna's case, Regan's former coworker, and the fifty-year-old woman from 1981.

"We should seriously consider this," Connelly said. "But I don't want to lead on to his defense team that we might be interested in something of this nature."

Donna brought up her concern that perhaps Regan would get off on the kidnapping charge in her case because, as she put it, "the victim had not been moved."

Connelly agreed. It would be tough to make that charge stick. And if they couldn't, then what charge were they left with?

"The defense will also argue that the DNA was not obtained properly in your case, Donna, because, according to Regan, it was consensual sex . . . If we go for a plea of twenty to twenty-five years, which is the max, they have no reason to agree. They might as well fight it out at trial. We need to be realistic here. Fifteen years might be the right number."

Donna was floored. The rights that the perpetrator of such violent crimes had at his disposal were enough to make her sick.

I was so frustrated. It was maddening that John Regan could not be arrested for the crime of sexual assault in my case, and the ripple effect was that the SA couldn't risk going to trial. Regan had powerful attorneys. Connelly said that if Regan was arrested for rape in my case it would have been a slam dunk and he would have gotten forty years. The charges of kidnapping in my case were going to be difficult to prove. I felt sick learning that his New York and Connecticut sentences would be served concurrently. Ultimately, I had little say and had to defer to the SA and my attorney. This whole experience compelled me to fight to remove the statute of limitations on sexual assault cases involving DNA evidence even more. It was ridiculous. Our laws needed to match the science and technology available. After all, when these particular laws were written, no one knew about DNA evidence.

—◆—

"What does that mean, though?" Donna asked. She wanted hard numbers. "Let's say the guy gets twenty years. In the end, what does twenty years actually amount to?"

"It means that he would serve, for your case, twelve and three-quarter years out of fifteen. We could add on potentially five years of 'special parole' and five more years of probation. They might go for that . . ."

The other major factor here was that even if Regan was convicted at trial in New York, Connelly would be forced to exclude that conviction from Donna's case because it happened after Donna's assault.

Score another round for the bad guys.

"And if your case is tried first," Connelly explained, "they couldn't use it in the New York case because they are not similar enough."

Neil piped in, saying, "The victim in what we'll call Regan's first case—in 1981—would *never* testify. I am certain of that."

"I have to leave for a few days, but I plan to be in touch with Regan's lawyers on May 15. Think about this seriously, Donna, John," Connelly said, looking at the two of them, "but let's not tell anyone we're discussing it."

Chapter Thirty-six

The Narrow Gate

On Friday, May 19, 2006, John Regan was ushered into court wearing a blue denim jacket, a green, prison-issued two-piece jumper that resembled hospital scrubs, handcuffs, and shackles. He looked old, well beyond his forty-nine years. Regan had dark, puffy half-circles under his eyes and a desultory look, his face ashen and devoid of any sentiment besides embarrassment, perhaps—a look more of a man accepting punishment, rather than taking responsibility. He never looked at anyone except his attorneys (no family was present at Regan's request, because, he later said through his attorneys, he "didn't want to submit them to the media").

In what some reporters later tagged as a "surprise move," Regan pleaded guilty to second-degree kidnapping in the case of Lindsey Ferguson; a plea under what prosecutor Jim Murphy said was "not a deal" or "lesser charge." Sentencing was slated for July, but word was that John Regan was only going to get twelve years.

"Basically, we achieved the highest conviction without having to put the victim on the stand," Murphy astutely explained to the media. "She was ready to go, but we were able to obtain the same result without having to put her through that trauma and confront Mr. Regan a second time."

A win at trial, Murphy said later, was not going to yield any more time than the plea bargain. This decision to plead the case out was the best deal for everyone involved. He was certain of it.

"I was fine with it," Lindsey said later. "And knowing that I never had to see him again made me very happy." Lindsey had not only bounced back from her attack, but also went on to become one of the top cross-country runners in the United States. With offers from universities all over the nation, she chose to attend Notre Dame.

With the plea agreement wrapped up, Chief Ed Moore could smile. He was satisfied with the outcome and gave credit where credit was due, telling the press, "Art Kranick and Ray Harrington are the real heroes."

Kranick and Harrington, two underpaid and under-celebrated teachers, had done the right thing in chasing down Saratoga's Halloween monster. Their tenacity, diligence, and courage had changed the lives of so many people, including, certainly, any potential future victims of John Regan.

Walking out of court, one of Regan's attorneys told a small crowd of reporters that the proceeding was the "first step" in "resolving matters." He called the New York case against his client ". . . by far the strongest."

Back in Waterbury, Regan's attorneys ratcheted up their defense. Through constant communication with the media, they "maintained [Regan's] innocence" regarding the Connecticut charges.

A multiagency task force assigned to track down cases and determine if Regan could be responsible for other rapes or even murders throughout New England had come up with nothing extra with which to charge him. This boded well for Regan's argument that both cases in Connecticut were consensual. Still, the woman from 1981, twenty-five at the time, told her story of Regan forcing her into his truck, locking the doors, and trying to make her give him oral sex. This was not a charge that would ever stick (especially if the woman wasn't willing to testify), but it spoke to the type of crime Regan was known to commit.

In July 2006 Regan once again shuffled into a Saratoga County court, his familiar look of despair—turning away from the cameras, staring up at the sky or down to the ground—this time to hear his sentence.

The convicted criminal was given the expected twelve years. Regan stared at the flag behind the judge's bench the entire time, never looking at anyone, almost as if he was doing the court a favor by being there. Rocky Regan had been known for his square jawline and his tough, hard build. Yet here, on this day, stood a broken man whose life had distilled down to a series of attempted sexual assaults and attempted kidnappings, a man whose actions were thankfully stopped before escalating into the unthinkable crimes of a madman. If nothing else, John Regan was a convict who would soon be forgotten by the public, labeled with a number in a system that viewed him as one more offender doing time behind bars, taking up the state's space, spending taxpayer money.

In a predisposition plea/sentencing report filed by the Saratoga County Probation Department before Regan's sentencing, summing up their "evaluation analysis," probation officer Christine Pusatere and probation supervisor Mickey Mahoney called Regan's crime a "brazen attempt to abduct a . . . student." They said Regan's criminal behavior "shocked and terrified an entire community," and noted that police believed, after investigating the case (searching Regan's van), he was prepared to "perpetrate unimaginable horror upon his young victim." What's important to note within this report is the fact that Regan "declined" at any time "to give a statement . . . [and] gave no indication of contrition . . . offered no apology and no regret was expressed." Concluding the report, both probation officers agreed that "for a significant period of time, the community will be safe from the likes of John Regan . . . [whose] abominable behavior was a painful invasion of [Lindsey Ferguson's] sense of safety and well-being . . . the type of invasion that can leave long, lasting scars . . ."

Despite the harsh reality of Regan's crimes and the impact those crimes had on his victims and the community, Regan's defense attorney,

E. Stewart Jones, told reporters after the sentencing that his client would soon be heading back to Connecticut to plead guilty to charges that would, in turn, be exchanged for a sentence fewer than the twelve years he had been sentenced to in New York. And the Connecticut sentence, Jones stated definitively, "would run concurrently with his sentence in New York."

Concurrent sentences. Not consecutive.

When the SAO in Connecticut heard of Jones's claim, a spokesperson for the office said, "That's news to us. There is no specific deal that's been made."

The SAO released a statement saying it was looking forward to having Regan back home and in court, where he faced the potential for one hundred years behind bars if convicted at trial.

Alcohol addiction became a factor driving Regan's defense now as he and his legal team headed into the Connecticut charges. Attorney Jones spoke of a client who was addicted to "drinking a fifth of liquor a day." Jones called alcohol "the devil" that did "damage to John Regan."

What was interesting about the revelation that Regan was a chronic alcoholic was that on the day he tried abducting Lindsey, Regan had not been charged with DUI; he was as sober as a snake.

"He was not drunk," Chief Moore told reporters.

In addition, Regan had refused a field sobriety test at the scene where he was arrested in Saratoga, saying he wouldn't take it "unless my attorney is present." Later that evening, at the Saratoga Police Department, Regan passed a breath-screening test.

Here again was Regan shirking any responsibility for his crimes. Now it was alcohol driving him to commit such cowardly acts against women. And, inexplicably, he had many people fooled. Scores of letters of support for Regan from friends and family flooded into the Saratoga County Probation Department from Jones's Troy, New York, office.

Rocky Regan, although accused of and charged with some of the most vile crimes imaginable and an admitted kidnapper, was, according to those who knew him in Waterbury, a "gentle man" and a "very present and involved dad." Regan's wife chimed in, saying that she had "loved him since" she was a "young girl." She said Regan had never "acted or tried to act in an inappropriate manner." The "happiest day of" her "life" was the day she married John Regan in 1981 (the same year he had allegedly tried to force a woman to give him oral sex).

Next his wife wrote about her husband's "heavy drinking" and how it had destroyed their lives. But she had stuck with him then, just as she was doing now. Finally, Regan's wife concluded that her husband was a "loving, caring human being who has done a lot of good on this planet." She asked that he be "forgiven" for "his faults."

Each of the letters hit on this same "gentle giant" theme, with a routine ending that focused on Regan's supposed alcohol problem and the treatment he needed for it.

Denial was rampant back home in Waterbury. It was as if the demon inside John Regan, urging him to commit these egregious, heinous, and violent crimes against women, was not something any of his friends or family could fathom or face.

Some family members blamed the media, saying Regan did not have a voice anymore, but that "the media's characterization of him does not do justice to the man that he is . . ." It was "the system," wrote one man related to Regan, that had "silenced John's voice . . ."

It appeared that nobody could make the connection between Regan being a serial offender and the same person they had known. It was a fact that his DNA had matched one victim and he had been caught in the act of another potentially serious crime. But nobody wanted to see it. Instead he was "a wonderful son" and a great "coach." He had a "lifelong love" for his wife. Some said they'd have no trouble leaving Regan with their teenage daughters. He was not "capable of *any* crime."

Not one letter mentioned the victims of his crimes.

If one were to read these letters, not knowing the crimes to which Regan had pleaded guilty, or of which he had been accused, one might think the man was being considered for canonization instead of incarceration.

CHAPTER THIRTY-SEVEN

Showtime

DATELINE PRODUCER SUE SIMPSON CALLED WATERBURY OBSERVER publisher John Murray to inquire about that lengthy story he had written. Simpson first contacted Murray back in December 2005, showing an interest in doing a story about John Regan. Basically, NBC was wanted to produce a full-length, hour-long Dateline on John Regan, with the narrative thrust of the show focused on Donna's story. Obviously, the potential to interview a survivor like Donna— i.e., Rachael—and get her exclusive story on camera was something NBC knew could bring in big ratings.

Simpson told Murray she had read the Observer stories online and was wondering if Murray could put her in touch with Rachael.

John Murray said he'd make a call.

During the conversation Donna had with Murray, she agreed to meet Simpson at the Observer offices in downtown Waterbury to discuss the possibility of appearing on Dateline. Donna was still on the fence about fully identifying herself on the show. Was it the right thing to do? The episode could not air until Regan's court proceedings in Connecticut were fully adjudicated. Donna needed to be certain that NBC would wait until the entire case was closed—it would have to be a prerequisite. Donna also stipulated several requirements of the meeting in a letter of agreement she asked Simpson and NBC to sign beforehand.

—◦—

Susan Simpson, a representative from Dateline NBC, *will be meeting with the victim of the 1993 rape case in Waterbury, Connecticut. The victim's name will be referred to as "Jane Doe." Jane has agreed to meet with Ms. Simpson for the purposes of exploring a potential segment to be featured on* Dateline NBC *sometime in the future. By signing this agreement, Ms. Simpson understands that anything Jane Doe says for the purposes of this initial meeting is totally off the record. None of what Jane Doe says shall be used in whole or in part by Susan Simpson,* Dateline NBC, *or any other media outlet without prior written consent by Jane Doe.*

—◦—

Simpson's signature on this agreement gave Donna a sense of security.

So they met.

Not once during that meeting, which lasted several hours, did Donna tell Simpson her real name. Simpson never knew—that is, until Simpson recognized Donna's photograph in a full-page *Observer* ad for Donna's business.

At the conclusion of the meeting, Donna told Simpson she needed more time to think about it.

By now, Donna had conceived of what she called the "Jane Doe No More" initiative. She was in the early stages of creating and developing a website dedicated to her story, including her goal to change the way law enforcement responded to sexual assault crime scenes, among other things, along with launching an online destination for victims of sexual assault who have been hiding behind a curtain of anonymity or too scared to come forward. Donna figured if she stepped out from behind the curtain and became Jane Doe *no more,* introducing herself to the world as Donna Palomba, it would serve as an example to victims afraid of reporting rape and sexual assault.

Coming out to a national audience on *Dateline* certainly felt appealing. A marketer by profession, Donna knew that with NBC she could get the most bang for her interview. The problem she faced now was the adjudication of her case against John Regan. The SA was imploring Donna to step back and wait. John Murray used the word "muzzled" when referring to how the SAO had advised Donna regarding appearing on *Dateline*, adding how "unwise" it would be "to talk about her case before Regan went to trial."

⌐⌐

My desire to come forward and make change was growing stronger. I could no longer keep my two worlds apart and they were beginning to collide. Once I make up my mind to do something, I like to get going. I used this time—between the Dateline *interviews and Regan's cases being fully adjudicated, to do a lot of heavy lifting in creating the not-for-profit Jane Doe No More, Inc., and the website, working with my attorney to file articles of incorporation, building the team, recruiting board members, and building content for the website.*

⌐⌐

Donna and Sue Simpson stayed in touch, but the last thing Donna wanted to do was give Regan any more ammunition than he had already. Near the end of the summer, on August 31, 2006, as talks between Donna and *Dateline* remained in limbo, Regan's Connecticut charges heated back up. With his case in New York complete, prosecutors there were eager to release any evidence they could offer Connecticut to help prosecute him in Waterbury. Regan was facing three separate charges: 1981 (the woman he tried to force to give him oral sex inside his truck); 1993 (Donna's alleged assault); and 2004 (the stalking and assault case brought by his coworker). As the summer came to an end, there was some talk that Regan would appear in

Waterbury court to plead guilty to the 1981 case. But that case bogged down as negotiations centered on bundling the three cases together, with Regan pleading to all three to avoid three separate trials. September came to a close and a pretrial date was set for October 19.

SA Connelly had explained to Donna that Regan's attorneys were hoping to nail down a fifteen- to twenty-year plea bargain, if pleading was the route they chose. Twelve years, the SA confirmed, was "unacceptable," if his attorneys thought they could begin at fifteen and slide the twelve by, much like they had in New York. Even twenty years for the three cases was light. But twenty plus the twelve (if the SAO could negotiate consecutive sentences) from New York, and Regan was looking at being an old man when—and if—he was ever released from prison.

On Wednesday evening, October 18, Regan was transported from New York to Waterbury and held inside the WPD's in-house jail. Word was that he would be brought into court the next day and served any new warrants to make it official.

John and Donna got up early the next morning and were at the courthouse by ten o'clock, waiting for the proceedings to begin. Donna had been told that Regan's former coworker would meet her there, so they could sit in solidarity together.

Shackled and handcuffed, Regan was brought into the courtroom. It had been a year since he had stepped foot in Waterbury. He was balder, had put on more weight, and had a look like he wanted to get things over with and get his sentence so he could start working on that time ahead of him. He walked into the courtroom, his eyes on the floor, nodding to his attorneys—a yes here, a no there—ready and willing to plead his cases and serve his time.

The proceeding was brief and, as expected, the cases were postponed until the following week, October 26.

As Donna sat inside the courtroom listening to Regan's case being discussed, she noticed Sue Simpson from *Dateline* sitting in the gallery. They "made eye contact" at one point, as Donna later wrote in her notes, and Simpson "signaled" that she wanted to meet with Donna and talk after the proceeding.

"Hi," Donna said softly, and then turned back around. Donna noticed at one point that Simpson was speaking to Regan's attorney, no doubt asking him about appearing on the show and maybe even trying to convince him that Regan should also do the interview.

Donna and John soon got up and walked out of the courtroom. There was nothing more for them to do here. Donna had no intention of speaking with Simpson, especially in public. She was having a difficult enough time with Regan being in town and was constantly worried, family and friends later said, that Regan would somehow escape and come after her. The meetings and discussions she had with NBC were supposed to be private. Donna had clearly spelled that out in the agreement Simpson and NBC had signed.

As Donna walked out of the courthouse with John, Simpson made what Donna called a "beeline" for her, calling out, "Rachael . . . Rachael."

Simpson followed Donna and John as they walked toward the street.

"Rachael," Simpson said again, raising her voice.

Donna ignored her.

"Rachael . . ."

Donna turned, looked back at the producer, and said, "No."

⬤～❧

Donna and John had their say in court on October 26, 2006, which had become sentencing day for John Regan after he decided to plead guilty to two of the three cases (Donna's and the coworker's). That third case, from 1981, SA Connelly had explained to Donna and Regan's former coworker, had to be dropped. Connelly never said exactly why, but the speculation was that with the woman unwilling to take it any further and the case built around a he said–she said argument, without her, the case would have fizzled. Why waste the court's time and the taxpayer's money on what would be a losing proposition.

Unfortunately, on this day there would be nothing to celebrate by the time everyone left the courtroom. Regan pleaded under the Alford Doctrine, which gave him the opportunity not to admit any wrongdoing. The Alford Doctrine has been in American courts since 1970 (*North Carolina v. Alford*). In that North Carolina case, according to the Supreme Court ruling: "An individual accused of crime may voluntarily, knowingly, and understandingly consent to the imposition of a prison sentence even if he is unwilling or unable to admit his participation in the acts constituting the crime . . . a defendant intelligently concludes that his interests require entry of a guilty plea and the record before the judge contains strong evidence of actual guilt."

Regan was saying he didn't do it, but that he believed the SAO had enough evidence to prove he did. He had already finagled his way out of the 1981 case. Now, it seemed, he was worming his way out of Donna's and his former coworker's cases too. How appalling. How disheartening.

—~—

I felt powerless over the situation. It was maddening to think that we had irrefutable DNA evidence proving that John Regan [was at the scene of the crime] and yet he could not be arrested for, or charged with, sexual assault. Makes no sense. I knew that he would likely have gotten forty years in my case alone had he been arrested for the crime of rape, which we all felt that he had committed. Ultimately, it wasn't my call, and I was frustrated by the loopholes and conditions that protect predators and disregard victims.

—~—

There was a brief interruption in the middle of the court proceedings when a fire alarm went off and the entire building was evacuated. Most everyone from the courtroom walked across the street to Library Park. As Donna and John stood with Maureen Norris, waiting to go back into the courtroom, she worried anxiously that Regan would somehow escape from custody, that maybe the alarm was a ploy of some sort to allow him to get away. It was frightening and disturbing, Maureen later described, to watch Donna continually victimized by Regan and his presence. This was what Donna as a sexual assault victim faced every day, not to mention the revictimization she had suffered at the hands of the WPD. All these years later, she still didn't trust the WPD with Regan.

When everyone was allowed back into the courtroom, Donna finally had her chance to speak, addressing Regan's crimes publicly for the first time. To her credit, Donna Palomba took the high road and kept her comments brief, expressing herself strongly and eloquently: "Your honor, it is not for me to judge," Donna said, her voice resolute, firm. "I believe John Regan's ultimate fate will be decided upon by God. John Regan is a repeat offender. He is calculating and dangerous. And I pray that he never has the ability or the opportunity to harm another person for the rest of his life."

And that was that—Donna Palomba was finished.

John Palomba, however, had a few more words than his wife for the man he had once thought of as one of his best friends. He started by calling Regan a "punk," finishing that part of his statement with "coward." He said Regan was a *"disgrace* to his family and friends." There was genuine anger in John's voice; it was clear that Regan had taken up way too much of John Palomba's headspace over the years, and it was high time for Regan to hear his former friend's voice ringing in his ears along that lonely road that lay ahead.

"I urge you to make sure this creep," John said, addressing the judge, "is kept in prison for as long as possible because he *will* attack again."

Regan stood with his head bowed, as usual, a look of indifference on his face. He acted as if he was disgusted and inconvenienced by having to listen to Donna and John talk about him in this way.

He had pleaded guilty to kidnapping, unlawful restraint, and stalking. That was the deal Regan's lawyers had negotiated. The charges were based on Donna's and Regan's coworker's cases packaged as one. Had John Regan gone to trial and lost, he would have faced what some reports estimated was up to thirty-six years in prison. This deal would set him back fifteen years. He would also have to register as a sex offender for ten years.

SA Connelly told reporters he believed this was the best the SAO could do and the stiffest possible sentence they could achieve "under the circumstances."

The biggest shock was that Regan had plea-bargained his cases into a concurrent sentence—meaning that he would only have to serve an additional three years for the Connecticut cases. He'd serve twelve years in New York and then owe Connecticut three years upon his release.

One of the more dramatic moments of the proceeding came when a victim's advocate read a letter written by Regan's former coworker, who was too scared to read the letter herself. The coworker had been re-traumatized by the discovery of those eerie photographs (of her) that had been found in Regan's van and at Wal-Mart, which clearly proved how obsessed Regan had been with her, even *after* being caught and out on bond in Donna's case. A small portion of the letter she had written put it all into perspective: "He has come after me twice and I fear for my life." As that sentence echoed throughout the courtroom, the woman began to shake and broke down in tears. She told reporters later that she suffered from heart palpitations, post-traumatic stress, and anxiety attacks. Her life would never be the same.

Of course, Regan had zero reaction to those chilling words, at times only shifting his weight from one foot to the other, acting as if the court was wasting his time.

Not one friend or family member showed up in the courtroom to support Regan.

It was surreal and anticlimactic. It was maddening seeing Regan standing there with no remorse. The Alford Doctrine is the wimp's way out. He never said anything other than one-word answers to the judge's questions. His . . . attorneys spoke about his rights and [one of them] wanted it to be stated that Regan could appeal the decision that mandated he be registered as a sex offender.

Chapter Thirty-eight

Change

With John Regan's Connecticut cases fully adjudicated, it was time for Donna to make her decision about *Dateline*. Even after careful reflection, she still wasn't sure whether coming out and being a voice for rape survivors was the right choice for her. And John Palomba wasn't so thrilled about going public with the story and his wife becoming the spokesperson for sexual assault victims. In fact, John was mortified that private Palomba matters would be aired to such a wide, national audience.

Still, it was Donna's call. She had gone through the hell that had become her life after that night Regan had maliciously changed things in the Palomba house forever.

"Donna was lucky that she had a strong family, a loving husband," Maureen Norris later said. "This sort of thing would have destroyed other families—*certainly* other marriages."

A week before Thanksgiving, Sue Simpson contacted Donna with a request. Sara James, the *Dateline* correspondent who would conduct Donna's interview on air if she agreed, wanted to meet with Donna, answer any questions, and talk things through. James, a seasoned journalist and popular NBC personality who had been with *Dateline* since 1994, was prepared do whatever she could to help ease Donna's mind. James was no talking head or television figurine with a pretty face placed in front of a camera because she looked the part. She had won an Emmy award, several Gracies, and a Headliner, among others.

Ironically, James had scooped up the Headliner award in 2004 for a *Dateline* segment she did on the last September 11 victim to be released from the hospital—a segment titled "Meet Jane Doe."

The meeting went well. James was sincerely interested in Donna's Jane Doe No More cause and listened empathetically as Donna sat and talked about what she wanted to do. In the end, Donna walked away from the meeting feeling good about appearing on *Dateline*, yet she still had several concerns she needed to work out with Simpson, in writing, before she would officially agree.

—◆—

This scared me terribly, as anyone might imagine. I believed it was the right thing to do. Still, I had been Jane Doe for so long. I felt ready to come out, yet my husband had reservations and my family was grow-ing increasingly concerned. I was impressed by Sara James's and Sue Simpson's professionalism during that lunch . . . so in the end, I decided the hour had come for me to help victims. It was that, or all of the suf-fering I had gone through would have been for nothing. It was time for me to step out from behind the Jane Doe curtain. Among the things I insisted on with agreeing to the interview was to dovetail the airing of the segment with the launch of the Jane Doe No More initiative.

—◆—

Maureen Norris had been there for Donna throughout the past ten-plus years. When it came time for Donna to decide on doing *Dateline*, she went to Maureen for both legal and personal advice.

"I felt that it was Donna's decision," Maureen said later. "If she felt that's what she needed to do—come out as Donna Palomba and not Jane Doe on national television—and she felt strong enough to do it, then she should. Look, she made a big decision that she was no longer going to hide behind a curtain . . . and, in the end, it was great for her. I think it kind of stopped her from feeling like she had done something wrong."

It empowered Donna and allowed her to take back her life, which, in turn, opened her heart, mind, and soul and allowed her to help others.

"She had felt that this had happened to her for a reason," Maureen added. "And maybe that reason was that she had to fight for other people."

After rescheduling the *Dateline* interview because of a terrible bout with the flu (which must have scared Simpson into thinking Donna was getting ready to bow out), on February 9, 2006, Donna and John met with correspondent Sara James at an inn near their home.

~

John and I sat next to each other as John was interviewed. It was very emotional for both of us. John was choked up as he talked about the struggle between his spiritual and human side. He relayed that story of when he went for a walk with [his friend] one night and said that he had to kill Rocky. They interviewed John for a couple of hours. He left, and we broke for lunch. Then it was my turn, and I was interviewed for about three hours. I felt that it went well, but by the end I was completely drained and felt like I didn't talk enough about the initiative. I also did not talk about the policy and procedure changes I was after—and the fact that pursuing the Jane Doe No More initiative and having something good come from something so evil has been a part of my healing. But it was done, and I had to let go. Above all, I wanted it to be a story about hope, and I believe that came through. *

~

Fourteen months went by before the *Dateline* episode (titled "The Man Behind the Mask") aired. Donna did not come out as herself for the first time on the *Dateline* episode. Her big reveal from behind the Jane Doe mask came on Friday, April 27, 2007, on NBC's *Today* show to

---

* To watch the *Dateline* episode, "The Man Behind the Mask," in its entirety, please go to www. msnbc.msn.com/id/18405518/ns/dateline_nbc-crime_reports/t/man-behind-mask.

promote the *Dateline* episode airing that Sunday night. Donna had been told on the Wednesday before, April 25, that she was scheduled to be live on air with Meredith Vieira during the highly rated 7:35 a.m. slot.

"It really shook me," Donna said. "The thought of being live in front of what was then the largest audience on network news television was intimidating."

—∾—

They aired a two-minute set-up piece (footage from the Dateline *show that was to air on Sunday), and I asked that the monitor not be in my view. They obliged, but I could hear the audio, and it startled me, especially the clip from the 911 call. As it was happening, I could look outside the studio and see the crowd of people (mostly women) gathered in the street. They were simultaneously watching the video clip and watching me sit with Meredith, waiting to be interviewed. They saw that I was startled, and the crowd began to give thumbs-up and many of them put their hands over their hearts in an expression of love. It was really wonderful, and I knew instantly that I had made the right decision.*

—∾—

The two-hour *Dateline* segment brought in nearly eight million viewers that Sunday night, April 29, 2007. It was one of the highest ratings *Dateline* had seen in years. Donna's JaneDoeNoMore.org website took tens of thousands of hits after the episode. Many victims/survivors of sexual assault and rape shared their wrenching stories of being raped and not believed on the JaneDoeNoMore.org message board. There was hope in many of the posts, not simply despair and pain. It was as if the victims who were out there feeling alone now had someone listening and fighting for them. Survivors of rape had a voice. There was a place on the web they could congregate and talk. Donna had achieved one of her foremost goals: to get the word out that victims of rape and sexual assault should not feel alone or condemned because somebody didn't believe their stories, or they were too afraid to come forward.

Donna's message to first-time visitors on the site was pure and on point.

—~—

Jane Doe No More is born out of my experience as a victim of sexual assault. Crime is an unfortunate reality in today's society, and I was unprepared for what was ahead after the attack as, I believe, is the case with most victims. I was mistreated by the very system put in place to "protect and serve" the innocent. On top of the pain and suffering associated with the crime, the abuse afterward rendered the healing process all the more difficult.

Through perseverance and the support of my wonderful family and friends, however, along with law enforcement and legal professionals who have believed in me, there has been an amazing turn of events . . .

I am Jane Doe no more; I am Donna Palomba. It was my decision to come forward to break the social stigmas associated with this misunderstood crime and help other victims heal. I believe we learn most from our greatest challenges, and I want to share what I have learned. Yes, I am a victim, but I am also a survivor, and I have gone on to have a wonderful life both personally and professionally. I look forward to a bright future.

—~—

Donna Palomba never gave up. She faced her attacker and accusers and stood firm in what she believed, never wavering.

On August 21, 2007, a truly historic day for sexual assault victims in the state of Connecticut, Donna was able to fulfill one of the dreams she'd had from the moment she realized John Regan would not be prosecuted fully for what she believed he had done. Standing at a lectern inside the WPD, Connecticut Governor Jodi Rell and WPD Chief Neil O'Leary standing like pillars beside her, Donna announced that she had officially gotten the statute of limitations for several sexual assault crimes involving DNA evidence in the state of Connecticut removed.

Her tenacity and perseverance within the legislative system had paid off.

It was time to celebrate.

Then the governor addressed the crowd, saying quite unequivocally and frankly: "Make no mistake: Sexual assault is a violent crime. It is not a crime of passion. It is violence of the most personal and devastating kind, as brutal in its own right as murder. And it deserves not only harsh punishment but our very best—and unswerving—effort to bring the perpetrators to justice. Today Connecticut takes another step in that direction."

The law Rell signed into effect that day "eliminate[d] the statute of limitations on six of the most serious sexual assault crimes if the perpetrator had been identified by DNA evidence and the victim notified authorities of the assault within five years."

It had been passed that July during a special legislative session.

"She has made changing the law in Connecticut her personal mission," Governor Rell said of Donna. "Her advocacy for this change has made her a true Connecticut hero."

—~—

I dream big. We live in an uncertain world in an uncertain time. It is up to good people to stand up and take action if we want to make a better world for our children and our children's children. And I do believe what goes around comes around; so many incredible things have happened on this journey, and I try to focus on priorities and what God wants me to do. It has become part of my healing process. I am learning every day, and it has inspired me to share that knowledge with others.

Epilogue
BY DONNA PALOMBA

ACCORDING TO MY RESEARCH, SOMEONE IS RAPED EVERY TWO MINUTES in this country. Most victims are between eighteen and twenty-four years old. One of the biggest obstacles I face every day is simply uttering the word and getting people to understand that rape is a crime we need to talk about.

It is not only okay to say the word *rape,* but necessary in order to understand its repercussions within the community and break the taboo of talking about it with friends and family. Consider this fact: 95 percent of rapes committed on college campuses go unreported. Now consider that the perpetrator will likely rape again. With that information alone in mind, we can no longer turn a blind eye to sexual assault. There is no such thing as "this doesn't happen in my neighborhood." In all likelihood, you or someone you know has been the victim of a sexual assault and there is reluctance to talk about it. The time has come to end that silence.

⸻

By 2009, Jane Doe No More had grown to the point where I decided it was time for me to leave the marketing agency I cofounded and devote myself entirely to the Jane Doe No More initiative.

As I reflect back on the past years, I am overcome with a sense of peace. It is a comfort that comes from the fact that I am doing exactly what I am supposed to be doing in this world, and feel I am exactly where I am supposed to be. Back in 2007, when I decided to come forward on *Dateline* and break out of that Jane Doe cocoon in which I was living, I understood there would be no turning back. What I didn't know—and how could I, really?—was what God had in store and where the road ahead would take me. I reached out to the brightest and best people I knew to serve as board members and advisors of our newly formed not-for-profit, Jane Doe No More, Inc. We had no office. No endowment. Not one grant. And no financial support from anyone other than friends and family. Mind you, it was 2007—the beginning of a recession. Yet what I recognized not long after taking this leap of faith was that what we lacked in funds and timing, we more than made up for in passion and perseverance.

My dream was that we could be a catalyst for change to break the stigma and end the silence about rape, which I feel is the most misunderstood and underreported crime in this country. I want each victim of sexual assault to feel confident enough to come forward, knowing he or she will be treated with dignity and respect. Think about this: Just thirty years ago it was unthinkable to talk about breast cancer. Then former first lady Betty Ford came forward and told the world she had it. Mrs. Ford was the catalyst to remove the shame and disgrace around publicly talking about breast cancer. Over the next three decades, Americans learned about breast cancer, which opened up the floodgates to billions of dollars of research funding. Because of Mrs. Ford's courage to talk about what is a dreaded disease, countless lives have been saved through education, awareness, and early detection. Today, during the month of October—Breast Cancer Awareness Month—there are pink ribbons, numerous activities, buildings lit up in pink, and Major League Baseball players swinging pink bats.

We at Jane Doe No More are determined to do the same for the crime of sexual assault.

If the past is any indication as to where we are heading in the future, it looks bright. In just four years, Jane Doe No More has:

- Successfully advocated for the removal of the statute of limitations on sexual assault cases involving DNA evidence in Connecticut and New York, using my story as the foundation for such legislation;
- Created and provided more than 2,500 copies of enhanced training to law enforcement in the form of a roll call video, *Duty Trumps Doubt*, showcasing sexual assault survivors and law enforcement professionals;
- Trained survivors to speak publicly through our R.A.P.E. (Raising Awareness through Personal Experience) Outreach Program;
- Presented our policy recommendations and procedure changes, along with our core message, at the International Association of Chiefs of Police Conference for two consecutive years (2010 and 2011);
- Trained hundreds of women and young girls in self-defense through the Escape Alive Survival Skills program in collaboration with East Coast Training Systems;
- And much more.*

I firmly believe the secret to our success can be found in the passion, commitment, and drive of our entire Jane Doe No More team. Every day we receive inquiries from students interested in an internship, while others contact us and wish to volunteer their time and talents. We are improving the way society responds to victims of sexual assault. We are committed to a new and innovative culture of ensuring that victims of sexual assault are allowed to heal and become members of a vocal, vibrant, and visible survivor community. We are gaining momentum. It is infectious and electric. I have been blessed abundantly by the amazing people that are part of this grassroots campaign to create lasting change.

Personally, I understand that each day is a gift filled with opportunities to make a difference. If you feel the same, please visit our website and join our team, send us a friendly message, and like us on Facebook.

---

* Please go to www.janedoenomore.org for a complete list and more information.

Acknowledgments

Listing the people responsible for the production of a book is always a challenge. With a project of this scope, thanking such great people becomes about focusing on those individuals who worked hard to get the story into print. First, I want to thank Donna Palomba for her desire to open up and tell her story.

I think the two most important people to acknowledge with regard to this story are Keith Wallman (my editor) and Janice Goldklang (publisher) from Lyons Press. Janice and Keith looked past the stigma attached to rape and believed that this project was worthy enough to override any possible obstacle down the road. There remains a public aversion to the crime of rape. Many large publishers did not want to touch this story simply because, according to them, the word *rape* carries so much ugly baggage along with it that readers and booksellers steer clear of anything related to the subject. I never expected this when I decided to work with Donna. I believed a good, evocative, and significant story—regardless of the subject matter—sold itself. But the following actual rejection became a common theme from editors reviewing the project: "Thank you for the opportunity to take a look at this. Donna's story is horrifying to imagine, but what she has done to overcome the experience and to help other rape victims is inspiring. That said, we fear that we would have a difficult time finding a broad audience for this so, sorry to not have better news, but we're going to pass . . ."

Over and over, Donna was praised for her tenacity, determination, and the great work she is doing with Jane Doe No More—all while, metaphorically speaking, being ushered out of publishers' offices with a pat on the back.

So I need to point out that Lyons Press, an imprint of Globe Pequot Press, deserves credit for not being afraid to publish a meaningful, important story, about which book buyers deserve the opportunity to make up their own minds. I also want to point out that I appreciate project editor Meredith L. Dias's hard work on the book.

Beyond the book, I want to extend my immense thanks to Andrew "Fazz" Farrell, Anita Bezjak, Therese Hegarty, Geoff Fitzpatrick, Alex Barry, John Luscombe, and everyone else at Beyond Productions in Australia who have believed in me all these years, along with my *Dark Minds* road crew: Colette "Coco" Sandstedt, Geoff "Sausage" Thomas, Jared Transfield, Julie Haire, Elizabeth Daley, Jeremy Adair, Paddy, and Jen Longhurst; along with my producers at Investigation Discovery: Jeanie Vink, Sara Kozak (senior vice president of production), and Sucheta Sachdev. David Schaefer (director of communications) has become a great mentor in all things media, and I appreciate Dave's love for and dedication to *Dark Minds*. Likewise, Nancy Wilson and Heather Lyons are great assets to the ID team; both have become great friends. A special shout-out to Henry Schleiff, president and general manager of Investigation Discovery, who has been behind my show since day one.

I would be negligent not to mention all the booksellers throughout New England and beyond—the indie stores and the chains—who have supported me and talked up my books to their customers (thank you from the bottom of my heart); and my readers: You are the most wonderful people—thank you for sticking with me all these years!

Lastly, thanks to my immediate family (Matty, Jordon, April, and Regina), who have stood behind me forever.

Finally, Donna Palomba would like to express her appreciation.

First and foremost, I must acknowledge that it is through God's grace and love that I have been able to persevere.

My sincere thanks go out to M. William Phelps for his desire to tell my story and for his belief in me and the importance of my work. When I set out to do something, I immerse myself in it. In many ways, collaborating on the book was difficult—I felt very vulnerable as I shared things never before revealed and was reminded day after day of all the disturbing details that had become my life. M. William Phelps understood that and helped me to, as he said many times, "embrace the process." I tried my best, knowing we had to get through the tough stuff in order to share a message of hope. And M. William Phelps's incredible work ethic and engaging writing style enabled the process to stay on a great track. I am forever grateful that he stood by the project even while some believed it would be better off not in print. In the end, I feel Lyons Press was meant to publish this work and, like M. William Phelps, I want to thank Keith Wallman and Janice Goldklang for standing by my side throughout.

Of course, I wouldn't be here today were it not for the love and support of my family and friends: my husband, John, our beautiful children, Sarah and Johnny, my mom, and my sister, Maria, my aunts, uncles, and cousins. Even though my father is no longer with us, he lives in my heart always.

I also wish to thank all of John's family and our dearest friends, Lisa and Santo Sampino.

And finally, to everyone on our growing Jane Doe No More team (staff, board of directors, volunteers, and supporters), thank you for sharing my dream and working with me to make it a reality.

So many people have voiced astonishment that my husband and I were able to stay together through it all. To us, there was no other way. We held each other up and, surrounded by our loved ones, our marriage grew stronger. It is fitting that I leave you with the lyrics to our wedding song thirty years ago:

'Til I Can Gain Control Again
written by Rodney Crowell
(Reprinted with permission of Rodney Crowell)

Just like the sun over the mountaintop
You know I'll always come again
You know I love to spend my morningtime
Like sunlight dancing on your skin

I've never gone so wrong
As for telling lies to you
What you see is what I've been
There is nothing I could hide from you
You see me better than I can

Out on the road that lies before me now
There are some turns where I will spin
I only hope that you can hold me now
'Til I can gain control again

And like a lighthouse
you must stand alone
Landmark the sailor's journey's end
No matter what sea
I've been sailing on
I'll always pass this way again

Out on the road that lies before me now
There are some turns where I will spin
I only hope that you can hold me now
'Til I can gain control again

Index

ABOUT THE AUTHORS

CRIME EXPERT, TELEVISION PERSONALITY, AND STAR OF INVESTIGATION Discovery's *Dark Minds*, investigative journalist **M. William Phelps** is the national best-selling, award-winning author of twenty-one nonfiction books. Winner of the 2008 New England Book Festival Award for *I'll Be Watching You*, Phelps has appeared on CBS's *Early Show*, truTV, The Discovery Channel, Fox News Channel, ABC's *Good Morning America*, The Learning Channel, Biography Channel, History Channel, *Montel Williams*, Investigative Discovery, *Geraldo at Large*, USA Radio Network, Catholic Radio, Ava Maria Radio, ABC News Radio, and Radio America, which calls him "the nation's leading authority on the mind of the female murderer." He is one of the principal stars of the hit Investigation Discovery show *Deadly Women*, now airing its fifth season. He's written for the *Providence Journal*, *Hartford Courant*, and the *New London Day*, and has been profiled in such noted publications as *Writer's Digest*, *NY Daily News*, *The Sun*, *Newsday*, *Albany Times-Union*, *Hartford Courant*, *Connecticut Magazine*, *Advance for Nurses* magazine, *Forensic Nursing*, and *NY Post*. He has also consulted for the Showtime cable television series *Dexter*. He lives in a small Connecticut farming community and can be reached at his author website, www.mwilliamphelps.com.

The face and founder of the education and advocacy group Jane Doe No More, Inc. (www.janedoenomore.org), **Donna Palomba** is recognized nationwide as a powerful voice for survivors of sexual assault. Since first telling her story on a 2007 episode of *Dateline NBC*, Donna has become a sought-after public speaker and media resource, logging appearances on local and national television and radio shows, including NBC's *Today* and Biography's *I Survived*. She is the driving force behind Jane Doe No More's mission to improve the way society responds to victims of sexual assault.

Donna successfully lobbied for legislative changes that protect the rights of sexual assault survivors and was instrumental in the creation of Duty Trumps Doubt, a training video used by law enforcement agencies throughout the United States. Through her national nonprofit Jane Doe No More, Donna established Raising Awareness through Personal Experience (RAPE), a groundbreaking outreach program that trains sexual assault survivors to touch the community as motivational speakers and mentors.

Donna Palomba was named Woman of the Year by the Business Women's Forum and Working Woman of the Year by the Connecticut Department of Labor, Westfarms Mall, and L'Oreal Paris. She has received awards and accolades from local bar associations, Boys and Girls Clubs, the Chamber of Commerce, and Toastmasters, to name a few. She is a current and founding board member of reset Social Enterprise Trust and a member of Naugatuck Valley Community College Regional Advisory Council. She has served on the board of directors of Special Olympics Connecticut, the United Way, and the Non-Profit Assistance Initiative.